ליקב"ו - שיל"ת

ישיבת בני נביאים

קס"ז
לעד

ללמוד תורת הפרד"ס

הרב אריא'ל ב"ר צדוק, ראש הישיבה

www.KosherTorah.com

‒◄O►‒

שמירה מרע

Protection From Evil

‒◄O►‒

Kosher | Torah
שויתי ה" לנגדי תמיד

Also by HaRav Ariel Bar Tzadok:

Walking In The Fire

A manual of classical Torah/Kabbalistic Meditations, Practices and Prayers

ISBN- 978-0-9791601-0-3

Sefer Yetzirah ~ The Complete Course

A 40 hour audio course covering the meditative aspects and usages of this ancient text.

Available exclusively through **www.koshertorah.com**

שמירה מרע

Protection From Evil

Exposing & Neutralizing Harmful Spiritual Forces
in Light of Torah & Kabbalah

Originally Entitled:
Occult Mechanics

◄○►

HaRav Ariel Bar Tzadok
KosherTorah.com

PROTECTION FROM EVIL – SHEMIRAH M'RA
Exposing and Neutralizing Harmful Spiritual Forces
in Light of Torah/Kabbalah

ISBN- 978-1-4507-2007-6

KosherTorah Publishers
A subsidiary of Yeshivat Benei N'vi'im

Operating through our website: **www.koshertorah.com**

18375 Ventura Blvd. Suite 314
Tarzana, CA. 91356 USA
Tel. 818-345-0888
koshertorah1@yahoo.com

KosherTorah.com
Torah/Biblical Studies
Classical Jewish Mysticism
Authentic Torah/Prophetic Meditation
Practical Spiritual/Moral Guidance For Everybody

KosherTorah.com offers a full selection of books, e-books and recorded lessons on CD and MP3 format in all areas of Judaic/Biblical studies, specializing in spiritual practices and the proper integration of classical Torah and Kabbalah.

NOTICE ABOUT APPROBATIONS: *Due to the continuing controversial politicization of many religious issues and divisions among Rabbinic figures, Yeshivat Benei Nviim, KosherTorah.com and HaRav Ariel Bar Tzadok choose not to endorse or approve of the traditional usage of Rabbinic approbations (haskamot) in any of our works. We cannot include everyone, therefore we choose not to exclude anyone. By not taking any political position, we hope to avoid offending anyone with inferred selective, de facto endorsements. All of our Torah works thus stand on their own merit. Anyone feeling the need to seek approval to study our materials should consult their local Orthodox Rabbi.*

Layout, graphic and cover design by: Dovid S. Brandes
dzyndit@gmail.com
PROUDLY PRINTED IN THE USA

To my dear mother,
Always faithful, always strong,
Memories live on.

Supportive through all
Always alive in our hearts,
We will all miss you.

In loving memory of my dear mother
Martha, daughter of Sarah
May G-d give her soul rest and peace
in the Garden of Eden.

Table of Contents

Opening
—◄o►—

Let me start off and say right here that this is not a book about religion and it is not written exclusively for members of any one religious community.

Although I am an Orthodox Rabbi and my area of expertise is Torah and Kabbalah, this book is not limited to these domains.

This book documents certain facts about fundamental human psychology and parapsychology. Whenever we speak about the realm of spirituality, we must understand that we are talking about the realm of the mind and human consciousness.

This book discusses issues that affect us all in the spiritual, psychological and parapsychological domains. No one is immune from these influences- no one!

All of us as human beings share common experiences: one of these being the exposure to evil. Experiencing evil has nothing to do with religion; it is a spiritual and psychological reality that cannot be denied.

At one point or another in our lives we have had encounters with those who are harmful and with those who may seek to harm us. Confronting this evil and defending ourselves against it is why I have written this book.

Religion has its answers for those who are religious. Yet, not everyone is religious. Not everyone wants to be. I understand this. Nevertheless, with or without religion, evil still exists. This is because it is a part of us. The potential for evil exists within each of us because it is part of our human makeup.

From my religious point of view, I believe that we are all human beings created in the "Image of G-d" as spoken about in the Bible/Torah. I also believe that although we have the potential to rise to the greatest heights of the inner Divine reflection, I also believe that we can sink to the terrible lows of animalistic depravity.

We, ourselves, cause most of our own harm. We are usually unaware of the harm we cause ourselves and we seem to be equally oblivious to how we are open to allowing others to also harm us.

I have written this book to help us all stay safe. I reveal herein things that many people already know but may be afraid to admit. I also will reveal to you new things, like how the psychic mind operates and what we can do to build our psychic strength.

I will go into great detail to expose how others, however unconsciously, use psychic mind power to reach out and harm others. We all are subject to this. Yet, most are unaware, and even more are helpless to resist.

This is a book about resistance. This is a book about strength training, about training your mind to overcome outside psychic attacks, from whatever source they may come.

I speak in the language of Torah and Kabbalah because this is how I was trained. But you will see that I do not waste your time and mine with a bunch of religious platitudes and symbols.

As I said above, this is not a book about religion and I made sure that there is no religious agenda herein. You will be able to navigate my mention of Torah and Kabbalah teachings without being intimidated by them and without a feeling of being coerced.

We live in a much larger and more crowded world than you can presently imagine. When you have finished reading this book, you will no longer be able to view the world again with such naïveté and narrow psychic vision.

Be prepared to have your eyes opened...

Chapter 1

◄◦►

Introduction,
The Proliferation of the Dark Arts

We have all heard about them; white and black magic, the occult, Satanism, Santeria, Shamanism, Voodoo, and Wicca. The list goes on and on, but who can name all the spiritual traditions that are based upon the manipulation of the human mind/soul and the "other forces" that alongside us inhabit our world?

Regardless of what an individual's religious beliefs are, almost everyone today has at one time or another experienced such "dark forces" like the evil eye, a curse, bad luck, or something much worse. While adherence to organized religion of any kind has plummeted and millennia-old cross-cultural moral standards are being chipped away piece by piece, belief in the arcane dark arts has skyrocketed to never-before seen levels. Western society is in a love affair with the arcane and the occult.

The popular media is filled with books, movies, television programs and computer games all about sorcery, magic and witchcraft. While many believe these to be benign forms of entertainment, the followers of the dark arts recognize no such limitations. Good and evil are defined very differently in the lexicon of the dark arts than how they are understood within the contexts of every classical religion from around the world. Every religious tradition throughout time and from every place on the globe has had to confront an "Other Side" that sought to cause harm, just as the religion itself sought to do good.

Confronting the dark "Other Side", therefore, is not a matter subject to just one people, one culture or one religion. Every human being has had to fight this battle. Every religion has had to confront an evil within its midst. Western religions, as eastern religions and native religions, are all faced with the same problem. Evil exists and is manipulated by evil people. They need to be confronted, fought and defeated.

Evil is not defined by opposing theologies. Religious beliefs have nothing to do with this fight. What you believe and how you serve Heaven is not here the issue. The issue is not what one believes, but rather what one does. Actions always speak louder than words. This is a true statement held in common by all religious systems throughout time, even those that are faith-based.

Unfortunately, we must acknowledge that there are good and evil individuals within every religion and every culture and this has always been the case. Confronting the dark "Other Side" therefore is the issue, not the debate over academic theological and philosophical issues.

One of the grand rules of all spiritual reality is the law of attachment. In brief, the law of attachment states, *"once one has any contact with a thing, however small or benign, that contact leaves an indelible spot which serves as a point of connection for further contact and acts as a bridge and an opening to get deeper into the person, even without the person's awareness or consent."*

This spiritual law of attachment is also found within Torah. The slightest contact with something "tumah" (Biblically impure) can render whatever it has contact with equally "tumah." The negative tumah energy is contagious and contaminates on contact. Even in modern medicine, we understand this concept regarding bacteria and viruses. What we fail to recognize is how the powers of the dark "Other Side" can contaminate and infect in the same way as does Biblical tumah and as medically-recognized bacteria and viruses.

Therefore, we have an entire generation that opens itself up to a psychic infection without even being aware that they have been infected and what damage this infection causes. Because almost everyone turns a blind eye to this infectious spread, it jumps, leaps and bounds to never-before seen heights of proliferation. Unfortunately, like with all other disease, the dark "Other Side" kills.

We have only begun to see the initial stages of its poison in our society with the random acts of violence and murder perpetuated by those under the dark spell. We have not yet realized how many physical and psychological illnesses suffered by the masses have in fact been caused by occult influences more than by physical circumstances. Indeed, many physical ailments that have inflicted people have done so because of personal choices these people have made. Little do those people realize that their choices (or lack of choice) are a direct result of subtle dark "Other Side" influences upon their minds.

Another grand rule of the realm of spirit, similar to the "law of attachment," is the "law of greater influence." Simply stated, this law postulates that *with an open connection between two points (people, places or things), the influence of the stronger will always dominate the weaker.* Therefore, on the dark "Other Side", there is always an ongoing battle for control. In Torah, this law is reflected in the laws of Kashrut and is called "tatah gavar," (that which is below absorbs from that which is above).

Masters of the dark "Other Side" have since ancient times used methods similar to military warfare in order to place themselves into a position of ultimate dominance and control over others. These psychic, occultic manipulations are almost identical to the subtle and deceptive movements found in political and military maneuvers. Indeed, modern military practices of psychological warfare can be historically shown to have their origins in the teachings of the occult. Simply stated, the dark "Other Side" seeks to control the mind of the individual and through control of the mind, controls the person's body and actions.

Manipulations of the mind to control behavior are certainly not limited in scope. Our entire western civilization is based and built upon the public entertainment media, all of which is based on the premise of entering the individual mind, for the sake of manipulating individual behavior. Why else do you think companies spend billions of dollars each year on advertisements? Their sole purpose is to create a performance that will grab your attention with the intent that it should persuade you to purchase their product.

Modern advertisement uses the ancient art of subtlety, placed ever so cautiously throughout all forms of public entertainment (movies, television, radio, computers) to silently compel us to accept and embrace what it is they are selling, whether this be a product for money, or ideas and beliefs to influence our thoughts and behavior. We so proudly proclaim how we live in a free society. We are so terribly blind to the truth as to how much we are really enslaved.

In order to understand the mechanics of how the powers of the dark "Other Side" work, we must first understand some standard laws of natural physics. The fundamental principle of all is that the dark "Other Side" operates by manipulating the laws of nature, both those commonly known and those less commonly known. Ultimately, all the dark "Other Side" does is manipulate natural law. Although some will refer to occult powers as supernatural, the term supernatural has to be understood as a relative value. In other words, we define the term supernatural to refer to those things that operate outside of the forces of nature. However, there is nothing in creation that operates outside of nature.

Everything is in nature; it is just that our definition and perceptions of nature might be very limited. For example, two centuries ago to have spoken about airplanes, computers and cell phones would have sounded supernatural because the technologies underlying them were completely unknown and unimaginable. Today we can speak about, what for us may be fantasy/supernatural inventions, but in another two hundred years time might be everyday reality.

Much of modern psychology and mind manipulations used daily in the media have their source in the occult. What was understood by very few long ago is today understood by many more. Instead of guarding the secrets of how the human mind works and interacts with impressions of sound and light, these once secret, occult teachings are now taught openly in universities under the names of science. The results are unfortunately the same today as they were centuries ago. Those who learn the ways of manipulating the human mind take control of human behavior.

The human mind, that house of consciousness and the soul, still operates within the organic chemistry of the physical brain. The brain is an organism like all others. It is influenced by stimulations coming from outside of it. Brains are influenced by sounds, lights and brain wave projections, all emanating from outside. The human brain cannot turn itself off; it is always open to receiving these stimuli.

An adept trained in recognizing how his brain works makes great efforts to recognize all influences to which he may become subject. This training requires an adept to delve within the recesses of his mind to explore whatever thoughts and feelings reside there. He is taught techniques how to investigate without emotion and to analyze with clear and coherent rationale what is actually happening within his own inner space. Inside his own mind the adept comes into contact with his own true self and becomes conscious of a reservoir of information and knowledge that has flowed into his mind (usually at the unconscious level) from sources other than the normal external stimuli accessed through the consciousness centers of the brain.

Adepts learn, even as later Jungian psychoanalytical research has discovered that the human mind/soul actually has access to realms beyond the limitations of the physical brain and thus can travel freely in time and space. In other words, an adept can train his mind to travel into realms detached from physical reality. This does not make such experiences supernatural. On the contrary, this is very natural, it is simply an aspect of nature that has not yet been cultivated by and incorporated into the masses.

Adepts learn that while exploring the recesses of their own inner space that they can just as easily access the inner space of the minds of others. Therefore, with the proper alteration of consciousness and directed focus of thought, the adept of the occult can project his own thoughts into the mind of another, all the while making the victim think that the new thoughts or feelings are his own. The adept is able to conceal his tracks and thus he can influence other minds from a distance completely undetected. The one under such influence has no idea that he is thinking thoughts not his own. The one under such influence may sometimes feel compelled to act in certain ways, often out of one's character. Only afterwards does one wonder what "possessed" him to act in such a way. This can be true on both the individual and collective level, depending on the force of influence.

The exploration of the inner workings of the mind takes the consciousness of the adept into new and previously unknown places. A full explanation and description of these is beyond our present scope. However, one point every adept learns very early along his path is that in his travels, he is certainly not alone. Just as our physical world is inhabited by numerous others, so too are the other realms into which the mind travels also inhabited by indigenous beings of those places. In religions, these others are given names like demons and angels, yet these mythical terms do almost nothing to describe the actuality of the different races that one can encounter. We will learn much about these "others" in later lessons.

We live in a large universe and all that great distance in outer space is easily and quickly traversed by traveling through a medium different from space. Travel at the speed of thought is instantaneous throughout physical space. When one travels into the inner space of the mind, one accesses doorways that actually enable one to travel through consciousness to other places in the universe as well as into other dimensions of parallel being.

While all this will sound mystical to many and nonsensical to others, the occult adept just responds with a coy smile, knowing how uneducated such comments are and how easily he can enter into the mind of the ignorant and cause them untold havoc. Indeed, dark "Other Side" adepts usually train by picking an unsuspecting victim and project thoughts into that one's mind until that one succumbs and does as commanded, all the while completely unaware that he or she has fallen victim to such a psychic attack.

This type of behavior is ancient. We even find references to this in the Bible. In the days of Jeremiah the prophet, there were witches living in Jerusalem. These dark "Other Side" adepts would hire out their services and use their psychic training to tap into the souls of the unsuspecting and slowly but surely drain out of them life and the will to live. Today, with the growing proliferation of psychological depression and baffling diseases like Chronic Fatigue Syndrome, one should ask just how much of a dark "Other Side" component is active here.

Knowledge of dark "Other Side" activity is a closely guarded secret. One who has an advantage never lets others know of his advantage. He guards his knowledge and thus protects his secret. If everyone else knew what he was doing and how, they would be able to learn to do the same and protect themselves from the malicious attacks from others. Such knowledge and defense would break the back of most novice dark "Other Side" practitioners. Of course, the masters have even greater knowledge along with allies and associates to support and reinforce their activities.

The reality of the occult is often dismissed and even mocked by the ignorant. Unfortunately, we have no shortage of ignorant individuals amongst us. Even more unfortunate is that the ignorant are often leaders in academia who believe in the supreme value of their logic and rationale. They have no idea what they are missing and how open they are to the very powers they deny exist. Judging from the despicable behavior we often see coming from members of the overly rational academic community we can wonder how many of them have already fallen victim to the ire of some offended occultist.

In religious circles today, almost all Rabbis are ignorant of the occult. In Biblical and Talmudic times, mastery of occult knowledge was a prerequisite for an elder to take a seat in the Sanhedrin. This knowledge was at one time required learning by all Sages, to recognize and know how to combat malevolent occult forces. Unfortunately as Torah learning was transformed into an exclusively rational endeavor, knowledge of the occult fell to the wayside. As such, entire communities were left powerless to recognize occult forces working to destroy them. In the end, as we all know, European Jewry, the crown of religious rationalism, fell victim to the Nazis, a movement founded in the occult and dedicated to enacting its tenets.

Amongst Rabbis of Middle Eastern and oriental origins, where the infection of European rationalism had little sway, knowledge of the occult and how to deal with it has remained intact since Talmudic days. Numerous books on the various subjects are available in many Jewish bookstores. However, even those who buy them and read them seldom understand them.

Some knowledge however accessible can remain a closely guarded secret until one is taught how to understand it properly. For this one needs more than just the book, one needs a teacher. The teacher passes on knowledge that no book can provide. The student's job is to receive it; he is the receiver. Does not Kabbalah mean, "to receive?" Now you know where I am coming from and to where we will be going in future lessons.

Let me conclude by assuring you, if you think you are safe and have nothing to worry about, then it is probably already too late to save you. Only those who are open can receive. Those who are closed will have to be opened with a pry bar, just as was the case in Europe. You do have something to fear. Acknowledging it is the first step to defeating it.

Chapter 2

◄O►

Understanding the Psychic Mind & Reading the Original Story

The methods of implementing psychic mind control for spiritual self-defense are numerous. Yet, they all share a common denominator. They all use the natural order of how the organic brain and the ethereal mind/soul receive and integrate information.

Remember this great rule: light is life and life is sentience. Sentience is essentially self-awareness and self-awareness requires information and knowledge. Life is in everything and everything contains information vital to itself. Everything in creation, simplified to its most basic form, is basic information. Information explains and tells everything what it is and more importantly what to do. Everything needs an understanding of what it is to do; otherwise, it could not come into existence, maintain its existence and serve its purpose.

Not everything understands itself and has choice to override its initial programming. Everything exists to be, not everything exists to know. This is how we human beings exist. We are born, live and die, all according to a natural organic design outside of our conscious control. We are unaware of our collective purpose in the universe and we certainly have no control over how our race grows and matures here on Earth.

While we all hope for a better world and a utopian society, the way to collective betterment comes about through the conscious enlightenment of individuals, one at a time. Transformational information, the type that transforms collective societies, never comes from an outside source. In others words, the necessary new information comes from within, not without.

Humanity awaits a personal savior, a special human being, who with special powers of persuasion, will show us all how to acquire higher knowledge. However, this is not the role of the coming Messiah. The hope for someone else to come and do the job of finding the higher way for us is scapegoat escapism. It is the job and destiny of each individual to find the secrets of redemption within oneself. Only when the individual finds the higher path within oneself will one awaken to recognize what we refer to as the inner *spark of messiah*" within each of us.

No external, magical savior will ever come. The bringer of higher knowledge is always ourselves. As one individual becomes enlightened then so does a second, then a third and so on until the entire collective human race shines like the radiance of the sun. Needless to say, this process will take a very long time. Granted in many world religions we find the concept of the coming of a Messiah. Yet, the messianic character is not the bearer of Divine Light or higher consciousness; he is rather the enforcer of Divine law. He comes to impose a new world order, to reward the already enlightened and to punish those who still walk in their individual darkness.

Prophecies about the Messiah ushering in a utopian society culminate a long process of the human evolution of consciousness. While this inevitable outcome is longed for and welcomed by the religious, the dark forces of the "Other Side" look at the advent of the Messiah as the end of their game and power. When Heaven intervenes on Earth and takes control, those here who have manipulated things for so long will no longer be able to function in that capacity. Indeed, they will be brought to trial, judged for illegally manipulating the minds and lives of others and punished accordingly by the now new imposing authorities.

Therefore, many devotees of the "Other Side" will manipulate anything they can to forestall this inevitability. Granted, they may have limited success, however, in the end, the more energy they exert to prevent the coming of the

Messiah, the greater the opposite energy will be to speed his coming and to impose his rule. Essentially their opposition only works to make the Messiah even more powerful. However, I have digressed here enough. This is not the time or place to discuss Messianic prophecies. We must return to our discussion about information.

Information is knowledge. Knowledge is encased in life-force energy. Energy vibrates as sound. Sound is the vehicle through which our universe was created, as it says, "Let there be" and there was. Let us take this famous Biblical statement out of myth and understand it scientifically and we will understand the fundamental principle of how all spiritual/psychic powers work.

At the most fundamental level, our universe comprises sub-atomic particles. These "itsy-bitsy" tiny particles are relatively distant from one another at their sub-atomic level as planets are distant from one another in our big universe. This leaves a lot of "empty" space and vast distances to traverse. Yet, something tells these "itsy-bitsy" particles, you go here to form this atom and you go there to form that one. This "voice" of instruction directing these particles to be and to form what they do is the primordial information that underlies everything in the universe. This information, or what I refer to here as the "primordial voice," is what Torah refers to as the Voice of G-d creating the universe through speech, again as it says, "Let there be" and there was.

The Torah later teaches that man was created in the image of G-d. This image has nothing to do whatsoever with our physical form, although our human body in a way does reflect the supernal pattern. The image of G-d in which we were created is a reference to our human consciousness. The "image of G-d" is the unique combination of creative forces that are the individual parts of what we call the human soul. In Torah language these parts are referred to by different sets of metaphors, the most popular being the Ten Sefirot and the five parts of soul called NaRaNHaY.

An understanding of our own internal human parts provides for us insights how we operate within ourselves, how we connect to the universe and thus, with everything in the universe and ultimately how we connect to G-d. In religion, the connection to G-d is emphasized. On the "Other Side," the connection to everything in the universe is emphasized. Through the powers innate in the human mind/soul we can access the innate information existing in every sub-atomic particle and like G-d "speak" to it, through the power of combined thought and speech (so-called magic words) and thereby influence its structure and integrity. This is the underlying principle of all occult operations.

As we have mentioned in the previous essay, the human mind is not limited in scope to the confines of the organic human brain. Thought can travel everywhere. While we call "thought travel" imagination, we often find that the things we are dreaming about or imagining sometimes are real and come true. This is so because the conscious mind when unfettered from its organic brain prison can indeed see other places and other times. More than this, it can influence events in those places by the combined power of thought and word. This is how psychic powers work and this is also how prayer works. Both operate using the same "spiritual" or mental apparatus.

The human mind projects its power through a combination of mental image and physical sound. One is the soul of the operation, the other is its form. Everything in the universe needs these two components, force and form, soul and body, light and vessel, they are all the same. The two act together in a unique way creating the third element, which is the desired result.

This triad relationship was discussed centuries ago and actually put into writing in the opening words of the ancient Sefer Yetzirah, the Book of Formation. For centuries, this book was rumored to contain the secrets of creation, that one could use it to create a Golem, an artificial life form. Yet, if one reviews all the standard Hebrew commentaries to the text, none of them seem to shed any light on the techniques how to perform these operations. This is because most of the commentators only dealt with the text academically and never practiced its deeper meditative teachings.

Sefer Yetzirah is a guide to meditation and the recognition of the subtle energies encountered by the mind traveling through the not so unreal world of the imagination. The text opens by stating that G-d created His world with three books. Yet, here is where proper understanding means everything. What are these three books? The text offers us a peculiar, almost code-like choice of wording. Three words are used to describe what G-d used and because these three simple words have never been read correctly, they cannot be translated correctly and thus, not understood properly. In order to explain this initial important concept we will have to use the original Hebrew terms of the text.

First, the text speaks about the 32 wondrous paths that G-d used, through His many Names, to create the universe. The text then states that G-d created the universe with a sefer, a sefer, and a sefer. Most interpret the word sefer as book, thus the metaphor and the rise of myth. However, the first mention of sefer in the text should be rightly translated as book, yet the second mention, while spelled the same, actually is pronounced with different Hebrew vowels giving the word an entirely different meaning. Instead of the second mention being sefer, like the first, the second should be read as "sapar," which actually means the one who reads the book, or if you will, the storyteller. Finally, the third mention of sefer curiously adds the Hebrew letter Vav between the last two letters Peh and Resh. This turns the word sefer into sippur. This is the Hebrew word for story. Now, we have the actual meaning of the three words. They are book, storyteller and story. This is how G-d created the universe and this is our metaphorical way of understanding the creative process.

Information must first be received from its inherent pre-existing source. This is the book. This explains the ancient teachings of our Sages that G-d looked into the Torah and created the world. In other words, creation followed an already pre-ordained pattern. Even in the teachings of Kabbalah, it speaks about how our universe is merely a copy of an already pre-existing higher universe and how our story of creation is only one of many. The pre-existing knowledge is the book. One must be able to gaze upon it first in order to accomplish any creative act. Unless one can touch the components of creation, one cannot create anything.

No creation is something out of nothing. Only G-d creates something out of nothing, and this we call emanation, not creation. All creation at our level is something out of something. We must first know and embrace something before we can manipulate it and turn it into something else. Thus, we must first know what we call the story, the already pre-existing reality. Without mind travel and expansion, we never see the true story (reality) of the universe. Therefore, all spiritual/psychic training begins with learning the principles of what underlies creation, the laws of physics and the psychological parameters of the human mind. This information is the "story" which we read and learn how to manipulate.

Torah speaks about the universe being created with the "twenty-two letters of the Hebrew alphabet." In religious circles, many interpret this literally and actually go so far as to attribute meaning and significance to the shapes of the individual letters. Yet, the letters themselves are archetypal representations of ethereal energies, or ideas. Their physical shapes may indeed be used to extrapolate meanings, however, those meanings and the letter shapes are subjective and, as we say, in the eye of the beholder.

The initial "story" underlying creation, again are the laws of physics that govern all worlds. By all worlds, I include the realm of the psychological. Torah and many other spiritual traditions teach that the realm of the human mind/soul is equally subject to the laws of creation as is everything else. By understanding inner human dynamics, we can extrapolate and understate the universe. When we say that we are created in the Image of G-d and that G-d created the universe, therefore the universe, in its concentrated state, exists within the human psyche. All we need to do is access it. Accessing it is reading the story. This is the meditative process of mind exploration practiced by every authentic spiritual practitioner, be they of the side of Light or of the "Other Side." Therefore, from the story we proceed to the reading.

Reading the story does a whole lot more than merely reciting words. Words by themselves can be dry and boring. When, however, the mind and the imagination of the reader reads those words he embellishes them with feelings. It is the feelings of the reader combined with the words of the story that merge into yet a third entity. This is the story itself. The reader transforms the words of the book into a living tale. The reader bonds with the book and thereby makes the story his own.

In brief, I have just explained the procedure of how sefer (book), sapar (reader) and sippur (story) work together. At the same time, although I did not outline it, I also explained the procedure of how the Light of G-d shines through the Ten Sefirot. We have so many metaphors, so many words to describe things. We all too often become distracted by the descriptions and forget what it is we are describing. This is only one of the many dangers of learning mysticism, or for that matter Kabbalah.

We must begin with knowledge, proper knowledge; yet we must never convince ourselves that knowledge alone has any power. Unless one knows how to use knowledge, knowledge remains impotent. All the power and force in the world is useless without the proper knowledge to know how to use it. Therefore, we see that knowledge and power must be joined for either to be used. Knowledge is learned from one's teacher. Power is generated through passion. Passion is generated through the performance of specific rituals.

The power in question here is the power of focused emotion. Nothing translates from potential to actual other than through the power of emotion. The mind is the engine but the emotions are the gasoline that makes it run. The mind is the book; the emotions are the reader who embellishes the book giving it life.

In Kabbalah terms, the mind is the upper triad of the sefirot Keter (Crown), Hokhma (Wisdom) and Binah (Understanding). The emotions are the six sefirot of Zeir Anpin: Hesed (Mercy), Gevurah (Strength), Tiferet (Heart), Netzah (Victory), Hod (Glory) and Yesod (Foundation). Only when these are combined can we manifest Malkhut (Kingdom), the never-ending story of life and creation. I am not interested here in digressing to discuss details of Kabbalah. I will not be using the Kabbalah metaphors here in this book. Kabbalistic metaphors often distract one from the very meanings they imply. Understanding the metaphors is less important than understanding what they actually mean and how they are meant to be used.

Spiritual mind control begins with learning how the mind works. This is learned through the studies of both psychology and psychics. Both of these disciplines were known in ancient times and considered essential and guarded traditions within mystical schools of knowledge. Once one knows how to operate, one can then implement the operations.

Torah tradition is full of such psychic/spiritual traditions. Unfortunately, most modern Orthodox Rabbis, especially those of European/American backgrounds have never realized that the general principles underlying Jewish Law were all founded upon psychic/spiritual principles. Why else do you think our Sages established what, to some, seem to be arbitrary rules. Arbitrary, they are not. Torah law was established to safeguard the Jewish people from the evil, occultic forces of the "Other Side." Judging from the centuries, the wisdom of our Sages has been proven correct on countless occasions.

Before one can learn how to channel psychic energy through the medium of sound, one must first be able to generate that energy and then be able to control it. Without the generation of power, nothing can be done. Without the control of power, nothing is safe.

Therefore, step one in manipulating the minds of others is first to learn how to control one's own. This requires discipline. One must learn both the laws of inner and outer reality. One must learn how to control one's desires at the same time that one learns about the true nature of those desires in oneself and in others.

One must learn the ways of reality, the laws of universal truths, these are the foundations of all Torah, all science and the mind. Seek these out in the words of our Sages. Strip them down to their bare essence. See the psychic profundity in the most simple of their sayings. Strip away all the religious hype and cultural nonsense that has crept in over the years from the schools of the rationalists.

Once one develops an intuitive sense for recognizing true knowledge, then we can build upon it. This will take us into the next lesson where we can review practices that will use sound to arouse emotions and merge the sefer with the sapar. This is no mere academic concept. This is a process that merges mind with heart, thought with passion and mental image with focused intent. Only then can we take this generated force and project it through the vehicle of sound to traverse time and space to manipulate our chosen targets.

Chapter 3

—◄○►—

Magic Words & Holy Names
That Are Not So Magic Or Holy

"In the beginning," the Torah states that G-d spoke the universe into being. The concept of sound is hereby introduced as being a conduit for creation. G-d spoke "words." Words are nothing more than combinations of sounds. Yet, words are specific combinations of sounds that represent a thought and a mental picture. Essentially, words are the physical manifestation of mental constructs. Sound creates. Therefore, words bring into being the physical reality of the mental construct they represent. This is how G-d created the universe. His mental power congealed itself into specific sound combinations that when "spoken" into physical space gave rise to all forms of existence.

One of the great spiritual rules is that *"as it is above, so it is below."* If sound can be used by G-d to create a universe and we human being are created in G-d's Image, then we too should be able to learn how to harness the powers of sound and to become co-creators. This is the underlying rule of how all spiritual powers operate, be they what we call the powers of magic and the occult or the powers of holiness and miracles. This is how prayer, magic and mind control all work.

Thought is expressed through sound. When sound is received in an appropriate receptacle, the thought it represents is received in the mind and consciousness of the receptacle. We all know the truth of this at the physical and conscious level. What we do not recognize is that sounds can be made inaudible, beneath the threshold of conscious hearing. Images can also be projected through sounds though not necessarily associated with words of a recognizable language. In other words, the brain can pick up sounds or voices that are not physical and that are not verbal. This means of communication some would call extra sensory perception.

The human mind holds within it enormous, untapped reserves of power. There is so much that we human beings can accomplish. Yet as a race, most have never conceived of what latent powers lie buried within us. As a race, we truly have great potential for developmental evolution. When I use the term evolution, I do not mean that we will adapt and change into something other than what we are right now, rather I mean that we will come to realize what we have had inside us all along.

We develop our inner mental/spiritual powers, similar to how we develop large muscles through physical exercise. Mental exercises develop mental muscle; extra sensory exercises develop extra sensory "muscle." This concept should be easy to understand and accept. We each have the power within us to become what by today's standards would be called "super-human."

However, in reality, today's super-human is nothing new. Rather, it is something old, very old and very original. Tomorrow's superhuman will actually be yesterday's Adam, before the fall. G-d's great plan for humanity is that we as a race eventually overcome the proverbial "sin of eating the forbidden fruit" and return to how we were originally created in the "Garden of Eden." Torah tradition is very clear on this point, that the original physical form of Adam (and thus the indigenous natural state of humanity) was a body of light, not one of flesh and blood.

We never lost our original body of light. It never went away. The result of the "sin" was that our light body became encased in a body of flesh. Our consciousness became split between that part which stayed conscious of our light body and now a detached part, which became entrapped in the body of flesh. This is why today we have conscious and unconscious parts to our mind/soul. This is also why we have two bodies, one being our physical body, the other being what today many call, the astral body. This astral body is our true indigenous form. In the language of Torah, this astral body is called the Haluka D'Rabbanan.

It is this "astral" body that comes down to this world at inception and brings together both the ethereal and physical forces to create the physical body in the mother's womb. It is this "astral" body that casts off the flesh at the end of life in this world and returns to where it came, for better or worse, depending of the nature of one's sojourn here on Earth.

It is through the medium of our other "inner" body that all spiritual forces work, be they for good or evil. The "inner" body transmits and receives information in accordance with the laws that regulate its being. This "inner" body is nourished by the life-force energy that is called by many names. In Hebrew it is called Nefesh and in Chinese, Chi. Regardless of how we refer to life-force energy, it and our inner bodies are subject to tremendous influences being exerted upon them by the actions and behaviors we each individually perform with our bodies of flesh. Although the bodies exist in parallel dimensions, their connection is an intimate one. Our action either strengthens or weakens one body or the other. All forces of holiness and uncleanliness operate according to these principles.

What we do physically has an immediate and direct effect upon our inner aspects. This is why we human beings can bear deep psychological scars from actions involving our physical flesh. The flesh itself can heal and show no scarring whatsoever, whereas the inner self, can bear scars from lifetime to lifetime. One must learn to recognize one's inner self, recognize that it has a body all its own and that it is not physical like flesh, although it bears a similar image.

Our inner bodies are nourished by life-force energy. When we perform certain behaviors, we drain ourselves of life-forces, weakening ourselves, often to the point of death. This is why addictive and abusive behaviors are a poison to both body and soul. When we perform even the most benign physical activity, it has an effect upon us internally, regardless of our level of awareness or sensitivity.

Torah Law outlines for us prohibited activities such as eating forbidden foods, and certain sexual activities. These prohibitions protect one's life-force and enable one to strengthen oneself. Violations create openings in the "inner" body that allow life-force energy to drain out. Worse than this, if such openings were coaxed by one who serves the dark "Other Side", such an opening can be exploited allowing the dark practitioner access to one's "inner" body and one's unconscious thoughts. Ultimately, the best protection against negative spiritual forces is our own self-defense, as outlined by Torah.

The "inner" body is in actuality a field of energy. This is why it is called "light." This body is like every other energy field; it resonates a specific frequency of energy. It is also highly subject to the influence of sound. Sound itself is nothing more than oscillations of energy. Thus the "inner" body and sound waves all resonate within similar frequencies and thus one can have a profound effect upon the other. G-d created the universe through sound and we in turn can use sound to influence G-d's universe and to carve and mold our own universes. Yet, sound, in and of itself, however powerful, remains relatively useless unless one knows how to use it properly. This now leads us to a discussion about the usage of chants, holy Names and magic words.

Proper formations of sound give form to mental constructs. Mental constructs when properly focused using emotional energy can be channeled into the correct sound formats and used to transmit the mind of the individual, and used for either good or evil purposes. Mental imagery, emotional energy and proper sound combinations together are the building blocks of creation. These are the three books we discussed in our previous lesson. Mental imagery must be precisely focused. Emotional passion must be harnessed and strong. We will discuss both of these as we proceed in future lessons. Now, let us focus on sound techniques and how they work.

There are words that have power and there are words that have no soul. While many search to find the right combinations of sounds that they think will perform "magic," the adept knows that the power is in the speech and not necessarily in the words. Almost any combination of words or sounds can be transformed into power projections

45

of thought. It all depends upon the level of focus of one's thought and the power of passion in one's speech. Words are like an engine and the focus and power are like the gasoline. One can have the most powerful engine in the world, but without gasoline, it will forever remain useless.

In Torah tradition we have numerous "holy Names" that are said to be powerful enough to perform miracles. Many of these "Names" are readily available in Hebrew books, some of which have even been translated into English and other languages. In one or two cases, the translations are actually accurate. Still, I laugh when I hear that the readers of these books think that they now have a powerful "magical" weapon at their disposal and that by merely reciting these so-called Names, they will perform "magic." I laugh again and invite them to try. The holy 72 letter Name, the 42 letter Name, even the many forms of pronouncing G-d's Biblical name YKVK, one can see written in books. Yet, none of these books, including the original Hebrew sources explain the proper procedures and preparations necessary to perform prior to one attempting to use such Names.

I see the foolish repeatedly running after their dreams and fantasies, without ever waking up to the fact that they are wasting their time. I cannot prevent the foolish from following their folly, I can only make sure that they do not bother me, or take up my time when they do so. There is an old saying, learn it well; *"The right means in the wrong hands will always make the right things work in the wrong way."*

This is a simple and basic rule. It cannot be broken. If one wishes to use holy Names properly then like everyone else before them who used these Names properly, they will have to go through years of rigorous training. For Jews, this begins with full observance of Torah and mitzvot and continues with a life-long commitment to Torah study. For everyone, Jews and non-Jews alike, we must every day work hard to refine our personalities and devote hours to long and hard mental training in the fields of meditation.

Holy Names and Power Words work not because of themselves but rather because of the one who is wielding them. Train yourself to become strong in these operations and every word you speak can become a Power Word. When focus of mind is properly united with emotional passion and channeled in the right way, usually through silence and calm, then the simplest word can become a tool of tremendous power. This is the secret of the blessing.

When one goes to a Sage, Rabbi or Kabbalist to receive a blessing, the Sage does not merely mumble words, he does not merely wish that good be bestowed upon you. Rather the Sage takes a moment's pause, focuses and then in a few short words projects the power of his powerful mind through his speech into you. This is usually accomplished through a medium of placing his hand on your head or by previously blessing some food that has been placed before him and he then offers you to partake. If a Sage or true holy and Orthodox Kabbalist ever offers you something to eat or drink, never be so foolish as to decline.

Rabbis and Kabbalists devote their entire lives to Torah study. They therefore develop the focus of mind and passion of heart naturally through their pursuits. They do not need to practice certain types of meditative exercises that others might have to learn. Not everyone can devote their entire lives to the study of Torah. Most of us will have to go out and earn a living and thus be distracted by the needs of everyday life. This is only natural. However, this does not mean that the everyday person cannot learn the necessary techniques to use mental powers. While one may never become as strong as the Sage or Kabbalist, one can still nonetheless develop some skills, and these can be rather helpful in one's life.

Sound techniques begin with the mind. The words used are subjective. They must become a focal point of concentration, where mind and heart merge into one. In other words, one must find a phrase or group of words that have personal meaning and then one must make use of the following techniques.

First, one must focus on what it is that one wishes to accomplish. Is one seeking guidance, a soul-mate, avenues of financial gain, healing for a physical ailment or a psychological one? There are numerous pursuits, as many as there are individuals. Step one is that one must focus on what one wants and pursue this specifically, without allowing any distractions to cloud one's concentration.

Once one has decided upon what one wishes to focus on, one then chooses which words to use to help channel this focus. In Torah tradition, our way of focus is to use a verse from the Jewish Bible or a saying of one of the Sages recorded in the Talmud. We choose the verse or statement that most accurately expresses that which we ourselves are seeking at the moment.

Our choice of verse should not be merely academic; one should have an emotional feel for the verse, a sense of it being important and personally special. One has to pick something and feel as if one "owns it," as if this verse or statement was originally spoken centuries ago just for you at this time. You cannot academically define this, you have to feel it. Following your feelings in choosing your chosen verse or statement is the first step to activating it with power. It will be the inner voice channeling into your conscious mind from your inner "body" that will guide this selection. Step one is to open this connection.

The following steps will define how to reinforce the opening. The conscious mind is wired in such a way that it hates repetition. The conscious mind likes to do one thing, one time and be done with it. The inner mind does not work in this way. Actually, it works in the opposite fashion. Therefore, the key to circumventing the conscious mind and to awaken the inner mind is to use our chosen verse or Rabbinic saying as a repetitive chant, which in Eastern traditions is called a mantra. Repetitive recitations bore the conscious mind into closing itself off and thus enables the inner mind to express itself. The focus of mind is achieved through the repetitive recitations. If one has chosen correctly then the words being said should produce an emotional affect, which becomes greater with every repetition.

I will now give you an example of the verse that I personally use as a device for mental focus. Often throughout life, we are faced with many decisions that we cannot rationally ascertain what is the right thing to do. Under such circumstances, I pause to recite this verse numerous times with an additional prayer that I made up. This verse enables my mind to focus on what it is I am asking of Heaven and also provides for me an emotional outlet for my feelings of frustration, confusion and longing for solution. This is the verse, Proverbs 19:21.

"Many are the thoughts in a person's heart, but it is the council of HaShem (RaMaB'Ih'Wah Yo'Hi Ta) that shall rise."

This verse works for me. Each individual must choose a verse that has special meaning to them. The technique for usage is as follows.

First, one must focus on what it is one is seeking to accomplish. Second, one must give up any notion of expecting answers or results to come in the form and way one expects.

The unconscious mind is not subject to control by the conscious; it is the other way around. Those who endeavor to control their unconscious by manipulating the forms of answers they seek will be in for a rude awakening, one that can include mental illness and physical harm. Do not dictate what you want and how you want it, rather humble yourself before Heaven and ask with an open and sincere heart for that which you desire. As the verse says, G-d will not hold back good from those who ask with innocence.

One must have a clear mental image of what one seeks and then one proceeds to recite one's verse or saying over and over again, each time saying it with more passion and fervor. When one is saying the words, one must have in mind what one intends. With every repetition, one should focus more and more and allow one's passions to rise to a pitch. This procedure enables the conscious mind to bow out of the picture and for one's unconscious mind to express itself. I always recommend using one of G-d's holy Names in one's chosen verse or saying.

This adds independent power to what one is doing. In a way, it gets G-d involved. There are many different Names of G-d and many other combinations of letters that form what we call Holy Names. I have included an example in the verse stated above.

The name *RaMa B'Ih'Wah Yo'Hi Ta* is simply formed by combining the initial Hebrew letters of the words in Proverbs 19:21. This abbreviated form makes no sense to the conscious mind and therefore the conscious mind pays little attention to it. However, as a representative symbol, the unconscious mind recognizes well what it means and is strongly attracted to it. Therefore, one of the techniques we use to draw out the inner mind is to use an abstract form of Torah, according to one or more of many different formulas. These will have to be discussed at another time.

Aside from using the verse and any forms of holy Names one can also form one's own sort of prayer or affirmation, again reciting it repeatedly for affect. The wording of this prayer or affirmation can be of one's own choosing, however it should be easy to recite and repeat. In order to make it easy and repetitious, such prayers or affirmations are usually formed as rhymes or poems, often stating the desired thing in rhythmic fashion repeatedly. Here is one example that I use with the above verse.

> *"Many are the thoughts in a person's heart,*
> *but it is the council of HaShem*
> *(RaMa B'Ih'Wah Yo'Hi Ta)*
> *that shall rise."*
> *Arise HaShem, let there be no surprise.*
> *Enlighten me I pray, open my eyes.*
> *Show me that which I wish to see.*
> *Please I pray hear my plea.*

"Many are the thoughts in a person's heart.
Please HaShem, make me smart.
May Your council arise.
Let there be no surprise.
Enlighten me I pray, open my eyes.
Show me that which I wish to see.
Please I pray hear my plea.
"Many are the thoughts in a person's heart,
but it is the council of HaShem
(RaMa B'Ih'Wah Yo'Hi Ta)
that shall rise."

We find this similar type of device often used in traditional Jewish prayers. For example, in our bedtime prayers we recite a simple prayer for protection that in the original Hebrew is rather rhythmic.

It states, *"At my right be Mikhael, at my left Gavriel, before me Uriel and behind me Rifael and above my head the Presence of G-d."*

This is recited only once in the traditional prayers, although some have the tradition of reciting it three or seven times. We often find Hebrew prayers or verses that are repeated numerous times. This is all to create a certain effect emanating from the inner mind.

Remember, the unconscious mind is the mind of the "inner" body. When it comes to the forefront of action and takes over, it alone has the power to express itself through the words being spoken and to influence things in its own realm and dimension. We call the "inner" body the Source body. Therefore, the inner mind is the Source mind. One can always influence the outcome of a thing when one can influence its source. The Source mind acts through the Source body through the physical voice of the flesh to influence both the inner and outer realms. This same technique is the underlying science that operates hypnosis.

The sound repetition itself works wonders; however, it alone is usually not enough to accomplish the full intensity of mental focus and emotional passion. We also often use some forms of symbolic visual representations. Gazing upon these symbols, specifically designed to baffle the outsider, creates a focal point upon which the mind can concentrate adding to the power being generated by the word recitations. Visual symbols are very important. They have been used for millennia to abstractly represent many things. I too have developed specific ones that have powerful meanings. These we will discuss in our next lesson.

Chapter 4
◄o►
The Power in Symbols

The eye is the window to the soul. The soul is actually your mind. Therefore, the way to influence the mind is through what the eye sees. This is why Torah teaches us to guard our eyes, for it is they that lead the heart astray. Nothing can lead the heart astray unless it is first seen with the eyes. In other words, the mind cannot consider the performance of any negative activity other than that which it already knows, recognizes and understands.

Understanding must precede desire. One cannot desire that which one does not know or understand. This is why many times people have a yearning and a longing for something or someone that they do know. The inner mind recognizes what is missing, however the conscious mind cannot conceive of it because it has no vessel through which to congeal the unconscious thought. Once the eyes see and understand what it is seeing, then the conscious mind can receive input from the inner mind, cognize it and arouse a desire to put into action, leading to manifest behavior.

This natural process of recognizing content from the unconscious mind is common to all. What we do not realize, however, is that not everything that arises out of the unconscious mind has its source within us. Some unconscious influences and impressions can be implanted into our minds through subliminal seduction, hypnosis, or other forms of mental manipulations. When we are commanded to guard our eyes, we are in essence being taught to guard our minds, both our conscious minds and our unconscious minds. The processes of guarding the mind are many. We will review some of them now.

The mind is a two-way door. Influences enter that can be harmful and influences enter that can be helpful. As always, we can often choose which we allow entrance. Granted, our world is so full of harmful things that to completely bar negative influences into the mind would require of us to live in a comatose state. Yet, however much our surroundings are full of harmful influences we can surround ourselves with helpful influences. These require the use of symbol and metaphor.

The human mind reacts in a strong way to a symbolic representation of a thing. One merely needs to think about the power of a religious or political symbol to understand this. What Christian does not understand the symbol of the cross? What patriot does not understand the symbol of his national flag? In and of themselves, a cross is merely two joint lines and a flag just a piece of cloth with pretty colors. Yet, in the mind of those who recognize the symbol and embrace its meaning, they become far greater than the materials used to create them.

The human mind can extract from a simple symbol tremendous academic and emotional meaning. A symbol is a message in concentrated form. Many representative symbols have universal meanings that touch the mind and heart of almost anyone. Other symbols require knowledge of their meaning. Those symbols that have universal significance are called in psychology, archetypes. Although their specific interpretations can differ, the general meaning of certain symbols, nonetheless, are shared in common by almost everyone. Such symbols as the rising sun, the human fist, the faces of a lion or tiger, or a budding rose will affect almost everyone in the same way. There is an underlying tone to each of these and many more like them. Of course, each can be embellished with many more meanings; nonetheless, their fundamental meanings are understood by all.

For example, one who wishes to express a sentiment of peace and love would not use the image of the clenched fist to symbolize it. Instead, one might use the drawing of the heart shape or possibly a budding rose. A fist symbolizes power and strength, its image represents power and possibly conflict. Therefore, it might come to represent a group or idea that represents such a struggle, but never a group that represents love and peace. Hippies, for example, are recognized by the flower. Militant organizations, on the other hand, often are represented by the fist. Hippies are by nature soft and passive, like the flower; militant organizations want to be strong, like the first.

Therefore, each group takes an archetypal symbol that best represents their ideals and goals. Universal symbols are used throughout every society and world culture. They have a power all their own. However, more powerful than the universal symbol is the unique symbol, whose meaning and purpose is understood by only the small group that embraces them. Such symbols, undecipherable to outsiders, become the bonding agent that takes individuals of like mind and gives them a means of identification and association unknown to others. Such secret symbols help to form a strong bond between individuals that transcend almost any outside influences. This type of symbol is often used in religion and especially within secret societies of all types. The secret symbol, when understood is a powerful tool and has the ability to defend the mind from outside influences that express opposite sentiments.

The secret symbol is the perfect tool for protecting the mind from outside contrary influences. It acts as a protector for that place where mind and heart, thought and passion merge into one. When the mind and heart become exposed to contrary influences and one is tempted to act in ways that one would normally find objectionable, one can pause and take a moment to visualize one's secret and "sacred" symbol. All of a sudden, all of its inner concentrated meanings rush into the mind filling it, not with intellectual remembrance of academic concepts but rather with passion, zeal and resolve for everything that the symbol represents.

The mind uses the symbol as a tool for concentration. The symbol does not need to evoke remembrance at the conscious academic level. The symbol works by activating all the meanings stored within the inner mind of the unconscious. This way the symbol works almost instantaneously and immediately arouses the necessary emotional energy to push out of the heart any contaminating influence. Do not underestimate the power of the symbol. It can make you strong at the moment of weakness and can save your life in times of danger. The symbol does not work magically; rather it works because of the natural psychology of the human mind.

The "sacred" symbol speaks in the language of the inner mind. This explains to us the meaning of the old saying that "a picture is worth a thousand words." Such sacred symbols are found in every culture around the world. Yet, in order for a sacred symbol to have power within the private psyche of the individual, it has to have a personal meaning and significance.

For example, the symbol of the Nazi swastika is ancient and has been used in cultures around the world for millennia. Its origins had absolutely nothing to do with Germany, white supremacy or hatred of Jews. Indeed, in ancient times the swastika was even known in Biblical Israel. While it was never a Jewish symbol, its meaning, from the Orient from which it came, was recognized, known, and not feared. When the Nazis came along, they adopted the swastika and injected it with a meaning all their own. It became the symbol of their nation, their religion and the hate and evil that they represented. The symbol took on a life of its own; one that lives on today as powerful as in the recent past. Today, all who see the swastika associate it with its recent Nazi meanings. Its original ancient meanings are lost to all except a small group.

The Magen David is today considered the symbol of the Jews and Judaism. However, there is no real historical connection between the two. This is why the so-called "Jewish star" is really nothing of the sort. As such, it only has a subjective power within the minds and hearts of those who choose to embrace it. Being that its meanings are nebulous and not clearly defined, it does not have the innate power to arouse the inner mind to express passion or zeal. Israelis might feel a certain passion for the symbol because it has been emblazoned on the Israeli flag and has come to represent the modern secular state. However, not all Jews are Israeli and not all Jews have good feelings towards the secular Jewish state. Politics aside, the secular state of Israel is not the home for all Jews worldwide and therefore its symbols do not reverberate in the hearts of all Jews.

The original symbol of Biblical Israel was always the Temple Menorah. This symbol, more than any other has always represented the ancient past. Yet, we have come a long way in time and history since then. Even the Menorah has lost its archetypal place in the Jewish heart. Today, there are not many Torah related symbols that have such archetypal meanings. Nevertheless, the importance of such images survives. Since the days of the Temple, two very important types of symbols have maintained themselves within Torah circles, both of which have very profound transformational affects. The first of these are the holy Names of G-d and the second has been the visualization of the face of one's teacher.

Unfortunately, both holy Names and images of Sages have a rather limited scope of influence. A holy Name is a mere pictorial symbol. For those who do not recognize the letters of the alphabet used to spell the name, all the more so what the Name itself is supposed to represent, then its power is neutered. The face of a Sage may indeed hold reverence for those who have a positive relationship with that person. Yet, both the holy Names and sagely image, while arousing academic acknowledgements seldom alone are powerful enough to solicit emotional response.

I must emphasis that it is the emotional output that creates the psychic barrier of mental protection. Without sincere emotional expression aroused by the pictorial image, not only will there be no protective barrier generated, worse, one will believe one has done all that one needs to do and proceed with a false sense of security that will surely lead to one's downfall. We see exactly this happening today throughout the world's religious communities that are expressing mere platonic shows of faith and passion, whereas underneath at the unconscious level, there is little to no attachment whatsoever.

People fool themselves all the time. Let me say this a bit more clearly, people lie to themselves and to others on a regular basis. The lies we tell others can be spotted rather easily. The lies that we tell ourselves we usually never see, and it is these same self-delusions that lead us to a living hell. Without sincere inner transformation, no religious concept, belief or symbol can have any affect in protecting our minds and hearts from the ominous and predatory forces roaming our world looking for us to be their next victims.

Be as religious as you wish. Unless your religious devotion is real, deep and sincere, you are nothing more than a walking target, waiting to be hit by the forces of evil. The forces of the dark "Other Side" know very well the levels of hypocrisy prevalent amongst religious communities today. This is why religious people are often the targets of severely harmful psychic attack. The evil force or individual seeks to corrupt the behavior of the religious individual whose heart is already full of hypocrisy. Such attacks are easy.

To trip up a hypocrite and make him fall into the worst types of deviant behavior is rather easy. Heaven does not interfere in these affairs. Hypocrites are hated by all forces in Heaven and on Earth. Whatever bad things that happen to them is a matter of course and is never a matter of concern, and certainly never a matter to be avenged. Mind you, the definition of hypocrite is defined by what resides within one's heart, by one's level of religious arrogance.

Sincere individuals have the ability to learn new techniques that can protect them from all types of psychic attack, those emanating from practitioners of dark arts and an even worse type that emanates from the hypocrites. Attachment to power symbols can have a remarkable affect upon those who bond with them. Unfortunately, we do not have many such symbols of this nature readily accessible to us today.

Torah power symbols are usually so academic in nature that they do not lend themselves to easy usage by the masses. As such, their power is severely limited to those who can understand them. Mind you, with power symbols, the old saying holds very true, "there is strength in numbers." The more people who can use them and who do use them, the more powerful the symbol becomes. Secret symbols become powerful because tiny little groups all adopt them with such passion and vigor that the symbol serves to strengthen the group. Here, it is the symbol that strengthens the group, not the group that strengthens the symbol.

Simple symbols such as the Christian cross or the Nazi swastika have a known power. Jewish symbols such as the Star of David or the Menorah have a power, but cannot solicit the necessary passion to enliven them. Kabbalistic symbols such as the Tree of the Sefirot or certain Holy Names, while having tremendous power, also require tremendous amounts of academic knowledge in order for one to understand them and unleash their inner passion. This makes Kabbalistic symbols too complicated for the masses, thus their complexity weakens them.

There is however, another way we can approach Kabbalistic power symbols. We can extract very complicated meanings and put them into newer, simpler forms. We can extract the tremendous power of the Kabbalistic holy Names and symbols and present them in modern, simple and still secret forms, knowable only to those who wish to be so initiated into their secrets. However, these new symbols must reflect the proper and true nature of the sublime truths that they represent in order for them to serve as actual sources of power.

Most students of Kabbalah today only know the teachings of the theoretical schools. As such, they have no emotional connection to anything and can therefore never comprehend the potent emotional archetypal nature of symbols. The Kabbalistic theorists, therefore, never generate such power symbols. To say it simply, while they have a great academic understanding of Kabbalistic concepts, the teachers of the theoretical schools of Kabbalah do not teach their students anything about the actual workings of the inner mind. As such, everything they touch only impacts the surface of things and can never touch the depths of a thing.

I have used the age-old teachings of the prophetic schools of Kabbalah to create some new forms of Torah/Kabbalah power symbols. In our coming lessons; I plan to share with you two of these new power symbols and their basic significance. They are the secrets of 167 and 250. They are much more than mere Gematria (numerology). Their shapes and colors all represent many things.

Chapter 5

◄O►

Union with Heaven: The Symbol of the LAMP 250

T he human species is a composite organism. We are
made up of many parts, not all of which are indigenous
to our Earth. Our minds, both individually and collectively
originate from another dimension where life is very different
from how we know it here. The human mind, or as others call
it, the soul (Neshama), is not an organic physical component
of our bodies, therefore it is not subject to physical law or
what we call the natural order. Of course there is an order,
a rule of law that operates in the realm of mind, yet that
dimension follows its own rules.

Although the dimension of mind is foreign to our physical
space, it is not foreign to our humanity, because we spend a
good deal of our time in that alternate dimension. Every time
we close our eyes to imagine, sleep and dream, we enter into
a realm of thought that can take us to alternate, but actual,
places in space and time. Our imagination can become so
real that it can overcome our physical circumstances. This is

how mind control and hypnosis function. One can train the mind to believe that one is relaxing on a warm sunny beach somewhere in the South Pacific and totally lose awareness of the fact that one is instead in the dentist's office undergoing root canal work. The power of the mind is so strong that through one's imagination one can totally negate the awareness of one's actual physical surroundings along with any stimulations being produced on the body there.

Once in such a state, one's imagination can become so real that in essence one's reality becomes that new place. Under such circumstances, life here on Earth ceases. In such a case, we would find the dead body of the individual, with the death being attributed to either a heart attack or unknown causes. The Talmud discusses a number of these incidents and we have also seen them in modern times. Do not underestimate the power of the human mind to control both life and death.

The power of the mind is strong from both ends, both from the conscious side working in and the unconscious side working out. However, the two opposites work in different directions and speak entirely different languages. One who learns the operational language of the unconscious can, in essence, program oneself with powerful mental messages that can be activated and enacted with a simple mental image.

The unconscious mind does not operate within the context of rational verbal communication. The unconscious mind thinks and communicates in accordance to its original manner outside of our space-time continuum. The unconscious speaks to our conscious selves in the same language that infants use to communicate with the outside world prior to their developing the ability to communicate rationally and verbally. The inner mind communicates with our conscious selves with a series of archetypal images instead of with words. Our unconscious minds project imagery into the conscious mind, yet it uses a highly individualized set of pictorial images that can only be understood by the individual. This is the foundation of our human enjoyment of art.

Biblical prophecy was an art form. All Torah discussions about prophecy state clearly that no two prophets ever saw the same spiritual reality. This is because spiritual reality is not something that can be visually seen. It does not exist within our space-time continuum. It has no physical form as we understand them. Therefore, in order for our minds to grasp a form of formless reality we have to use an intermediary gap to bridge the difference between the two faculties of mind. As we say, both beauty and ugliness reside in the eye of the beholder.

We can easily tap into our unconscious reservoir of mental strength by approaching the unconscious mind in the language it speaks; this is the language of symbols and imagery. Therefore, the symbol is powerful and in a moment speaks a thousand words. Yet, in order for a symbol to be potent, it must be understood and the simpler the better. The unconscious mind does not need, desire or appreciate academic complications. Simplicity is always best.

Many forms of art, however detailed and complicated still manage to project an impression, one that is felt deep in the heart. Yet, however, deep each impression is felt, upon examination, each feeling and interpretation will be found to be unique to each individual. Imagery content is not understood by the unconscious mind with academic recognition. It is understood intuitively and actually felt emotionally. This is why there is a big connection between intuition and emotion. One leads to the other, often, but not always bypassing the rational cognitive intellect. The symbol speaks to the heart, the deepest place within the mind, where knowledge and passion meet. It is therefore vital that the symbols one chooses to embrace present something deep and dear to one's heart.

This also explains the highly subjective nature of visions. Have you ever noticed that anyone who has experienced any type of a vision always sees an image or an entity based upon their own cultural beliefs and pursuits? An individual from one religion never has a vision of an entity or icon from another. No Protestant has a vision of the Virgin Mary. No Jew has a vision of Mohammed. No Hindu has a vision of Eliyahu HaNavi. Each individual sees what their culture, religion and faith have trained them to see. This is even true of atheists. They see modern visions of extraterrestrials, whereas in ancient times, religious individuals had visions of demons.

We are left to ponder the question, what is going on here? Are there numerous "Heavens" each with their own set of gods, angels and demons, or is there only a single "Heavenly" reality and we all perceive it differently, each of us in accordance to our own preset mental constructs? Needless to say, the second answer is the correct one. The unconscious mind of the individual presents to the conscious mind the nonphysical reality of the dimension in which it interacts through the only medium that can comprehend it. This is through the academic intellectual and the subjective images of the individual conscious mind. The alternate reality is objective and real unto itself. However, due to its absolute different nature, the conscious mind knowing only construct physical realty can only perceive it in its own specific unique individual way. Therefore, no two prophets ever see the same spiritual vision. This is clear from the Bible when one compares the visions of Isaiah to Ezekiel.

This is all the more so true when one compares the visions of an individual from one culture to someone from another. They are not envisioning competitive realities in Heaven. They are seeing the same things, each within their own context. And it is the individual human mind that misunderstands this and creates the divisions that divide us and harm us.

True spiritual visionaries, from all walks of life, from every culture and religion, transcend their apparent differences, recognize the subjective nature of what they are seeing and delve into its essence, perceiving the true message, regardless of how it is culturally packaged. This is how the Biblical evil sorcerer, Bilaam was able to have a clear and true prophecy from G-d.

This is the secret of overcoming all occult forces and evil influences. All the perceived imageries of devils and demons, of evil and mayhem are nothing more than subjective mental constructs projected onto an individual in a style similar to hypnosis with the intent to trip up the individual and to get them to succumb to the images that their minds perceive. Bottom line, the occult operates by spreading fear, panic and mental illness. Judging by how such illnesses proliferate in our society today, the forces of the occult are growing by leaps and bounds.

It is clear from the Biblical Book of Daniel that even the Watcher Angels punish wanton human beings in this same way by creating the mental circumstances that lead to psychiatric illness. Angels (and other entities) attack human beings by projecting into the unconscious mind all types of frightening imagery, fears and nightmares until the mind cannot take it any longer and goes insane, not being able to tell the difference between the outside physical reality and the internal bizarre images. This is the spiritual reason underlying schizophrenia.

This is exactly how the Book of Daniel describes how the angels punished King Nebuchadnezzar. They struck his mind and he went insane. This is the same way angels operate today and the same way how occult practitioners attack their victims. Everything works through the unconscious mind and how unconscious content is perceived by the conscious rational side of the mind that deals with life in this physical world.

Protect the mind and one stays secure. There is no greater protection for the mind than the source of the mind. This, of course, is the Creator. This explains why everyone, regardless of our religious origins, that calls upon G-d the Creator always receives renewed strength, regardless of one's cultural affiliations. This too is spoken of in the Bible in a prophecy given to Malakhi. G-d looks to the heart, not to the mistakes of the intellect. Therefore, power symbols that represent archetypal spiritual imagery that can be embraced by all and not just a few have great strength. Their unique use of colors and numbers can have a remarkable affect.

I have developed one such symbol that I will introduce to you now. It has multiple meanings, the basics of which I can explain here, but their deeper meanings I will leave for you to contemplate. The number 250 is special because of its Hebrew numerical significance. This number represents the LAMP of G-d. This number shines the Divine light. Yet, it does not do so merely because I say so. Rather, it is the LAMP because G-d is in it in a unique way. Let me explain.

We human beings are generally constructed of three basic parts. We have our minds, our hearts and our bodies. Each of these three areas operates in their own spheres of influence. Each of these therefore needs to become subservient to Heaven. How does one subordinate one's mind, one's heart and one's body to Heaven? The answer is by allowing the Source that rises up from within the unconscious mind to pour into the conscious mind and to influence each of our three parts. Remember, it is the unconscious mind that controls all three elements within us. Therefore, it is through the unconscious mind that they can be influenced.

The source of the unconscious mind is G-d. G-d's revealed holy Name in Torah is YKVK. Some call this Jehovah, others Yahweh. Neither of these pronunciations is accurate and no pronunciation of the Name is necessary. The power of the Name stands for itself. So powerful is the Name of G-d that the concept alone has tremendous power even without its form in the original Hebrew. G-d's Name is an art form.

The Name of G-d emanates from the realm of the unconscious. As such it is above intellect. Therefore, it is not subject to rational analysis and intellectual diagnosis. The holy Name therefore has no one pronunciation, for all pronunciations are included within it. The Name YKVK is the Power. It alone stands against all forces and it alone can conquer all foes. Therefore, when combined with other similar forces, we only strengthen the manifestation of its already limitless power. There are other names of G-d used throughout the Torah. Each of these Names has specific meanings and subjective applications. Certain Names are attributed to certain human functions and emanate and dominate these functions.

The holy Name Ehyeh, "I am what I am" spoken by G-d to Moses at the burning bush correlates to the realm of the mind. The holy Name Elohim, "G-d," used in Genesis, when G-d created the Heavens and the Earth, correlates to the heart. The holy Name Adonai, "my L-rd" used often by the prophets to refer to "my L-rd YKVK" correlates to the body.

We have three holy Names of G-d, Ehyeh, Elohim and Adonai; one each corresponding to head, heart and body. Each of these Names has their source in YKVK. Each of these Names receives their sustenance and support from YKVK. When YKVK is united with each of these Names, it imbues these Names with power and thereby fills the corresponding parts within us with the Divine power.

Unite YKVK with Ehyeh to strengthen the mind. Unite YKVK with Elohim to strengthen the heart. Unite YKVK with Adonai to strengthen the body. This process of strengthening is performed by a simple mental exercise of visualizing the Names and by joining them together. Remember, the unconscious mind is influenced by imagery. When we create a holy imagery within our minds, this creates an actual reality in the unconscious. That unconscious reality then comes back into us, in this case giving us instant intuitive power for our minds, hearts and bodies.

If one were to look at these holy Names numerically, we will find that in Hebrew numerology (Gematria) the Name Ehyeh equals 21, the name Elohim equals 86 and the Name Adonai equals 65. Now, we add YKVK which is equal to 26. Yet, we do not add the Name YKVK just once. No, we must unite it with all three Names. Therefore, we unite YKVK 26 with Ehyeh 21; we unite YKVK 26 with Elohim 86 and we unite YKVK 26 with Adonai 65. Together then we have 26, 21, 26, 86, 26 and 65. Together all six numbers add up to 250. This then is the LAMP of G-d.

The LAMP is formed by three specific forms of union. Therefore, when we visualize the number 250 we superimpose it over three concentric and overlapping circles. Each circle represents one of the three spheres that form the LAMP, these being mind, heart and body. The colors of each are distinct and represent a merging of the YKVK element with the individual elements of each sphere. Thus all three spheres are a combination of very specific colors to express the individual unions occurring in each sphere.

When one who understands the symbolism of 250 gazes upon its image, replete with all its colors and significances, one is actually at the unconscious level, calling for the active Presence of YKVK, the Creator, inviting "Him" into one's mind, one's heart and one's body. Therefore this simple number and its representative symbol becomes our tool for meditation, enabling us to call upon, merge with and be renewed by the power of Almighty G-d.

A simple number and three overlapping spheres is now a secret power symbol. It will be recognized by the unconscious mind as representing all the material I have just described. Regardless of what the conscious mind remembers or understands about it, the unconscious mind "has got the picture." It understands the image. Therefore, from now on, one wishing to gaze upon it, or wear it as a lapel pin (available through our KosherTorah.com website) can be enriched by its presence and well as recognize others who share the same beliefs and knowledge.

No one else will know what you know, no one else will understand. You will have an advantage to cultivate a strength, focus and power that they will not be able to comprehend. This is how sacred symbols operate. You are now empowered to speak the language of the angels, using the same form of communication as they do.

This is also the secret of the prophetic arts, the occult arts, the martial arts and all art in general. It flows from within you and has a life and energy all its own. Every artist will understand exactly what I am saying. Every non-artist will continue to be baffled. Just remember this; scientists Nicola Tesla and Albert Einstein were artists in the same way as were Rembrandt and DaVinci; in the same way as was the ancient Chinese military philosopher Sun Tzu and the warrior monks of Shaolin and in the same way as were the Biblical prophets Isaiah and Ezekiel, and the Rabbinic Sages, Rabbi Shimon Bar Yohai, the Ari'zal and the Ba'al Shem Tov. All these men, from divergent walks of life, all used their minds in similar fashion, as I have described herein. I have revealed much here and concealed even more. The artist reader will be able to extract what I am saying from what I am not.

Chapter 6

◄◦►
The Symbol "167 Forever!"

The conscious human mind is severely limited in scope. Our conscious minds operate best when they are focusing on only a single operation at a time. Granted, in today's business world multitasking is the chosen course of action. Yet, multitasking is by its very definition doomed to failure. Strong minds can indeed be trained to simultaneously observe different things and function in different ways, but none of it is actually simultaneous. We are always jumping from one thing to another. Our attention spans are extremely short. All this jumping does wear down the mind's ability to focus.

Ultimately no one can multitask with the same clarity and focus that they can when paying attention to a single project wholeheartedly. Compare human thought to a laser, when it is sharp and pointed it can cut through everything. When it is diffused and allowed to shine everywhere, it creates light, true, but it has lost its power of penetration. Our human consciousness was designed to be single focused. This is how it operates best. Everyone with a brain has experienced this, although those who are brainless will not accept it.

The unconscious mind, however, operates by a completely different set of rules of reality. Its natural orientation is multiple. The unconscious mind exists in a dimension not locked in by time and space. Its reservoir of comprehension far outshines the limited conscious mind. As such, what the unconscious comprehends in a fraction of a second, the conscious mind needs much time to be able to absorb.

From the point of view of the unconscious, the conscious mind is only a tiny speck of consciousness. It sees the conscious mind as being infinitesimally small. While we desire to consider that our conscious minds can encase the entire universe, this nothing more than arrogant illusion. Our conscious minds are but tiny specks of light encased in a body and world of darkness. Not that the body and world are inherently dark, because they most certainly are not. Rather, because our conscious minds have such an insignificant understanding of our world, all the more so, our own human flesh, everything around us appears dark, mysterious and dangerous.

Consciousness is the ultimate definition and gift of life. Life can be measured by how conscious something is. Our ancient Sages have taught that everything in the universe, even inanimate objects all have some semblance of consciousness.

Even entire planets themselves are said to be alive, self-aware and aware of the Presence of the Creator. It is through this menagerie of consciousness and awareness that we can be in touch with and communicate with everything in the universe. All we need to grasp is the common language.

The common language of the universe is not the subjective speech of any single race. Rather it is the universal message of consciousness. Through consciousness one can learn how to sense other things, to communicate with them and even to manipulate them.

In the Bible, we have a story told about Elijah the Prophet. He is told by Heaven to pray for rain, so he does. Yet, the manner of his prayers, as described is most unusual. He does not merely call out, "in the Name of G-d, let it rain!" and it rained. It most certainly did not. Elijah began to pray, stopped and asked his attendant if any rain clouds were forming. When told no, he went back to pray. Again, after a while, he stopped and asked his attendant, "Any rain clouds yet?" The attendant said he saw a very tiny one far away. Again, Elijah returns to pray, stops and asks the attendant for any sign of rain. The attendant says that this time the clouds are coming in. Again, Elijah returns to pray, and finally the rain starts to fall in buckets. This story reveals to us much about the nature and workings of the prophetic mind.

If G-d Himself were to send the rain, He certainly did not need the help or intervention of Elijah. Like in the story of creation, G-d could merely have said, "Let there be..." and there would be. Yet, this was not the case. The rain did not fall as did the parting of the Sea of Reeds. The rain was not brought about through the direct power of Heaven (although ultimately everything is from G-d). This time, the rain was brought by none other than Elijah himself. The prophet himself controlled the rain and brought it. This is clear from the above story, to those who have the consciousness to read it and understand it correctly.

Elijah was not merely praying to G-d asking Him to send rain. For if this were the case, G-d would have answered Elijah right away and rain would have miraculously fallen. G-d did not need to have an extended conversation with Elijah; Elijah did not have to convince G-d to send rain. All this type of thinking is primitive religious mythology. G-d is the one who told Elijah to pray for rain. Yet, it is the very nature of this type of praying that we fail to understand. Elijah was not merely asking Heaven to send the rain; Elijah himself was actually creating the rain and bringing it to his locale. Elijah's prayer was active prayer, not mere wishful expressions. Elijah did not speak words, he communicated with consciousness. He merged his own consciousness, with that of G-d and together then "spoke" to nature to combine all the necessary elements to create a rain storm.

Elijah went into his prophetic trance, through the use of many meditative techniques, some of which I am describing in this book. In his altered state, he bonded with the essence of G-d that is above the natural order and thus controls it. He then visualized in his mind, step by step, or as the Sefer Yetzirah would say, letter by letter, the formation of moisture. He communicated with the Earth, the air, the water itself and combined them as if they were clay in his hands. Yet, these things were in his mind. He combined these images in his mind and infused them with G-d's holy Name YKVK. This, in and of itself, should have worked, but as our Biblical story shows us, originally it was ineffective.

Elijah, as powerful as he was is still only human. His conscious mind was limited by his physical human faculties. He went through the entire mental procedure, concluding in his mind that the necessary combinations have been made and that his goal was accomplished. Yet, when he asked his attendant, where's the rain, there was none. So, back to the drawing board he went, repeating the mental process and doing it again, this time with deeper focus and greater mental power. Still, no rain came. So, he did it again and again, deeper and deeper until his inner vision of a torrential downpour finally came to fruition in outside physical reality. Elijah fist visualized the coming of the rain and only when his visualization was strong enough did it completely slip out of his mind and become manifest physical reality. This is the power of expanded consciousness to create as the Creator creates. Those trained and tested to wield this power are in Hebrew called a "Ba'al Shem Tov" (a master of the Good Name).

Knowing full well the extremely limited nature of human consciousness, Elijah had to go beyond it. He had to delve into the inner recesses of his mind where he could break free of the shackles that held his consciousness prison. He could use the common, universal language of imagery and speak with the forces of nature and they listened to him. Although G-d ultimately sent the rain, G-d used the faculty of the human mind and the will of one of His creations to execute His Divine Will. As it was with Elijah so can it be with us, otherwise we would have no need for the Bible to have recorded this episode.

Everything in the universe is interconnected. This is no mere statement of religion or philosophy; it is now a conclusion of the scientific "M Theory" of physics. It is through our interconnection that we can commune with all things in the universe, including the unconscious minds of other human beings.

We connect with the other consciousnesses in the universe by going beyond the limited attention span of our present scopes of consciousness shackled as it is to the sensorial stimulations of our physical world. We cannot commune with anything else in the universe all the while that we think everything else speaks our verbal languages.

Communication starts and ends with a different part of the mind. Accessing that part, therefore, brings us into the infancy stage of joining the greater universe.

Symbols, imagery, metaphors, music and art are all tools for the expansion, or should I say, the alteration of consciousness. The unconscious mind can communicate with a symbol, picture or image the entire complicated code of actual performance. As we know from human DNA, substructures can be extremely complicated with layers upon layers of structure and subtleties that we have only as yet grasped the surface.

Ultimately, our science will find that however deep they go and whatever discoveries that they make, there will always be more to discover and even deeper layers to expose. We will never reach the end. That is because there really is no end. The conscious mind through its scientific explorations that endeavor to make everything conscious and controllable has not yet learned the lesson of its own limitations and mortality.

The unconscious mind acts autonomously from the conscious mind. From the perspective of the unconscious, the conscious mind is nothing more than a tolerated speck of light. The unconscious mind tries to communicate with the conscious mind but finds the process extremely tedious because of the severely limited ability of the conscious mind to understand what it is the unconscious is saying. This is why our dreams and visions are often confusing, containing imagery and symbols that make no sense. One must be trained to penetrate these veils of illusion to grasp the underlying realities that they represent. Otherwise, every dream or vision is like an unread letter, or worse, a misread or misunderstood one. Only the properly trained mind, refined through exposure to music and art can possibly hope to transcend the severe limitations of rational intellectual consciousness.

The power of art and music to influence the mind is well known to the forces of the "Other Side." One need just look at the effect that certain types of modern music have had on the behavior of more than one generation of youths in western society. Then the album covers for music began to graphically display disturbing images of Satanism. What was once FELT and KNOWN to be wrong, slowly became to be accepted and embraced as being right. These influences are far from benign. This process we today call "brainwashing." It is used throughout the western world, specifically through its usage of the entertainment industry.

Television and movies at one time were mostly inspirational and entertaining, and then a new genre of so-called realism began. This introduced all forms of images of immorality and violence to the public. Correspondingly public moral decency and religious affiliations dropped drastically. One cannot view these phenomena and not see the connection between them.

The public media is the strongest tool of negative spiritual influence in modern society. Whether or not the individuals controlling the system do this with intent or not is a discussion best left for the conspiracy theorists. Just remember this, just because something is discussed within the arena of conspiracy theories does not necessarily make it untrue.

Just as the mind can be bombarded and influenced with imagery that can harm it, so too can it be influenced with imagery that can protect it and strengthen it. This is why we create holy symbols; those which are known by all and those known by only the few. The difference between them can be rather striking.

Well known images of holiness are often subject to attack by the dark forces. Their method of attack is to strip away from the holy symbol its awe and reverence. Therefore, if one wishes to attack the symbol of a religion, one attacks the religion; specifically the behavior of religious individuals is targeted. There is never a shortage of religious hypocrites. By exposing the immorality of isolated individuals, the forces of darkness create the image that the individual is bad because everything he stands for is equally bad.

Therefore, the terrible and harmful deception states that if a Christian, Muslim or Jew commits any kind of a bad deed, they did so specifically because Christianity, Islam and Judaism are themselves bad and are at fault. Needless to say, this idea and attitude is stupid, ridiculous and the height of arrogant foolishness. Yet, it is accepted almost all the time as truth. This follows the Nazi teaching that stated, "Tell big lies long enough and the majority will come to accept them as truth." This is nothing other than evil prejudice. This is one of the common forms used by the "Other Side" to cloud the minds of otherwise good individuals.

When well-known religious symbols are attacked they lose the unconscious force of their influence. The mind becomes filled with contradictions. On one hand the mind identifies the symbol with something holy and good. On the other hand, the symbol has come to represent hypocrisy and something bad. Not knowing how to interpret contradictory messages the mind simply withdraws any type of emotional empowerment from the symbol, leaving it bereft and powerless. This has already happened throughout the world.

Knowing well how symbols can be attacked and discredited many within the circles of Torah and authentic Kabbalah have long endeavored to keep certain symbols and their meanings secret. To this day they have succeeded with many. When a symbol remains a secret, the forces of the dark "Other Side" cannot attack it because they do not know what it means. They have nothing to throw at it. What they do instead is attack those who embrace the symbol, calling them cult members.

The negative image of cults is known to us all. However, just what is a real cult and whom we are taught to condemn as a cult or to attack for being cultish are very different things. Yet, we are convinced that certain groups are bad or cultish. We just FEEL it is so. We FEEL that whatever the truth may be, we STILL do not like them much. This is the power and influence of the dark forces within our very midst. This explains anti-Semitic, anti-Christian and anti-Islamic prejudices.

Secret symbols, known only to a few, stand the best chance for long term survival and also because of their shield of psychic protection generate a great reservoir of strength from the unconscious.

One such symbol that I have designed represents the proclamation of G-d's unity and Kingship. It is a simple symbol of a blue diamond emblazoned with the number 167 and beneath it the word "forever." The statement "167 forever" has a powerful personal meaning to me. It is a statement of my faith and my defiance in the face of secular atheistic attacks. When I see what I do on television and the movies, when I hear horrible things on the radio or read them on the internet; in the back of my mind I visualize the blue diamond and silently repeat to myself just for the moment "167 forever."

This number is simple to understand. Let me explain. The great statement of our Torah faith is that G-d is our L-rd and that G-d is One. This is the gist of the opening phrase of our Shema Yisrael prayer. We recite "Listen Israel, G-d is our L-rd, G-d is One" (Deut 6:4). Today, this cry is for the entire world to hear, not for Israel alone. The Hebrew words "Adonai Eloheynu, Adonai Ehad" (G-d is our L-rd and He is One) numerically equal 167. G-d is our L-rd and He is One, this we embrace and proclaim this "forever." This is the source of our strength.

Therefore, in our society where everything even remotely identified as having some Jewish element becomes subject to anti-Semitism, we extract the ancient call of faith from its ethnic origins and place it into a new and as yet fresh format. "167 Forever" is the call of faith and a proclamation that we serve Heaven. Some will condemn it as cultish, but we already know where that attitude comes from. Others will embrace it and allow the words of Torah to seep into their minds and consciousness circumventing all the subtly placed anti-Semitic innuendoes that modern society has placed on anything Jewish.

Our world is full of contaminating influences. It is about time we created some influences of protection to defend ourselves. Mind you, watch for the attacks of others. You will see that they will come. This only shows for sure how their minds are already subject to influences that they themselves do not know and certainly do not understand. Learn to stand apart or you will never realize when you have been absorbed into part of the crowd, i.e. *"the mindless masses."*

167
forever

Chapter 7

◄O►

Power Prayer

Understanding now the nature of the unconscious human mind to communicate with the language of symbols, we now can see why, at the conscious level, we are always drawn to perform symbolic rituals and the like. Whether it is to salute a flag or to dress or act in any certain way, we all surround ourselves with rituals of one sort or another.

Even in professional sports, we hear stories of athletes who will wear only a certain pair of socks, or adjust their gloves according to a precise procedure. When asked why they do this, they simply respond and say it's "lucky." Now, in reality there is no such thing as random luck. Nothing just happens haphazardly. Yet, when the athlete does perform his own little lucky ritual, he seems to perform a better job than if he forgot to do it. Why and how is this so? The answer has nothing to do with the ritual itself per se; rather it has everything to do with the faith that is imbued in the ritual.

Here we come to the crux of the matter. All our rituals are mere symbolisms. By themselves they are nothing more than mere meaningless acts. However, when the act is coupled with a belief system in the mind, then the ritual serves as a conduit for channeling a deep reservoir of unconscious energy into the conscious world (and into one's physical performance). The ritual therefore serves as a tool of mental focus and psychic channeling. This explains why all rituals when bereft of inner devotion, attachment and faith fail to perform anything. On the other hand, almost every ritual, when imbued with psychic content becomes alive and can serve as a strong source of influence. This is the underlying value of all religious rituals and the source of the fervor underlying all religious conflicts.

Religious rituals are fully charged with psychic elements. Many religious rituals are expressions of the archetypal truths of a culture or society. Yet, other rituals can tap into resources much deeper than subjective cultural expressions. Some rituals express the archetypes of the collective unconscious of all mankind. Others only express the archetypes of the racial subdivisions of specific groups and still others are meaningless rubbish. Everything depends upon their point of origin and the faith of the individual performing them.

In light of this, even the most powerful rituals become emasculated of all power when performed without sincere devotion and faith. On the other hand rubbish rituals, which inherently are a joke, can become very powerful, once they are used by one with faith and fervor to express his inner unconscious content. The great rule is everything revolves around faith. This is a sound psychic and psychological principle found in both the Bible (Habakkuk 2:4) and Talmud (Macot 24).

Faith is simply accepting the influence of the inner mind over the contradictory input coming from the outside world. Although we cannot change external physical reality, we can change how we chose to perceive it and interact with it. Just be careful that you do not allow yourself to slip off into a dangerous fantasy world of self-delusion that can leave you vulnerable to psychic and physical harm.

There is a popular philosophy today about how positive thinking can create any reality. One just has to think and wish for a certain reality to be and thus it will be. This is false, dangerous and inherently evil. We are not masters of external reality. We cannot visualize ourselves healthy, wealthy or wise. Those who believe they can are as deluded as if they were in a drug-induced stupor. One can desire all one wants, but mere desire does not create an alternative reality. Faith without action has no conduit through which to manifest, and manifestation is everything.

Manipulating the fabric of creation is indeed possible. Manipulating the minds of others is also possible. Yet, if one is standing on the railroad tracks with a speeding train moving straight for you, all the manipulations in the world will not save one from certain destruction. Wish all you want for the train to go away and all that will happen is that you will go away (die) and not the train.

Faith will dictate that you open your eyes, see the train barreling down on you, realize that it will kill you if you do not move and finally faith will get your "bottom" in high gear to get the heck out of the way. You can wish all you want for the train to dissolve. This is not faith; this is foolishness. There is a very finite limit to positive thinking. It is always coupled with the rational mind that is fully aware of the natural parameters of the surrounding circumstances.

Ultimately those who teach otherwise how all consciousness is subjective and reality is in the eye of the beholder are dangerous charlatans who themselves are masters of the dark spiritual forces, who use their power to trap the souls of others. Beware of all those who claim to know "the secret" and any other such nonsense.

Spiritual power operates by accessing the inner mind to influence and manipulate that which can be so affected. It does not deal with fantastical matters. Spiritual power is not a wishing game. It does not give over something for nothing. Spiritual power can only be operated by the strongest minds. Those who are weak and try to wield this power usually end up seriously harming themselves. Worse, they usually become targets for unscrupulous individuals who can wield dark spiritual powers successfully. Accessing and unleashing the powers of the inner mind must follow the natural order of things. One must not falsely believe that one can circumvent the rules of mental psychic operations.

In order to safeguard the individual and to properly focus the mind, elaborate rituals have been devised in each and every culture. It is important to realize the absolute subjective nature of racial rituals subject to an individual group. Members of one group cannot perform the rituals of another and expect to receive the same results that indigenous members receive from their own set of rituals. This is why, for example, many Rabbis have warned that for non-Jews to observe specific Jewish rituals of Halakha (Torah Law) that this can actually damage their souls. This also explains why, for example, Jews have chosen death over conversion, which would mean for them to adopt a new set of rituals foreign to their origins. To do so, would kill their souls, and their bodies would follow soon.

Rituals are the language of the inner mind, the soul and the very essence of a person. This is why we are all so symbolically and ritualistically inclined. Without ritual, the inner mind has no access to the conscious world. When this disconnection happens a part within us dies. In the secular world, bereft of all meaningful ritual, we see numerous individuals who sink into depression and cannot otherwise lead normal lives. This is because they have lost the language of communication with their own selves. As such, they are cut off, lost and set adrift. This also explains why ritualistic religions are enjoying a great revival. Orthodox Judaism and Islam, two very ritually oriented life styles are seeing large numbers coming to their doors. Unknowingly, what the souls are seeking is a way back into their lost individual selves.

Although many do embrace a ritual lifestyle foreign to their origins, they can still for the most part benefit from it because many of the expressions therein are universal and applicable to everyone. This is why many times conversions from one religion to the next often satisfy the convert. Yet, this change of psychic expression does not come without cost. For just as one embraces a form foreign to one's source, at the same time, one's original set of ritual expression becomes even more far removed. In order to justify the embrace of the new and the rejection of the old, many a convert become extremist. This is the case in every religion. The converts are the most zealous. This does not have to be a bad thing, but it often turns that way, if the convert cannot make inner reconciliation between where one is and where one once was.

Rituals of a generic form play a vital role in accessing the inner mind and the unleashing of its inner force. Rituals include practices such as prayers, specific body postures, and specific symbolic acts, each with their own significance and meaning.

Prayers to G-d are a well known thing. Every religion has its forms and versions. The ancient Merkava literature of prophetic origins, revealed that even the angels in Heaven pray and that their form of prayer is a specific liturgy. Following in the paths of angels, Judaism has constructed a ritual liturgy prayer service that reflects the spiritual ascent (or more proper to say "descent") into the inner recesses of the unconscious mind, thus allowing the participant the ability to transcend physical space-time and commune with the angels in the service of G-d.

Since the days of the Temple, Torah Sages have designed a special prayer referred to as the Shemona Esrei. This prayer was meant to be recited standing, similar to how the angels are portrayed standing before G-d's Throne. In time, this prayer became known as the "standing prayer," better known in Hebrew as the Amidah. To this day, the Amidah is the standard form of prayer recited by Torah-faithful Jews three times daily. It was called the Shemona Esrei, which means 18, because it was originally designed to contain eighteen specific prayers (which are now 19 for a reason I will not now discuss).

These specific eighteen prayers or blessings are not haphazard selections; rather, as revealed by the later Sages, they form a bridge for consciousness to travel through the inner dimensions and to manipulate powerful spiritual/ mental powers. The Talmud has long discussions about the different practices and laws concerning prayer and even its relationship to prophecy. Traditionally, prayer by Talmudic definition, is specifically the recitation of the Amidah. When this prayer was designed, it was not meant to be a mere recitation of words, indeed, it has long been debated whether or not one fulfills one's obligation with a mere recital of words devoid of their inner devotion and meaning.

The Amidah prayer was to be recited silently. Some said the prayer should be recited as loud as a whisper, but no louder; other held that even a whisper was too loud and that one's entire focus should be internal, with only one's lips moving, without the emanation of any sound. All these different opinions have validity and applications depending upon the spiritual level of the one praying and his or her ability to transcend the outside world and penetrate to the deeper essences.

The Talmud records that in ancient days, the masters would meditate for an entire hour prior to their reciting the Amidah and then meditate for an entire hour afterwards as well. This was done three times a day for a total of nine hours in meditation and prayer. The Talmud records that this was the ritual practice that led one to the doorways of prophecy. One achieving such a level was truly a master of spiritual forces and could easily wield them in defense against the dark arts and their attacks. The Talmud is full of such encounters.

Today, Torah faithful Jews recite the Amidah three times daily. Most are unaware of the prophetic nature associated with the prayer. Most can never hope to achieve any level even close to prophecy. This is because most today only recite the words and have absolutely no idea about the meditations associated with those words. The power therefore lies dormant within their very speech. Although numerous Kabbalistic prayer books are available today outlining the meditations for the Amidah few ever study them, even fewer understand them and even fewer than this ever grasp the power and wield the great "sword of Moses."

Non-Jews cannot pray the Amidah prayer. The prayer requires that the one who recites it be connected to the racial subdivision of the collective unconscious of the prayer's formatters. Granted, foreign souls can be grafted in through proper conversions. Yet, I must emphasize here the word PROPER. Unless one completely embraces one's new psyche, one never really embraces it at all. This is why all conversions to Judaism that do not entail a full commitment to live a life following Torah Law and devoted to Torah study are not conversions at all. Conversion must happen at the psychic level before it can happen in the physical world.

The Sages say that prayer is one of the greatest and strongest things in the world. Prayer works because fundamentally it is the surrender of the lower self to a higher power. The higher power that one taps into before contact with G-d is contact with one's own inner reservoir of psychic strength. This is why prayer works for everyone regardless of their religion.

Never underestimate the power of prayer, especially those that contain what we call holy Names. Holy Names are symbols of power recognized by the unconscious mind. When we recite them we are activating awareness in the unconscious that opens a flow of psychic energy to the conscious self.

Such prayers create around the sincere soul a barrier of psychic protection that is not easily penetrated by the forces that seek to cause harm. On the other hand, those who try to use prayer to create for themselves such spiritual protection, but at the same time are seeking to maliciously harm others, cause the opposite to happen. Instead of calling upon unconscious resources for self protection enabling them to attack and harm others, the collective unconscious recognizes the malicious intent of the conscious self and seeks to subvert it. Indeed, the unconscious mind of the evil-doer is his own undoing.

The first of the many rituals used in prophetic incantations and also by the practitioners of the dark "Other Side" is prayer. To whom prayers are directed depends upon which higher power one wishes to connect with. In Torah tradition any prayers addressed to anyone other than to G-d the Creator is considered strange and foreign activity, a practice inherently unnatural to the human race. Such strange activity in Hebrew is called Avodah Zara (strange service) and is the traditional Hebrew term for idolatry.

Prayer rituals within the context of traditional prayer services or those recited in private or small gatherings can have a tremendous affect to safeguard one against negative psychic attack. Yet, prayer must be offered in sincerity. Prayer must come from the heart, the deepest essence of human desire. These are the prayers that are "heard in Heaven." When we perform any activity we should first devote it to G-d. We do this by reciting a small and simple proclamation. "For the sake of the unity of the Holy One, blessed be He, in love and awe, behold I am about to perform this action. Behold I do this for the sake of Heaven. May my actions be pleasing and acceptable in the Eyes of G-d."

This can be recited prior to anything and everything; yet it must be done with sincerity and meaning and not just a mere recitation of words. One's intent means everything. One's mere recitation of empty powerless words means nothing.

Another powerful set of ritual prayers are the Book of Psalms. These powerful words, many written by King David have a very soothing affect upon one's mind and soul. One in need of any type of emotional support should read Psalms regularly.

The more one is focused on G-d in one's daily life the greater is one's barrier of protection against attack from the dark forces of the "Other Side." Remember, the dark "Other Side" seeks to attack the unconscious mind with images and impressions of fear and worry. One who trusts in G-d on the other hand has no room for such fears and worry. If they were to come, one with faith in G-d recites prayers or reads Psalms to calm his or her nervous soul. In this way, the power within becomes manifest.

One's inner self in its unique dimensional plane, knows the way to "the Divine Throne." It makes the connection. One has to surrender not only the conscious mind but also conscious desire in order for the Higher Force to manifest. One's own personal desires are a hindrance preventing the inner Higher Force from materializing. Thus in prayer, we always recite, "not my will, but Your Will be done."

The dark "Other Side" occult practitioner instead wishes to express his or her own self over the minds of others. This is a form of attack and enslavement. Those equally trained in the proper good side usage of psychic/spiritual arts can easily defend themselves and strike severe blows to their enemies.

Biblical prophets were the greatest of these adepts. Yet, for simple people like us today, who do not cultivate the spiritual powers of the Biblical prophets, our best protection is the easiest of rituals. This is prayer, the surrender to G-d and to allow Him to fight our battles. While this is step one, there is much more that we can do to protect ourselves and at the same time draw closer to Heaven, thus in effect making ourselves spiritually stronger and more able to meet the onslaught of subtle psychic attacks we face daily.

We will continue our discussion in the coming lessons. For now, learn to pray. Everyone should read Psalms. If one is Jewish, then one should begin to recite the traditional Amidah. Open your heart to seek out and bond with Heaven. You may find the path arduous and long, but you will not find it disappointing. All that we will learn will revolve around this foundation. Everything we build from here on will be founded on the cornerstone of prayer.

Chapter 8

◄◦►

Life Force Energy
& Those Who Pursue It:
The Power of Prayer & Sacrifice

A ll spiritual power flows out from the unconscious mind into conscious reality. The unconscious mind taps into deep reserves within itself and by doing so also attracts the presence of other entities existing in those domains to which the mind can travel. All these forces touched by the mind express themselves in the language of the unconscious. This is why ritual behavior is a very potent spiritual force. Although at one level, rituals may well be symbolic, at another level they are actual conduits of communications between worlds.

One must understand a simple rule. The human mind operates according to a standard system. When one follows the natural path for the expansion of consciousness one will indeed tap into energy reserves yet unknown. These powers are completely OF the mind, but not limited to being exclusively IN the mind. One who develops the power of the mind can unleash these forces and use them consciously.

Whether such powers will be used for good or evil remains to be seen.

Indeed, when one reaches out through consciousness to attract other entities, one will naturally draw towards oneself those that are mutual and compatible. This is the law of magnetism. Therefore, a good individual will naturally attract good entities and an evil individual will naturally attract their like-kind.

The entities on the other side of consciousness are, mentally speaking, not all that different from us. There are those that are righteous and true and then there are those that are deceptive and manipulative. Even though one approaches the inner domain with a pure and open heart, unless one is also wise, savvy and suspicious, one can quickly and easily fall victim to a deceptive influence that appears good, but is in reality very evil.

We often see people who after a short time of dabbling with either prayer, religion or other rituals feel that they have been "contacted" by some "higher" force. Many believe that they have heard the "voice of G-d," others believe that they are talking to an angel or disembodied spirit. There may be some truth to a small number of these claims, yet the very vast majority of cases are nothing more than deceptive, possibly numinostic experiences.

Prayers and rituals are designed to unleash the inner reserves of mental powers. Yet, here is where psychology and psychic reality split ways. Psychology as a secular science has not yet acknowledged the reality of other entities experienced within, but not limited to the domain of the mind. Prayers and rituals not only open the inner mind they also allow for the calling upon and connection with other entities.

In religious terminology these other entities are given numerous types of names. Good entities are usually categorized together and called angels. Bad entities are similarly categorized and called demons. Such titles and categories are terribly restrictive and limited in scope. We human beings are certainly not the only intelligent entities in the universe. We are not even the only intelligent indigenous species here on Earth. In the physical plane we appear to be the highest evolved form of life. While this may be true, life does not cease to exist at the recognizable boundaries of physicality.

Life is consciousness. We have been taught that everything, in its own way, is conscious. Long ago our Sages have taught that even a single blade of grass has an angel standing over it making it grow. From their words we can understand the nature of some of these other entities. Just as we human beings have within us a mind, which is our higher self and our soul, so too does everything else in our world similarly have such an inner essence.

The inner essence of higher self within everything is, metaphorically speaking, its "angel." Practically speaking within everything there is its source of being, its life force energy, and its sense of purpose. This in essence is its consciousness or if you will, its soul, or angel. Through the power of the inner mind, we can tap into the inner dimensional plane underlying all life.

We can travel in the inner dimension through the power of mind and meet various other life force entities. Mind you, like their physical counterparts, not all are what we would define as benevolent or good. When we open our minds to travel in the inner plane we cannot transport ourselves by physical means. We cannot create a literal vehicle to get around in. In the inner dimension of mind, travel is accomplished through thought. Where you think is where you are at.

The speed of thought is instantaneous. Even modern research into particle physics has shown that the speed of thought is faster than the speed of light. This is because thought travels outside the limitation of physicality and is not hindered by mass. Yet, when traveling in a non-physical universe, how does one find one's bearings? How does one know where to go? This is where the law of magnetism takes effect. You will naturally draw to yourself and be drawn to that which is compatible to your present mental state.

In the inner realm, proximity is not defined by physical space. There is no such thing as physical space there. Proximity, therefore, is not defined by physical closeness, but rather by similarity. The more similar we are, the closer we are. The more different we are, the farther apart we are. This is the underlying cause why good and evil are so diametrically opposite. In a plane where similarity defines proximity, these two are as distant from one another as can possibly be. What is more, in that dimensional plane, the two have absolutely no chance to ever meet or interact. Their very natures keep them forever apart.

The only way then for opposites to meet and possibly influence one another is for them to exist within an entirely different dimensional plane allowing them access to one another all the while that they maintain their integrity. This is why we have a physical universe. Here, clothed in a physical body, dimensional opposites can cloak themselves and move about in accordance to a completely different set of rules. Here in physicality, absolute opposites such as good and evil can actually face one another and influence one another (for better or worse). In this way the stagnant, absolute reality of the inner plane can actually be influenced and even changed. This explains the importance of our physical universe. We are the bridge. We are the apex of the worlds. Here in our reality, all other realities can meet and change.

Our human souls come to Earth to embrace bodies and physicality so that we can learn, grow and mature. Some human souls are inherently evil. They can come here to learn to be good. Some human souls are inherently stupid and naïve. They can come here to learn to be smart and wise. Some human souls are inherently good. They come here to serve as teachers and role models. Yet, all souls, regardless of type or purpose, are subject to the opposite forces that would naturally seek to attract them. Just as good seeks out bad to change it, so too does bad seek out good to change it.

We live in a very crowded universe. There are various races of entities, each with their own agendas of operations. Human movement in the inner dimension of mind can be fraught with danger to the one unaware of the realities that wait there. Such unawareness is usually the result of one not knowing one's true inner self and what one actually draws to oneself, be it good or evil.

When one is truly good, one cannot but draw something good to one's side. When one is actually evil or acting with evil intent at the moment, one can do nothing other than attract evil to one's side. Now, here we have an interesting dichotomy. It is the nature of "good" to support, assist and build. It is the nature of evil to take for itself. Therefore, by nature this manifests as a lack of support, weakness, theft and outright murder (yes, one can be killed on the inner plane, just as one can be killed in the physical world).

The nature of evil is simply to take as much for itself as it can possibly acquire. When a physical entity reaches out into the mental plane seeking compatible mental entities, it naturally finds its companions. Yet, one must not look at this budding relationship from the viewpoint of the physical entity, but rather from the non-physical entity. We know that the physical entity seeks the non-physical to tap into its energy to use it for whatever purposes here in the physical plane. Yet, why would non-physical entities be interested in helping? What do they get out of it?

Non-physical entities cannot be bribed with physical valuables. However, there is one thing that is very valuable to them, the one thing that keeps both them and us alive. This is life-force energy, the true and only valuable commodity in the universe. These non-physical entities look upon life-force energy as a commodity worthy of acquisition. Therefore, when a physical speck of humanity calls out to them for their support in some (what is in their eyes) a foolish squabble, all they see is an opportunity to leverage their position to enable them to siphon off life-force energy from those who call upon them.

Life-force energy is in the blood. In Torah we call this energy Nefesh, in Chinese it is called Chi. It is the source of life itself. Without Nefesh (Chi) nothing can exist in this world. The amount of Nefesh defines the amount of power. Nefesh defines strength, dominion and authority of will. One with great Nefesh will always dominate. Therefore the acquisition of Nefesh is one of the great pursuits of life. It is the underlying cause for all wars, fought in both our physical universe and in the other dimensional plane of mind.

Nefesh is in the blood. Therefore blood becomes a very important, vital element in all contact with the inner plane. This is the underlying purpose of animal sacrifice. Long ago the Tabernacle and later Temple worship all revolved around blood sacrifice. There is solid reason for this. When one violated a law of Torah, one in essence stole Nefesh energy from either a person, the universe or ultimately from G-d Himself. Violating the Shabbat disturbs the natural flow of Nefesh. Eating non-kosher food causes Nefesh to flow in ways counterproductive. Sexual immorality causes Nefesh to become intertwined in ways it is not meant to operate. All these behaviors cause obstructions in the best course flow of natural Nefesh in G-d's creation.

One who therefore wastes the Nefesh has to restore it. Yet, how can one restore that which one has wasted? The answer is that one must give of one's own Nefesh to replace that which one wrongly used. Indeed, one can give up one's physical possessions. So we see how an individual can face a serious change of fortune and lose whatever wealth they have. They can also be affected in their bodies and suffer from a depletion of Nefesh energy, the resulting physical manifestation is illness. Yet, beyond all this, the ultimate source of Nefesh is blood. Life for life, blood for blood,

Nefesh for Nefesh. Theoretically, one should have to die to restore the Nefesh balance to equilibrium.

Now, if everyone were to die every time there was Nefesh imbalance, none of us would live very long. Therefore, Torah ordained for us a substitute. Animal sacrifices were allowed. In essence the animal died in our place. Its Nefesh energy was allowed to pay back our accounts. Now, in its own way, no animal Nefesh could ever possibly match the higher Nefesh of the human. The system is inherently imbalanced. Therefore, G-d subsidized the Nefesh restoral and realigned balanced with a healthy dosage of Heavenly grace and mercy. Without such a subsidy, no mere animal sacrifice would alone suffice.

How was Heavenly grace acquired? Simply, when the one who committed the improper act expressed true remorse for the behavior. When the evil soul changed and became good, this solicited a change in the law of attraction and therefore the repentant sinner attracted to him or herself an influence of good and benevolence instead of one of evil and selfishness.

As long as the good intent of the individual was present the animal sacrifices served their purpose in balancing the precious accounts of Nefesh equilibrium. If however a sacrifice was brought yet the inner intent was absent, if the individual did not make the necessary inner changes, to have sincere remorse, to actually change from evil to good, then the animal sacrifice did not perform its function. Such hypocritical sacrifices only served to strengthen the forces of evil. Selfish, hypocritical and evil intent only unleashed all that animal Nefesh into the forces magnetically drawn to it. This is why and how the Temple in Jerusalem became defiled and why G-d allowed it to be destroyed. Sacrifice was never just about the blood and the Nefesh; it was always about the mind and the inner domain of the individual.

Life-force is in the blood. That is why the price of involvement with entities from that domain is always paid for in blood. This is not only true of the forces of G-d, Heaven and the Temple; this is also true of the forces of the unholy. They too are sustained by blood and those who solicit their support always have to pay with blood. However, the forces of evil are usually not so willing to be compensated with mere animal Nefesh. They want the stronger, more refined human essence. This is why practitioners of the dark arts of the "Other Side" often shed their own blood and offer it to their demonic entities. More than this, the practitioners of these evil spiritual paths will often kidnap innocent victims to murder them, to use their blood in ritual ceremonies.

Violence and bloodshed is often found with practitioners of the dark arts of the "Other Side." Many recent mass murder/suicides have been performed by individuals trained in one of the many dark arts forms, with the specific intent of feeding their demon and then at death becoming part of the demonic brood. They were taught that doing so will give them great super-human powers. Only too late do they come to the realization that in death, rather than become a member of the demonic brood, they instead only become its slave. Such a fate is worse than death.

Blood sacrifice is still practiced by many dark arts forms, the most well known being voodoo and Santeria. These are usually of animal Nefesh, but there have been exceptions to this rule. Offering Nefesh brides to the entities on the other side to fulfill some feeble human fetish has been practiced throughout history, often even in the royal courts of Kings or in the secret closets of Presidents. It does have its power. It is real and it should very much be avoided.

Dealing with those entities who would accept Nefesh/ blood bribes is a very dangerous undertaking. Only the most unclean of entities would engage humans in this way and motivate them to do these things. These entities are the least to be trusted. They promise all kinds of physical rewards, some of which are rather easy to provide. It is easy to bend another person to your will. It is easy to manipulate another into a sexual encounter. These are the most sought after desires by wanton humans seeking the demonic forces for help. Again, stupid is as stupid does.

All these endeavors and communications with the lower base entities are forbidden behaviors because they cause a serious disturbance in the balance of Nefesh equilibrium. This type of activity is foreign work, the code phrase used in

Torah for idolatry. The penalty for these behaviors is simple measure for measure. One who messes with Nefesh loses his Nefesh, life for life. Dark Arts practitioners seldom come to a good end.

Today, the forces of good lack a Temple in Jerusalem to properly balance Nefesh flow here on Earth. The forces of evil are very happy with this arrangement for it allows them to gain more than their fair share. Politically speaking, this is why there is so much opposition to the existence to the State of Israel. As long as the State exists, no matter how secular and corrupt it can be, it can still change its ways, walk towards Torah, with the inevitable conclusion to rebuild the Holy Temple. This is why the nations of the world threaten world war if such an occurrence was seen coming.

For the entities behind world politicians, business is business; it's nothing personal; it's simply all about Nefesh wealth. He who has the Nefesh energy has the wealth. If Israel were to have it and return it to Heaven, then the forces here on Earth would not be able to continue to enjoy more than their fair share. Why should they want a demotion? Interestingly, but Messianic prophecies do state that when Mashiah comes, G-d will wage war against the angelic representatives of the nations, removing them from their dominion here on Earth. Now, we can understand why.

Our Sages have taught that for this period in which we live without a Temple we are in exile, physically for the Jews, spiritually for everybody. During this time, when no blood sacrifices can be offered to balance the equilibrium of the Nefesh, the only force still available to us is the state of inner remorse called repentance. Here now is the actual key to inner power.

As I mentioned above, blood sacrifice in the Temple was only a partial fix to the problem of Nefesh imbalance. Nefesh energy through the blood only provided a partial fix. The rest was brought about by Heaven through the expression of Divine grace. Now, with the blood sacrifice element gone, Divine grace can still be accessed in the same way it always was, through sincere remorse and a change of behavior. Instead of this being expressed today through blood sacrifice, it is expressed through words of prayer. Again, this explains why our Sages placed so much emphasis on prayer. Today, prayer alone is what seals the breach and balances Nefesh equilibrium.

The forces of evil are also aware of the power of prayer. Prayer simply is a communication, with what or with whom, depends upon the one initiating contact. Some pray to demons, some pray to make-believe entities. Some pray to real entities of power. Some pray directly to and only to G-d, the Creator. All prayers can be powerful. All prayers may be heard. All prayers may be answered, regardless to whom one addresses it. Therefore, the forces of evil, knowing well the power than can come down from Heaven through the prayers of the righteous seek to corrupt them and thereby make their inner frequencies out of alignment with Heaven. By doing so, the prayers of the righteous can only connect with what is truly inside themselves, thus compromising the purity of their prayers and thereby weakening those prayers.

The attacks by practitioners of the dark arts of the "Other Side" seek to maintain the status quo of illegal Nefesh imbalance. Spiritual mechanics explains how this operates. The forces of evil operate according to the same mechanical spiritual laws and principles as do holiness. Each serves its relative master. When the righteous use the power inherent within them, they can easily oppose and defeat the powers of the dark "Other Side." Knowing this the "Other Side" fights back with its most powerful weapon, corruption.

Corruption works better than fear to undermine the righteous. Corruption runs deeps. Unless it is rooted out using every means at our disposal, then we are fighting a war that we have already lost. Unless corruption is recognized for what it is and dealt with honesty and completely, it will forever dominate our destiny. It led to the destruction of the Temple in Jerusalem and has since then prevented its rebuilding.

Blood sacrifices will be restored in their time, but for right now, suffice it that we have Divine grace to fill the gaps. Sincere prayer is our weapon of choice. Rooting out our personal corruption is our task at hand. When we do our share, Heaven will match us in turn.

Chapter 9

◄○►

Mind Travel Through the Shadow Realm: Modern Forms of Demonic Activity & How To Defend Against Them

The power of a connection to G-d should never be underestimated. It can save an individual soul from countless negative encounters with other indigenous intelligent entities that share our Earth with us. Before we proceed to discuss other paths to expand consciousness, we must first delve into classical sources to explore who it is that also inhabits our Earth and what other non-indigenous entities one might encounter when pursuing expanded consciousness.

We are certainly not alone in our universe or upon our own Earth. We interact with these entities, often to our own harm. The practitioners of the Dark Arts often interact with these entities to harm others. We must understand the reality of these entities, the parameters of their power, the methods of their operations and their ultimate purpose in acquiescing to deal with human beings.

Long ago, using the Biblical metaphors found in Genesis, our Sages taught that G-d created a species of beings, just prior to the first cosmic Sabbath. When Sabbath began the process of creation ceased. This race of entities was left in a state of incompletion. They were not as fully formed as were the human beings created previously. This led to a racial animosity of these beings against their older brothers, humanity. This antagonism then has existed since the beginning. This race of entities are called Shedim, in English we call them demons and all activity associated with them demonic.

These entities were only "half" created. Our Sages taught that unlike human beings, which were created with four elements, fire, air, water and earth, the Shedim were created with only fire and air. Their appearance can be close to humans, yet they do not share with us the physical density that comes from being formed with certain composites of physical matter. Shedim do have actual bodies, like human beings they eat and drink, sexually procreate and eventually die. It is just that their bodies, if seen accurately, without any mental imagery applied to them to conceal their true form would look similar to ball lighting. This more ethereal form also enables them to be similar in some ways to higher forms known as angels, specifically that they can fly through the air, they can be invisible to the human eye and they can see the future for about thirty days in advance.

This original state of Shedim has been a constant source of disappointment for them. Ancient legends, from both Torah and other sources tell us how Shedim always wanted to be more corporeal and physical like human beings. Sharing as we do many characteristics, the Shedim realized that they could easily interact with human beings and essentially feed off of us. More than this, they came to realize that they could manipulate human thoughts causing sexual ejaculations in both men and women. They could somehow extract from the seed its life-force energy and somehow impregnate themselves. This gave birth to children who would share the characteristics of both parents, human and *shed*.

Such children could then use their *shed*-like powers to further mate with unsuspecting human beings, creating more offspring, which generation after generation would become more and more human. Such offspring would inherent all the physical traits of being human, whereas still maintain, what we could call a *shed* soul. We have been seeing more and more of these types here on Earth in recent decades. These are those human beings who perform such depraved acts of inhumanity, that we often question, "What kind of monsters are these?" Now, we know the answer.

Many a reader will not want to believe this information. Yet, reality exists regardless of whether or not it is self-evident or whether or not one believes it. One's personal beliefs cannot make a reality go away no matter how hard one tries. Shedim presence among us is real. It is ancient and its modern forms of manifestation are well known, however grossly misunderstand and mislabeled. In ancient days, *shed* activity of gathering seed was said to be caused by wandering spirits known as incubi. Today, we do not hear many stories of wandering incubi grabbing bodies in the middle of the night and causing ejaculations.

Today, we have literally millions of stories of other types of entities who come in the middle of the night and steal people from their beds. These poor souls are then thought to be transported to a space ship, where all types of medical and sexual experiments are performed on them. These experiences are all said to occur in the mental state between being awake and asleep. Then the person awakens in his bed, feeling drained and bizarre, knowing that something "out of this world" just occurred. In their ignorance, reinforced by the popular media, these people are led to believe that they were abducted by aliens from outer space. Yet, nothing could be further from the truth. These entities are the ancient shedim. They are doing what they have always been doing. It is just that now they are projecting into the minds of their victims modern images and thoughts, the likes of which easily deceive modern people.

Demonic activity is real. It is active and it is very dangerous. This species in many ways has advantages over mere humans and in many ways has many disadvantages. Their physical capabilities are at present greater than most of us. Only the best adepts trained in the mental/spiritual disciplines can enter the domains of these entities and not be harmed by them. In these realms, physical strength means nothing. Mental strength on the other hand means everything. Only one whose mind is strong and clear, who knows how to differentiate between good and evil, truth and falsehood can safely enter these domains and easily and quickly soar above them to more appropriate realms of mental communions.

Such higher realms, the true desire of the inner mind, are what we call the domain of the angels, archangels and spirits of the Sages. Yet, in order for the mind to travel to the higher planes it must first go through the lower ones and the lower planes are a naturally dangerous place for human souls to traverse. In the Biblical vision of Ezekiel, these domains were called the storm, the cloud and the fire. These are mental states designed to confuse the human mind inhibiting its advancement through the higher planes of consciousness. Even the Biblical record of Elijah in the cave speaks how he too saw a strong whirlwind and the like and how G-d was not in any of these. G-d was to be found only after all these levels had been dissipated. Then was the still, soft spoken Voice of Heaven heard within.

This process is experienced by us as a psychological phenomenon. This is the inner mental travel through what psychology calls the shadow domain of the unconscious. It naturally blocks the way to the Higher Self inner mind in the same way as the Biblical metaphor of the *"flaming sword that guards the way to the Tree of Life"* in the Garden of Eden. They are actually one and the same thing.

In the language of later Kabbalah, the shadow domain of the unconscious is called the Klipot, meaning husks or shells. This name helps us recognize the true nature of this domain. As a shell it always covers the inner domain and imitates its form. Many adepts have failed to distinguish between the shell and the true fruit within it. Mental imageries are confusing enough without outside forces creating further confusion. Yet, this is what they do. It is therefore incumbent upon us to learn how to thwart their designs and thwart them we can, if one follows the proper path of training and discipline. These alone are one's spiritual and mental protection against all types of malevolent forces that seek to enslave our minds.

Proper training and discipline begins with one's attachment to Heaven. It must be strong and it must be real. Mere academic knowledge or acknowledgment of religion has no force here. Cultural expressions of religious association and dress only serve to make one a greater target for spiritual attack. True spiritual strength does not come from one's academic acquisitions but rather through the development of one's moral character and one's inner sense of self control, discipline and sincerity.

IN OTHER WORDS, G-D IS TO BE FOUND IN ONE'S HEART, NOT IN ONE'S HEAD. NOT EMPHASIZING THIS ABOVE ALL OTHER RELIGIOUS TEACHINGS IS THE GREATEST FAILURE OF RELIGION TODAY.

Many attach to religion intellectually and culturally, whereas their hearts are still far away. Therefore, regardless of their appearance, such so-called religious individuals are as far away from G-d and true religion as one possibly can be. This is why this type of person often succumbs to all kinds of temptations to perform perversions and other forms of hypocritical non-religious behaviors.

True connection to G-d is the domain of the innermost recesses of the mind that we call the heart. This is the source of protection against any attack from shedim or adepts of the "Other Side." Indeed, many years ago, when I researched for my book entitled *"UFO's & Aliens in Light of Torah,"* I discovered a very interesting article in one of the UFO magazines, entitled, *"How To Stop An Alien Abduction."* To my surprise the author's research led him to state that if one feels the presence of any of these entities, one should immediately begin to sincerely pray to G-d, asking for His protection and if one can, to recite Psalms from the Bible. Apparently the entities seem to be repelled by prayers and especially by Biblical readings. Here is where I realized the true identity of this modern scourge.

If so-called aliens act like shedim and are repelled like shedim, then logic concludes they must be shedim. Whether or not they come from outer space or in a space ship is no longer a matter of importance. We recognize who they are and what agenda they have. We therefore defend ourselves accordingly just as we would defend our physical homes against thieves and other home invaders. If we were ever to spot a thief inside our homes, we would defend our property. We are not going to pause to ask, where does the thief come from, maybe he is an extraterrestrial? No, first we stop him, if possible we capture him, and only then do we interrogate him and extract from him pertinent information. Then he is handed over to the police and courts for prosecution.

As it is with human thieves so is it with shedim. If they enter our domains, and we are strong and holy enough to confront them, we definitely do so, capturing them. Throughout the centuries, including modern times we have numerous records of Sages being involved in such activities and they have written about such matters extensively. We have a body of literature that teaches us what they did and what we must do in order to secure our own safety.

Shedim have their own lives, societies and agendas. Just where they reside physically is a secret best left untold. Yet, throughout history we have recorded numerous encounters, not all of them being bad or evil. Our Sages even tell us that there is one group of shedim that acknowledge G-d and seek to serve him. These shedim are even said to be helpful to humanity. Others seek to entrap unsuspecting human minds by appearing in the forms of saints, holy people and angelic beings. Many an old fairy tale about the "forest peoples," elves, and the like may very well be based on actual *shed* populations. Legends from every culture around the world speak about the "earth spirits" or other "native spirits." Most of these are shedim.

Contacts between shedim and humans can continue for centuries. If one member of a family were to make contact or worse a pact with a *shed*, that relationship does not end with the death of the human being. Such a human soul is still bound by the pact and it (i.e., the pact), along with the *shed*, will follow such a soul from one reincarnation to the next, until the pact and relationship is severed. If for whatever reason the pact is severed, the usually angry *shed* attempts to reconnect with the closest available family member, siphoning off his or her life force. This can continue from generation to generation within a family. Usually a ceremony of release is required to break such a connection. These usually do not occur without great cost.

Since Biblical times, practitioners of the dark arts have approached shedim and requested their assistance in accomplishing specific tasks. Dark Arts practitioners are usually "hired guns." They accept money, gifts and bribes to contact the shedim and to arouse them to either help or hurt targeted individuals or entire societies. The mission determines the price the *shed* demands. Usually the price of *shed* acquiescence is the offering of blood. We have discussed the value of blood offerings in our previous essay.

I cannot emphasis enough that shedim have a racial hatred against humans. Their animosity is never-ending. When they look at us, all they see is a weakened race ready "for the slaughter." In their eyes, modern mankind is good for nothing other than food. Being that their source of nourishment is Nefesh life-force energy, they seek attachments to human beings in order to "milk" us of our life force. Indeed, in shedim eyes, humanity is nothing more than cattle, ready to be corralled, milked and slaughtered. This is why shedim activity always involves the use of sex, drugs and violence; any method that they can use to extricate their Nefesh source of nourishment, the better. Therefore no one can interact with shedim without being harmed by them unless they are specifically guarded by the holiness that comes to one through the embrace of G-d and Torah.

Legends about the shedim agenda are rather ominous. According to many ancient sources the shedim interbred with humans to become more and more like us specifically for the sake of infiltrating the human race for some ulterior devious purpose. Their intent is reported to be much more than to merely cause havoc in human society. According to the End Times legends of the Armilus/Anti-Christ, the main goal of the Shedim agenda is to place one of their own in political charge over all humanity, with the specific intent to keep mankind in perpetual psychological and spiritual bondage, similar to Pharaoh in ancient Egypt.

Today, stories abound about reptilian entities disguised as human beings in high places of power. Personally, I do not know of any real shedim/reptilian connection. However, the modern day conspiracy theories do relate a similar message that has been passed down through the ages through a number of different sources, Jewish and otherwise. The modern conspiracy theory, however, has taken a turn towards the anti-Semitic.

Many modern authors are stating outright that the evil race of alien demonic reptilians, dedicated to taking over the world are in league with the Jews. These anti-Semitic deceivers blame the Jews for all the world's problems and condemn the Jews for being demonic, reptilian and alien. As with most conspiracy theories, the ones pointing the finger are usually the ones behind the conspiracy. The ones who are blaming the Jews, using the Jews as scapegoats, do so to take suspicion away from themselves and to hide and cover their own nefarious tracks.

The truth of the matter is that the Jews and their Torah safeguard the one power that can protect humanity from the shedim influence. This power is the connection to G-d through His Torah. By attacking the Jews, the anti-Semites are actually doing the work of the shedim, arousing hatred and evil against the one source of holiness. This is the premier case of mind-twisting. The forces of evil have always been liars, since the days of the serpent in Eden. They endeavor to confuse people to such a point that they are willing to embrace evil, thinking it is good and to shun good, thinking it is evil. This is exactly what is happening today. This is why there is so much hatred in the world against the Jews, Torah and anything related to them. This is a clear sign of the shedim agenda amongst us.

Another popular form of shedim activity today is found in the spiritualist movement called New Age. There is a practice called channeling, where one endeavors to enter a meditative trance and then open one's consciousness to commune with and actually speak for some other entity that uses one's body, mind and mouth through which to communicate. This type of practice is ancient. We have record of its practice in many cultures from around the world.

The problem is that the entities contacted here are shedim. They can and do call themselves by various ethnic names and create elaborate stories about their age and origins (some of which may be true). They usually spin out a set of teachings or instructions for one or more to follow. Sometimes what they communicate sounds benign; sometimes it can even sound sublime and Heavenly. Yet, in every single case, the agenda of the entity is simply to get the human listeners attached to it, so that it can use the connection to siphon off their Nefesh energy, little by little, without attracting too much attention or alarm.

This ancient form of Dark Arts practice is practiced today by many who are deluded into believing that they are speaking with G-d or one of his angels or some other benevolent character. Yet, the real benevolent entities are not contacted in this way. The entire body of prophetic literature teaches us how true contact is made with benevolent sources. Those not privy to this information and dedicated to follow this arduous path of discipline can only contact something unholy, deceptive and manipulative.

Of course, the individual making contact will believe his or her contact is benign, special and good. That is the nature and expertise of *shed* deception. They know what they are doing. They always reinforce their message within the minds of their contacts, telling them how special they are and how no one else can possibly understand the "truth" as the contact does. The arrogant contact, wanting to believe him or herself special and unique falls for these lies and becomes permanently ensnared by them. Most Dark Arts adepts fall into this category. Mind you, once contact with the *shed* is sealed, the *shed* does guard its "territory" and seeks to attack anyone who tries to "rock his boat" and take away his source of food.

Shedim attack humans through the openings in our minds and emotions. When we experiment with drugs that affect the mind, we create openings that allow shedim to enter. They are attracted to individuals by the law of magnetic resonance. If someone opens their mind to being influenced, then no matter where they are, the *shed* can be drawn to them instantaneously. This is why drug addiction and alcoholism is so prevalent today. It all has a demonic component to it.

This is also correct with regards to sexual promiscuity. Whenever there is a sexual encounter, there is a release of Nefesh energy (through the ejaculation and semen); the *shed* is attracted to this free source of food. If the activity is safeguarded in holiness, the *shed* cannot touch it. If however, the activity is not properly safeguarded the *shed* has open access. It specifically intends to influence the minds of the individuals to become as sexually promiscuous and frivolous as possible. In this way, they create for themselves more and more free meals and at the same time more and more entrap the individual human in to following the *shed*'s subtle subconscious directives. This is the source of sexual addictions and perversions, pornography and the like so very prominent in our society today.

Any type of destructive, addictive behavior is a sure magnet to attract the attention of shedim. They are numerous. Indeed, our Sages have said that it is an act of mercy from G-d that we have not been given the eyes to see shedim, for we would go crazy seeing just how prevalent their presence is almost everywhere.

Let me remind you of one important fact. G-d created these beings. They themselves do not necessarily have to be bad. We practically provoke them by our wanton behaviors. When we do what we are supposed to do and act properly, the law of magnetic attraction naturally keeps the shedim away from our spheres of activity and influence. There is nothing to fear from these entities. Like us, they too are creations of G-d, and like I said above, some of them can even be good. Mind you, never let this be an excuse to seek contact with them. Like human beings, the bad ones always try to present themselves as the good ones. The good shedim do not seek human interaction anymore than good human beings seek out shedim. Both, good human beings and the good shedim are otherwise occupied doing what G-d originally intended for us to do. You will not come into contact with one of the good ones, period, so cast out of your mind any curiosity or desire to make such a contact.

Like I have said countless times in the past; guard your minds and now especially guard your bodies. Beware of any type of addictive self-destructive behavior. This includes over-eating and being obese. These also attract shedim. The disciplines outlined in Torah direct us how to live proper, decent, moral lives, built upon strong character, mental discipline and self control. These are the keys to protecting oneself from *shed* influence. Our modern society and culture subtly opens every gate imaginable to *shed* influence. We see all around us the destruction of our society because of the wanton behaviors of its members. This too is part of a greater *shed* agenda. We can choose to be part of the problem or part of the cure. There is a war going on here. You are not free to sit it out on the sidelines; thinking that you are already means that you have been lost to the dark "Other Side."

We are here on Earth to learn how to serve Heaven. We are here on Earth to learn how to be proper human beings. We do this by acting properly and transforming our inner selves, making them strong and angelic. This is why we are here. The shedim have their own agenda. Heaven will deal with them as a race and individually, similar to how Heaven will deal with us both as a race and individually. We are all on this Earth together. As long as we act as inferior entities, good only for food, then that is how the shedim will view us and treat us. We can make all the difference. As always, it is all up to us.

Chapter 10

◄o►

Earthbound Lost Souls

All entities, good or evil, benevolent or harmful, are contacted using the same mind-expansion techniques. Compare this, if you will, to the telephone. By itself, it is merely a tool. One who wishes to communicate with another simply picks up the phone and places the call. Who the caller ends up talking to depends upon who he called. We can use the telephone to call either good friends or bad enemies. We can even reach a wrong number. This is how it is with reaching out with our minds to connect with the minds of others, regardless of whether those others are angels, demons, or other human beings, living or dead. There is a single apparatus, using a single mental technology that works in all instances. Therefore, it is not that we call that makes a difference, it is to whom we call that makes a difference.

Non-human entities are not very accessible for human mental contact. Those humans who wish to make contact with them, for whatever reasons, must go through elaborate procedures just to merely open the lines of communication. Mind you, having an open line is no guarantee that one will achieve what one seeks. One might be heard by the other side, but that does not mean that they are listening. After all, these entities have "lives" of their own, with their own agendas, business and concerns. Communicating with human beings is not high up on their agendas.

There is however another form of entity that avails itself to human contact all the time. It is not right to say these entities are not human, because in a way they are, or maybe better to say, they were. I am referring to the earthbound lost souls of the unrighteous dead. These naked souls, as they are referred to in Kabbalistic literature, are more popularly known as Dybuks. They roam the Earth and actually seek out living humans with whom to communicate. Unfortunately, their desire to commune seeks only their own self interests.

Like shedim, these earthbound Dybuk souls also feed off of a living person's life-force Nefesh energy. Yet, unlike a *shed*, these earthbound Dybuk souls do not come and go, milking the human soul periodically. The earthbound Dybuk soul seeks a compatible living human host and takes up permanent residence. This is what we call a possession. In essence, what has come to be known as demonic possession rarely has any demonic element to it at all. Demonic possession is actually caused by an earthbound human Dybuk soul seeking another human receptacle through which it can continue to experience the physical pleasures of life. The term Dybuk actually means "clinging" or "bonded." The Dybuk seeks to implant itself into a new human host body and thus cling to it.

Such earth bound souls are essentially stuck here on Earth. They are not refined enough to enter into what we would call Heaven. Even Hell, also known as Gehinnom, does not accept them. According to Torah tradition, Gehinnom is a temporary place of refinement for fallen souls. After a soul is refined in Gehinnom it can then proceed to ascend into the lower Garden of Eden, our proverbial Heaven. Yet, often souls are so soiled that no manner of temporary refinement in Gehinnom will suffice. Therefore, they are left here on Earth to be hounded by a certain species of angels whose job it is to corral these lost souls and subject to them periods of rectification. For the lost souls, these periods are torments.

These souls lived and died wanting to be evil and now in death, there is nothing that has changed. They only crave to inhabit another human body through which they can continue their evil life-styles. Thus Heaven has ordained that these angels corral these lost souls, to protect innocent human beings and to help rectify these lost soul and to help them move along the path of spiritual evolution. Yet, in order for this to happen, these lost souls will many times find themselves being reincarnated into various forms of lower life forms, even including inanimate objects.

Seeking to flee their pursuers these souls long to find a compatible human host in which they can hide. When no human host can be found, often these souls will take up residence inside of an animal. These types of soul intrusions are most dangerous and harmful. They are often the cause of many illnesses, especially psychiatric ones. The procedure of removing these souls requires becoming involved in the rectifying of their blemishes and preparing them to surrender to the powers that be in order to process them into the experience of Gehinnom.

Mind you, not all souls are willing to undergo a process of this nature that for them is quite painful. In such circumstances where one has a very dangerous and stubborn soul refusing to exit the one that it is harming, stronger methods are used to exorcise it. These methods will no doubt free the possessed individual. However, unless that individual takes the necessary step to avoid similar openings, one can very easily become repossessed, if not by the same entity then by another.

Shedim seek the weak and open souls to siphon off their energy. The presence of a *shed* in one's life is experienced more as a sense of depression, weakness and a subtle nudge towards performing actions that provide greater access for the *shed* to the human's life force energy. A lost Dybuk soul on the other hand is much more blunt. Once it enters into its human host, it sets about right away to create a parallel personality. This is often the cause behind serious multiple personality disorders. The lost soul is much more pushy than is a *shed*. The two often can work together, both being fed by the human's weakness and dangerous behaviors.

Sheds and Dybuks are regularly fed through sexual intercourse and the capture of human seed, male and female. They are also easily fed by the shedding of blood, however small or large, violent or accidental. In order to create scenarios where the circumstances for feeding will occur, both the lost Dybuk soul and *shed* will motivate and push the human host to become involved with regular abuse of drugs and alcohol. Both these deaden the resolve of the mind of the human host, making him or her more and more open to influence from the siphoning entity.

While a *shed* pushes an individual only with moderation, a lost Dybuk soul will push the human host often to the point of death. The *shed* does not want to lose its source of nourishment, whereas the lost soul only wants more and more human stimulation. It therefore pushes the host to uncontrollable excesses of all type of sensorial experiences. This is the underlying cause of many addictions to sex, alcohol and drugs. No one can deny that these three behaviors are always overlapping. These types of behaviors lead the human host down the path to destruction and death.

Quitting, as any addict knows is extremely hard. Addicts often feel like they are being torn up from the insides. In a way, they actually are. The invading entity certainly does not want the host to stop behaving the way it wants to. Therefore, recurrences of dangerous behaviors are common without outside help. Generally speaking, twelve step programs that emphasis a relationship to G-d and religion have been successful in helping many people. It is the interaction with others who are similarly suffering that may give one the edge not to heed one's inner voices and the demons within that drive one to fall. Focus on the external often helps one to fight the irrational, emotionally felt compulsions arising from within.

Dark "Other Side" masters are trained to be aware of the presence of shedim and lost Dybuk souls. Dark "Other Side" masters use elaborate rituals to align with them, offering them what they want, more souls to siphon life from and more human hosts to push towards perdition. It is through these entities that dark "Other Side" masters gain access to the souls of others to cause them harm. The wise therefore, never allow an opening in their souls by becoming involved with behaviors that involve drugs, alcohol or forbidden sexuality. The truly wise stay far away from all these.

The arrogant, on the other hand, believe themselves strong enough to dabble just a little. Because they are strong, they think, they will not get hurt. It is these self same arrogant souls, who are so assured of their strengths that become the primary targets. Religious individuals especially who dabble ever so little with an occasional drink, or illicit intercourse can easily destroy their lives. We have seen numerous religious individuals from every religion who are, on the outside, meticulously righteous, yet who possess a secret craving and desire for some perversion. We have seen numerous religious leaders getting caught with drugs, prostitutes and the like. One cannot dabble and remain safe. This is simple and common sense. One who denies this and believes oneself stronger might as well paint a big red target sign on one's soul, because indeed, they become the greatest attraction for both Dybuks and shedim.

Once we are able to identify what sort of problem there is, we can then figure out the right solution. *Shed* attachment and earthbound Dybuk soul possession are two different things. They come from different sources, manifest in different ways and are also handled very differently. While the master dark "Other Side" occultist might instigate both phenomena, only a well-trained master of the holy arts can protect and heal inflicted souls.

Shedim are repulsed by holiness. Earthbound souls are repulsed by righteousness. Shedim cannot absorb the unadulterated light of holiness. Therefore, to negate their influence one should involve G-d and religion in every part of one's life. But this must be done with sincerity, not hypocritically. In a place where G-d resides, the *shed* cannot enter.

Earthbound Dybuk souls, on the other hand, are not repulsed by holiness. They could care less what one believes and, being human souls, they are not repulsed by the brilliant light of holiness. All they want is to experience the sensations of being back in flesh and blood. They nag and nag getting one to do something, however small, it can even be something permitted by religious law. Then, they push their host body to do the small thing over and over again, until it turns into something big, possibly something forbidden, always something dangerous. Earthbound souls feed off of human sensations. Therefore, righteous living that strictly moderates sensorial pleasures is a poison to these possessing entities.

The presence of a *shed* is experienced more like a feeling of depression or weakness. The presence of an earthbound Dybuk soul is experienced as if one has a separate voice talking in one's head. This does not mean that one is actually hearing inner audible voices, although this too does occur and is a sure sign of mental illness, which itself might be caused by a possessing soul. The inner voice of the earthbound soul always seeks to push one in the forbidden direction. Thus the inner conversation that goes on inside one's head might sound similar to this. "Why can't this be done?" "Maybe, just this once." "No one is watching." "No one will notice." "No one cares." When we rely upon mere human logic to decide our courses of action, we can justify the destruction of the world. Only one with a strong heart silences these inner voices by saying, "No, never, not a chance, period." This resolve does not make the inner voices any less, indeed, it might even make them feel stronger. Yet, in the long run, one with resolve will eventually wear down the inner voice, which will then proceed to exit and find more fertile territory for it to pursue its nefarious desires.

Possessions by earthbound Dybuk souls happen in a variety of degrees. Some can be very subtle and underwhelming to the point that one could be totally oblivious to their presence. These earthbound souls may not be the real malicious ones. They may simply be caught here and are looking for some place to hide from their tormentors. Mind you, those tormentors are not evil; they are angels sent by Heaven to gather up the earthbound souls, to take them "into the light."

Out of fear of losing the known pleasures of this world and fearing the unknown in the light, many souls simply run away. They keep running, with the angels pursuing them. Granted, this does not happen often, but it does happen often enough that it is a problem for unsuspecting living human beings. Only vice-free, righteous living protects one from becoming a magnetic target to attract such lost souls.

The really malicious earthbound Dybuk souls try to cause havoc in the lives of the ones they possess. In order to enter in, these malicious souls look for a psychological opening and often try to create one where none is found.

All they need is for someone to slip up even only once, however small, with something like getting drunk, allowing oneself to fly into a rage and anger, or getting involved or even becoming sympathetic to something that one knows one should stay far away from. However small an opening, the magnetic attraction draws the earthbound Dybuk souls like a big target sign saying, "Enter here."

Once in its new domain, the malicious earthbound soul tries very much to break the individual's personal resolve. The inner voice nags and nags to get the person to do horrible things. When the person can no longer resist the inner compulsions, the battle is won. The earthbound Dybuk soul does not care what the host body believes or does. It simply wants to know that it can take control at will to fulfill its own pleasures.

Many individuals suffer from this type of nefarious harmful ailment and yet are totally oblivious to it. They might think that they suffer from some type of psychological neurosis or even schizophrenia. These ailments are many times brought on by a Dybuk possession. This does not mean that mental illness does not exist also under other medical circumstances. For centuries, Sages have been very helpful in distinguishing which mental illness is organic and which is spiritually based. Yet, even when a proper diagnosis is made, convincing the individual so afflicted of the true reality is far from assured. Not everyone is willing to accept that they suffer from an organic malfunction of brain activity that needs to be treated with psychotropic medication. It is always more sensational to blame it on "another." Many want to believe themselves possessed in order to avoid the moral responsibility and consequences of their actions.

Then there are the radical secularists who are not willing to accept the existence of earthbound Dybuk souls and the possibility of an afflicted soul being a victim of Dybuk possessions. These radicals express opposition to everything spiritual and by doing so compound problems and make matters much worse. Their denials of spiritual reality do not make those realities any less real, regardless of their pomp denials and hiding behind their so-called sciences. In both cases, that of the spiritual person wanting to believe that their organic mental illness is spiritually based and the secularist who wants to deny all such realities, working for a doable healing is very difficult.

The secular world at large because of its adamant denial of anything spiritual or religious is the prime target for all shedim and earthbound Dybuk souls. Secularism has itself become a religion against G-d and against what it calls organized religion. Yet, it was these self-same organized religions that kept souls safe for centuries from attacks from both shedim and earthbound Dybuk souls. As long as one was sincere and truly devoted to Heaven, they generated the necessary fields of protection that kept them safe.

Now, with the secularist jihad, those walls of protection are being torn away. It is no wonder that as secularism rises we see correspondingly a rise in the use of drug, alcohol and sexual promiscuity. With a rise in these we also see a corresponding rise in widespread mental illness and a general sense of unhappiness and non-fulfillment in life in general. With all the clear signs proclaiming the truth, still the secularists, with religious devotion and fanaticism to their atheistic agenda, deny what is right in front of their eyes. They do not only make the problem worse; they are very much the greatest cause of the problem. When religion discusses how in the End Times there would be a worldwide society completely turned to evil and how that society would be ultimately destroyed, we can now see why.

In my opinion, reaching out to secularists is a waste of time. I prefer that they be left alone to face their inevitable destinies. I am not in the missionary business. I do not care to waste time trying to convince the blind to see. If the secularists wish to continue in their aimless lives and thereby become subject to all the sinister forces surrounding them, this is their choice, their free will, and I am all for one embracing the greatest human value of free will, to choose between good and evil. Every one of us will face the consequences of the choices we make, for better or for worse. This is true at the individual or at the national level.

Now, to address the issue of helping afflicted souls. Only those who believe can be helped. Those who doubt are beyond help. Faith in the power of G-d and in the strength of Heaven is essential here. One must believe that whatever has been made wrong, can indeed be made right. Heaven helps those who help themselves. No one is beyond help, not even a secularist. Yet, one must want help and be willing to sacrifice in order to receive it. Sacrifice is an essential tool here. One must be willing to surrender one's own will to Heaven, to adopt certain practices and life styles in order to create the appropriate safeguards to protect one's soul.

Above all, the greatest power to thwart both shedim and earthbound Dybuk souls is the gift of Divine grace. This can never be merited or earned. Grace is a gift from G-d. It is bestowed upon one just for the asking; yet the request must be sincere and the commitment to safeguard one's health must also be sincere. If Heaven intervenes to save one from a terrible fate and then one turns again to embrace dangerous behavior, even once, Heaven can remove its protection as easily as it was bestowed. Heaven is then not too agreeable to restore healing and protection to one who foolishly or weakly threw it away. Without protection and without any hope for further Divine intervention, such a soul will end up afflicted even worse than it was originally. We have seen this happen a number of times. We all have examples that we can give.

Do not underestimate the powers of the dark "Other Side." They work through subtle deception to trick you, to pump you up with pride, getting you to think that you are above these sorts of things and that you have the power and discipline to resist anything. Remember, "the bigger they come, the harder they fall." Arrogance and pride are a person's worst enemies. Humility and surrender before G-d are one's greatest allies.

Dark "Other Side" masters open up their victims by first making those victims believe that they are invulnerable to attack. "Other Side" masters use denial, mockery and even hypnotic-like stares to convince their victims that there is no such thing as the occult and that all its powers are nonsense. Once one believes that they are strong and that there is nothing to worry about, this is when the dark "Other Side" master sets in to do his or her dirty work. They can create all kinds of mental images and associate them with all types of things that attract shedim and earthbound Dybuk souls. Sooner or later the law of psychic magnetism takes effect and the unsuspecting arrogant fool becomes a target and a meal for a malevolent entity and the dark "Other Side" master receives his or her reward with the entity assisting the dark master in the petty request that he makes. This is how Santeria and Voodoo work and their popularity is on the rise in direct proportion to the rise of secularism.

The procedure for performing an exorcism is a rather involved matter. It would be best to discuss their details in a separate work. For now, let me share with you a prayer that each of us can recite. It is a prayer recited to release earthbound Dybuk souls from their torments. One who recites it regularly and with sincerity will show Heaven that one indeed should be bestowed with Heaven's grace. Mind you, Heavenly grace is not given to just anyone just for the asking. The theology that states G-d loves you and forgives your sins just for asking is more of a myth than a reality. Real work must be done in order to solicit the grace of Heaven. Like I said above, grace is free for the asking, but it all depends upon who is asking and how.

Taking care of oneself, protecting oneself from harm and always doing the right thing are a good way to be noticed by Heaven and earmarked for Divine grace. Taking care of others, providing for their needs and helping them in their hour of need is of even greater benefit. Praying for those who cannot help themselves is a powerful tool of protection for oneself. However, such prayer must be sincere for the sake of those for whom one prays.

If one prays just to seek favor, no favor will be given. One will instead receive scorn. One cannot deceive Heaven. One cannot hide from the forces of evil so prevalent in society today. One can however defend oneself and more than this help others to fight the good battle for their own safety and security. This is the definition of righteousness and it can save one from becoming a target of wandering earthbound Dybuk souls looking for a new home.

The Prayer for Lost Earthbound Souls

"May it be your Will L-rd our G-d and G-d of our ancestors, Father of mercy and forgiveness, He who shows mercy to all the worlds, may You show mercy to Your people and upon the souls and spirits of the wicked who are being judged in Gehinnom (Hell), and upon those who have been reincarnated into inanimate objects, vegetation, animals or humans and [especially] upon all the souls and spirits of the naked earthbound who are forced to roam from place to place, and who are pushed around from one suffering to another by the hands of their tormentor angels who throw them around like from the sling of a slingshot. Please include in this supplication the spirit and soul of... (if a specific soul is being addressed at the moment, then recite its name, so and so, son/daughter of so and so*).*

G-d, full of mercy, please show them Your grace, ease their rightful punishments, for You are the Master of mercy and forgiveness. Although they have sinned before You, intentionally and unintentionally, blemishing the worlds above and even the sources of their souls and spirits, there is still nothing that can stop You from rectifying their blemishes in your great mercy and pure grace. Wipe clean their slates of reckoning and cast all their sins into the depths of the sea. Hear our prayers. Blessed are You who hears the prayers of everyone."

Chapter 11

━◄◌►━

Protection from the Evil Eye and Evil Speech

While we have discussed the dangers facing human beings from non-human entities and from earthbound human souls, we must now discuss one of the most powerful psychic dangers in the hands of our fellow living human beings. While Dark Arts practitioners use all types of secret rituals to solicit their goals, regular everyday people commonly use a powerful psychic tool without even realizing that they are wielding it. Everyday people using this psychic tool of pernicious evil cause more harm to more individuals than all the dark "Other Side" adepts combined. The tool of evil that we must explore and understand is the common everyday usage of the Ayin HaRa, the evil eye.

The evil eye does not really have anything to do with the physical eye itself, although the physical eye may be used as its tool. The power of the evil eye rises from within the imagination. It can be projected upon its object, from a distance in both space and time. The evil eye is the force of malevolence and harm that comes forth from the unconscious mind.

The force of malevolence projects itself upon the image conceived in the mind. Through the mind the malevolent thought is projected onto the unaware victim. Again, I must emphasize, this is done daily by almost everyone and to almost everyone. It is done unconsciously and often unknowingly by the perpetrator and to the victim. Yet, regardless of the lack of conscious awareness the attack is still perpetrated and the harm most definitely done.

So prevalent and dangerous is the evil eye that our Sages have said that the evil eye is the prime cause of death, more than anything else. While one might succumb to accident or illness, the openings in one's soul that allowed these things to manifest were pried open by the evil eye that struck the person first.

At the level of the unconscious, all human minds are connected. As such, communication at the unconscious level from mind to mind is an ongoing process. We are always bombarded with the thoughts and impressions of others, be they from far or up close. What others think about us can affect us even if we do not know them or have never met them. All they have to do is think about us, or the image of one of us, seen anywhere, in any photo, still or video and instantaneously their projected thoughts are magnetically transferred through the dimension of mind directly to the object of their mental conceptions.

This mental process, we have discussed previously. This process of thought transference is the underlying foundation of all ESP. It is also the system how we transfer blessings and prayers; and of course, how we also transfer curses and the evil eye.

There really is not much of a difference between a curse and the evil eye. The major difference is that a curse is usually placed with awareness, that is, with words and some symbolic form of ceremony. The evil eye has the same effect as a formal curse, but without all the pomp and ceremony. Again, it is often transferred unconsciously, unbeknownst to both the one placing it and the one receiving it.

The evil eye can cause one all sorts of misfortune both in the immediate present and last far into the future. It can block and hinder one from having success in almost any of life's endeavors. The evil eye is like a malignant cancer. It must be removed with surgical accuracy in order for one to be cured and become well.

Usually one cannot in any way feel the placement of the evil eye. It does not strike with a bang. Its placement does hit one hard, but its presence is only detectable by what it causes. Therefore, by the time its malevolent power finds its first manifestation it might have already been there for a long time. Therefore, it is almost impossible to ascertain where the evil eye came from.

This is especially true with regard to anyone in the public eye, whose picture or image is prominently displayed. Once such an individual irks others, there will be an avalanche of evil eye upon them. This is why so many politicians and entertainment industry individuals suffer from so many personal problems, in their physical and/or mental health as well as in other areas of their lives. It is all due to the evil eye, projected on to them however unknowingly by countless numbers of malevolent wishes from the dark side of even otherwise good hearts. Mind you again, it is not only the rich and famous who suffer from this, but everyone.

There are two specific issues we must address. First we must learn what one can do to protect oneself from becoming an unknowing victim of the evil eye. Second, we can discuss ways to remove the evil eye upon one so infected.

To protect oneself from the evil eye is actually not a hard thing for the most part. Dark "Other Side" adepts and holy Sages alike are masters at avoiding the evil eye by the most simplest of methods. Remember what the evil eye is and how it is attracted. Remembering these precuationary measures one can easily take necessary steps to avoid it, if one is appropriately wise and disciplined enough to do what needs to be done.

The evil eye is attracted upon a person through that which one is most proud of. What one shows off to the world is the primary target that arouses jealousy and the evil eye. Let me give you a clear example.

Many years ago I was walking down a New York City street with a female associate. A very attractive woman passed by us walking in the opposite direction. Being single at the time and like most males of the species possessing a yetzer hara (evil inclination), her attractiveness caught my eye and I watched her as she passed to our left. Yet, as she passed I noticed something more stunning than the woman herself. I noticed that my female associate was staring at this woman, much more intently than I ever thought to. I understand when a man notices a woman, but why would one woman gaze at another? Then as the woman passed, my associate mumbled under her breath, "bitch," turned around and then we proceeded on our way as if nothing happened.

I was rather shocked by this response and turned to ask my associate, "Do you know this woman?" She replied that she never met her. Then I asked her in shock, why then would she call her such a horrible name. She looked at me and asked if I noticed how "put together" she appeared; such good make-up, accessories and poise. My associate said she makes other women, like herself, look bad in comparison. No sooner had she said these words that we heard a commotion behind us. Apparently someone was not looking when she was about to cross the street and walked right into a stopped bus. Like everyone else I paused to look. To my surprise, it was the attractive woman who just passed us by.

My associate, however unknowingly, placed the evil eye on this woman because of how "put together" she was. It had an almost immediate effect in that for whatever reason she alone of over a dozen people on that street corner did not see a rather large city bus and walked right into it. I did not stay to offer any medical assistance, there were plenty others to provide it. We continued to walk along and I learned a great lesson how the evil eye works in such overt form, in such a quick fashion and with such devastating consequences.

I do not believe that the attractive woman desired to attract the evil eye, but it was clear from her very attractive appearance that she did desire to attract attention, and that is exactly what she received, even though the attention was not the kind she solicited. This is a classic example of the evil eye and we can learn from this many things.

The evil eye is attracted to all those things that can be seen to the naked eye and are meant to be attractive. This includes one's appearance and one's possessions. These more than anything else can cause one serious harm. Now, looking good and having nice things, in and of themselves are not bad, however flaunting them is sure to attract unwanted and dangerous attention. The only way one protects oneself from such unwanted attention is to guard oneself by hiding from the eyes of others that which they have no business to see.

This is the underlying reason for modesty in both behavior and dress.

The magnetic law of attraction always works in both ways. It attracts what you want and what you do not want. No one can be immune from this, no matter how righteous or holy one is. Even one's righteousness or holiness, if prominently displayed can become a target for the evil eye. Many a public holy or righteous figure has suffered from numerous illnesses and mishaps all due to the evil eye.

One may rightly ask how come G-d does not protect His own from such evil occurrences. The answer is that G-d does indeed protect His own, but not by some magical power force, but rather by practical intelligent steps taken by the servants of Heaven themselves.

In ancient literature we are taught that the evil eye can only rest upon that which the physical eye can see. Hide something from sight and it is naturally protected. Pay attention here! There is always great wisdom in the act of concealment. One must be wise and learn how to conceal one's wealth, one's strengths and yes, even one's wisdom, all the more so, one's physical attractiveness. The simple act of concealment, keeping something under wraps, or under non-revealing clothing is the best protection against the evil eye and against many other dark "Other Side" devices.

There is an old saying, "loose lips sink ships." If you desire to keep something safe from attack, physical or psychic, you simply do not talk about it, AT ALL, to anyone, at any time, for any reason, period! This is always a great policy to follow throughout life. One should never randomly or haphazardly discuss any aspect about one's private life with anyone other than a completely tried and true associate. Our society today hemorrhages with information everywhere. There no longer exists the age-old concept of privacy. Idle chatter today is the norm where people gossip about the most intimate details about their lives and the private matters in the lives of others around them. How many people gossip about their mates sleeping or eating habits, how he or she is this way or that, for good or for bad? All this type of apparently idle chatter is cannon fodder for placing the evil eye. It causes so much damage that I cannot begin to relate it all.

Let me provide an example that I saw firsthand. Many years ago I was approached independently by two married couples seeking help to overcome problems with adultery. A member of one couple got involved with a member of the other couple and things got messier from there. One couple was newlyweds, married literally for just a few weeks. The other couple was married for years with children. Both couples were supposedly religious. The key between both couples was that the wives were lifelong friends, who shared all their secrets with one another. This is where "loose lips sink ships." Some secrets are not meant to be shared, especially amongst very close girl friends.

Soon after the marriage of the one couple, the two wives got together to discuss amongst other things, the one's honeymoon. The newlywed wife ranted and bragged about the sexual prowess of her new husband and related in graphic detail of how he pleasured her and brought her to the point of ecstasy. Without even realizing it, she set up her husband for a psychic attack.

After a few days, the unsuspecting newlywed husband was invited over to the house of his wife's best friend to supposedly help her with something that her own husband did not have time to address. Needless to say, this was a ruse. The newlywed husband was met by his wife's closest girlfriend who related back to him all the sordid details of his honeymoon and then said that his own wife wanted to share her joy with her girlfriend, but that in the decorum of the religious community in which they lived (not Jewish) it had to be done in this secret way. Knowing his newlywed wife truly did share everything with her life-long girl friend, and probably not being too resistant, acquiesced and gave the married woman an adulterous experience to remember.

The newlywed husband did not share this with his wife, nor did the married woman share this with her husband. Yet, when the two women got together again, "loose lips did sink ships." When the newlywed wife continued to brag, the married woman let slip two words. She simply said, "I know." Immediately, without having to say more the newlywed wife understood what had happed. She was furious; she felt betrayed and very much wanted revenge. Mind you, she was not angry with her best friend. She was angry with her husband. She was not a bit angry at her friend. She was angry that her husband kept this a secret from her.

Matters went from bad to worse, with both women now acting in ways with both husbands that need no explanation. Two pregnancies resulted. At the time of my involvement, the identities of both fathers were in question. The couples wanted to stay together and bury the past, but the husbands were having a hard time with this, whereas the two life-long friends wanted to put this all behind them. I was not involved in the resolution of this mess, but I have since come to realize that this type of behavior is certainly far from an isolated event.

When circumstances like this arise, the souls emanating into such children are derived from nefarious sources. This is how shedim and earth-bound souls find human hosts in which to incarnate.

The evil eye is not only passed on through what one sees, it is equally passed on through what one speaks. The evil eye is intimately connected with what we call evil speech (Lashon HaRa). Now, evil speech does not have to have malevolent intent. Any revelation of any information can be evil speech if it can be used or abused in any way to create a harmful outcome, as in the case above.

Not for naught has the military and intelligence community developed a term describing some information as being passed on only on a "need to know" basis. This is a tremendous idea that everyone should adopt in their own personal lives. No information, however apparently unimportant or irrelevant should be shared with anyone for any reason. Remember, "loose lips sink ships" and you never know how your most innocent intentions can be twisted and turned against you.

Malevolent intent is often fired up by jealousy. Jealousy is not always malicious in intent; however, it often turns malicious when one is willing to harm another just to get what one wants. Often one does not just want what the other has; one wants to have it and for the other not to have it. Thus jealousy also breeds selfishness. All these attributes are powerful magnetic attractors that draw shedim and earth-bound souls to cling to one, thus creating and causing more harm.

Protecting oneself from the evil eye does not require religious rituals. Rather, protection against the evil eye requires good common sense, strong moral values, and the ability to keep one's big mouth shut and for one to learn how to be private, even when completely, openly exposed. Being private in public is not as hard as it may sound. It simply requires one of the most praised religious traits. One must cultivate humility and make every effort not to do anything that will be exceptionally noticed by anyone.

Invisibility is the key. Anonymity is the key. Simplicity is the key. None of this means that one must be mediocre. On the contrary, one must become greatly exceptional. However, one's greatness must never be publicly exposed. One must not advertise one's prized possessions, be they physical, psychic or spiritual.

The greatest and most powerful of spiritual/psychic beings are the most simple and non-descript individuals. Dark "Other Side" masters know this truth very well. Authentic "Other Side" masters always seem to be regular everyday people. Those who dress up in pomp and ceremony are usually the charlatans and imposters. This is also true with regard to Rabbis and Kabbalists. The real powerful ones will pass you by on the street and you will never notice them. They know how to blend in. Even when you know who they are, they will always appear simple. True masters never embrace pomp and grandeur. Their might is in their actions and their actions are concealed from all prying eyes.

Living in simplicity, dressing modestly, speaking softly and acting normally; these are the great tools that deflect the evil eye and evil speech. The desire to be noticed and to stand out is one's worst enemy. Blending in, looking like everyone else and not advertising yourself is a safe course for all to follow. Targets stand out. That which is not noticeable is next to invisible. That which is invisible does not get noticed and therefore is never targeted to be hit. This common sense is one of the greatest secrets of psychic warfare. It is also one of the essential requirements for holiness.

Religious law has always dictated to us to guard what we say and to guard our eyes from gazing at dangerous images. The mind can only desire that which the eye has seen. The Ten Commandments themselves warn us against forbidden desires, also known as coveting. Coveting makes you crave that which another has. Such unfulfilled desires lead to the evil eye. This happens automatically and unconsciously. It cannot be avoided. As long as one's heart is impure so too will be one's thoughts and desires. Knowing well the frailty of the human heart, religious laws were instituted to protect us from ourselves.

Modest dress for both men and women save us from unwanted and unwelcome glaring stares. This is especially necessary for our children. Those who allow their children to dress like Hollywood whores place these kids in serious harm's way. I would go so far to call such permissiveness child abuse. Parents: guard your children; watch how they dress. Keep it simple and modest. Parents: watch your own behaviors. Your children will learn from you, not from what you say, but rather from what you do. If they observe that you place the evil eye upon others, they will learn from you to do the same. You will therefore become a partner in their crimes.

Even if you are very wealthy, this does not mean you have to flaunt your wealth with ridiculous superfluous spending. This is a sure way to draw the evil eye upon yourself. If you are attractive, you do not have to flaunt it to the world. Your attractiveness should be your special gift to your spouse and no other. Your spouse is your protection, not your source of harm. If you are wise or educationally gifted, do not flaunt your knowledge to the world. Academic jealousy strongly arouses the evil eye, especially in religious circles. This is why certain Sages grossly disrespect other Sages.

All these behaviors are outright evil in and of themselves. Worse than their being evil, they are also magnets to attract sinister shedim and earthbound souls. Ultimately a bad heart leads to bad behavior. Bad behavior leads to terrible outcomes. Terrible outcomes bring harm to many far and wide. This is how evil propagates. One is therefore either part of the problem or part of the cure.

The dark "Other Side" operates based upon the realities of human nature. The more we understand about ourselves, the better we will understand the realities of our world and the true nature of the evil within it and within ourselves. More than shedim and earthbound souls the greatest dangers we face come from ourselves. Dark "Other Side" masters know this well and manipulate our own weaknesses to their advantage.

Do not fear the dark "Other Side," those who master it or those entities that they can invoke. Rather be afraid of your own weaknesses and safeguard yourself against them by changing your behavior and your attitudes. I cannot over emphasize or repeat this point enough.

Chapter 12

◄O►

The Psychic Mechanic Operations of the Blessing & the Curse

The ultimate fate of every human being is certainly in Higher Hands than our own. This does not mean however that we have no influence over what happens to either ourselves or others. Through various means, such as through mental projections, but not limited to them, we can influence specific areas of our lives and the lives of others. These influences are what we can call blessings and curses.

One individual can certainly have a psychic influence upon another. As we learned in our previous lesson, the powers of the evil eye and evil speech are real and ever present. Yet, both of them usually are projected from one individual on to another because of some type of contact between the two. There is usually a spirit of jealousy involved when placing the evil eye or when speaking evil speech. These are forms of placing a curse, however, curses and their opposite, blessings, do not necessarily need to be placed through the medium of jealousy, or emotion of any kind.

While emotional expression is one of the easiest ways to project thoughts on to another, it is also one of the weakest ways. Thought projections projected through the higher realms of the unemotional mind are much more powerful and longer lasting. Their influence is more deeply felt and can last sometimes for one's entire life. This is true whether we speak about the positive influence of a blessing or the negative influence of a curse. Both can stand like clouds over one's head, one raining down showers of blessings and the other showers of misfortune. Both may be placed either by the Hand of Heaven or by the hand of man. Sometimes the two work in conjunction, sometimes even without the human being knowing that he is acting as Heaven's agent.

Blessings and curses both operate according to the same principles; therefore I will be addressing both of them simultaneously. It is important that we remember the mechanical nature of psychic processes so that we never forget that they are controllable. When we elevate psychic processes to the level of myth and superstition, we lose control of manipulating them, for either good or evil. When we understand a thing, we at least have a chance to analyze it and discover its operations. Not for naught are we human beings intensely curious creatures. Through our curiosity we can learn how to control the universe. When we abrogate our control and surrender it into the hands of unseen forces, we strip ourselves of our innate ability to help mold our environment. This contradicts the Divine plan for humanity.

Although we are always under the roaming eyes of the Watcher Angels and the Higher Hand of G-d, it is still the way of Heaven to enable us human beings to have great leeway in the way we live our lives. This is what we call "free will" and it very much is involved with our reception of either blessings or curses. The interaction of the seeming independent human mind and the controlling, guiding Hand of Heaven is an intricate web that I do not believe any human being has the power to accurately and comprehensively describe.

Although a full understanding of how Heaven works to control things may not be fully understandable, even within the context of our human free will, nevertheless, we should not delegate human fate to the realm of myth and superstition and mistakenly say, whatever Heaven wants will be. Although this is ultimately true, the attitude itself is passive and thwarts the natural state of aggressiveness that Heaven placed within the very essence of humanity. We are not meant to just sit back and let life unfold around us. We are not witnesses to circumstance; we are partners in its creation.

G-d helps those who help themselves. Although this saying is not in the Bible, it should have been, for its sentiments are surely what the Bible teaches. These simple words describe for us how a great portion of blessings and curses come our way. Although Heaven may very well intend for us to receive one thing, Heaven often allows us to receive something else, if and when we do not take the necessary steps to receive the right and proper things destined for us in the first place. This is how the Fate of Heaven and the free will of man interact. It is an intricate web, which no one can fully unravel.

Let me clearly state that it can be the preordained Will of Heaven that one receive certain blessings and those blessings not materialize. It can be the Will of Heaven for one to receive certain curses and have those curses nullified. While it is true that Heaven ordains, it is still us, humanity, that has a large say over what eventually befalls us. Our individual behavior plays a great role in deciding our individual fates. Ultimately, in the end, what we decide and the efforts we make to build or destroy are somehow always either complemented or challenged by Heaven. No human wisdom will ever fathom all this. Great power is in our hands and it is important that we realize this.

We must never allow there to be any room for myth and superstition in our minds and hearts. From the start, Heaven ordained that these be outlawed. Unfortunately for us, we often violate these laws and openly embrace fantasy, superstition and myth. We will often subscribe mystical powers to mediums, occult practitioners and even Sages and mystics, without ever acknowledging that the powers that these individuals might have, we too also have. Many will turn to an occult practitioner to place a curse; or to a Sage or Kabbalist to solicit a blessing; in both of these cases, the agent of evil or the servant of good will operate using the same mechanics, although working them in opposite directions.

Blessings and curses both operate through a single dimension, this being the human mind. Blessings and curses are influences, for good or for bad. These influences either open our eyes to recognize opportunities or close our eyes from seeing them. Blessings and curses manifest themselves within tangible realities. Attitudes and influences, by themselves are nothing; however, they tap into the conduit that transforms thought into action. Here is where they manifest their true power.

When one wants to act upon a thought or to manifest a certain reality, what one does and how one does it makes all the difference in the world with regarding how a thing materializes from the potential into the actual. When one can see clearly and acts with wisdom, allowing all appropriate emotions and mental clarities to each take their place, the outcome may be very much as one expects, or even better. However, when one does not allow all things to take their place and their proper turn, and instead acts impetuously, without wisdom, based upon emotions and without clarity of thought, then such a chaotic, creative process usually gives birth to chaos, instead of order. Therefore, let us ask, who created this chaos, Heaven or man? This is the power of blessing and curse in action.

It is also vital for us to realize that if we end up creating chaos, we do not have the recourse to turn to Heaven and demand that G-d clean up our messes. Heaven usually responds graciously yet firmly and tells us that it is our mess and thus our responsibility to clean up. If we would only decide to follow Heaven's counsel we can indeed clean up the mess and learn from our mistakes. However, this would require of us that we follow Heaven's instructions as outlined in Torah and the Bible. This would mean that we would have to act with discipline and become the best human beings that we can possibly become. Alas, for many this is a burden they are unwilling to carry. With impetuousness and selfishness many create chaos in their lives and are rarely willing to change their ways to create new opportunities for themselves. We thus find that many in the end are either a blessing or a curse unto themselves.

Granted, through their charms and spells dark "Other Side" practitioners can place a curse on someone. Depending on how powerful the practitioner is these influences might indeed be powerful. Yet, none of this should matter. No one should be frightened by this or express any concern over this whatsoever. Our world is full of indecent individuals who seek to take advantage of others to cause them harm. Business scams are everywhere. Just as we should be careful how we invest our money realizing that we can either gain or lose considerably based upon our investigations, so too is it with regard to psychic matters.

Curses are a mythological fear embraced by many, yet, these can be quickly and easily overcome by a mere change of attitude within the person. Yes, breaking a curse, even a powerful one starts with the person denouncing any negative influence having any power over him, and then acting upon this new-found faith. Mere verbal proclamations mean nothing if one still believes deep down that one is cursed and whatever one touches becomes tainted. It is this attitude that itself is the curse. It is the attitude that must change. The change of attitude is the breaking of the curse.

Of course, a change of attitude begins with a realignment of one's emotional core; but it must continue from here to manifest in a change of how a person looks at the world and interacts with it. Impetuousness must cease. Emotions and mental clarity must each be given their rightful places. Opportunities must be sought out carefully and analyzed with caution and care. One must learn how not to go either too fast or too slow with regard to anything. This is a learning process. No one ever gets it right from the start. Yet, if one's attitude is right, then one's actions based upon those attitudes will also be right. This is how Heaven showers down upon us its blessings. We have to believe; we have to have faith; and our faith has to be backed up with proper, rational and righteous action.

When we take control, then Heaven is in control. As funny and contradictory as this may sound, it is nonetheless true. Heaven only seeks our best interests and our good. These may not be how we interpret them or desire them to be. We should never be so arrogant to believe that Heaven wants for us what we want for ourselves. This blindness is surely a curse upon one's head.

Ultimately, one ends up with the chaos of one's own creation and has to live with it. Sometimes, one manages to do this; yet, most times, one's self created chaos ends up severely damaging one's soul, with results manifesting in ways of physical or mental health problems, as well as family and financial problems. All of these can come because one is under the power of a strong curse, one placed by and on oneself. Ultimately one causes oneself more harm than any dark "Other Side" practitioner would ever hope for. In the end, we must realize that we have the power within us, to either build or destroy; to either be a blessing or to be a curse.

When we believe that Heaven seeks our betterment and we act upon this without myth or superstition, we can dance through life, from one movement to the next, always finding that which Heaven has prepared for us. This is a life of blessing. It may provide for one great financial benefits and social status, or it may not. The blessing resides in the realization that money and power are not the sources of fulfillment in life. Indeed, the pursuit of wealth, prestige and power may be curses in themselves. Judging from the terrible things that have happened to those who pursue these things, their danger should be self evident.

Blessings and curses are matters of attitude. They usually never exist in absolute states. Each person often has some areas where he is blessed, and other areas where he may be cursed. Sometimes these parameters are ordained by the Hand of Heaven and sometimes not. In order to ascertain which is which, one must be willing to act in the proper course as described above. If one is doing everything right and still one is not successful in one's endeavors, then maybe one needs a change of course.

I have always said that I consider it a waste of time to knock on a locked door, when nobody is at home. Go to another door; knock on it. If necessary one will have to go from door to door, until one finds the right one that opens. And how does one know that it is the right door? Simply, if one is doing things the right way, then the right things will happen. This is Heaven's promise.

Fear is the mind-killer. Fear is what every curse is built upon. One must overcome fear with faith. Remember, the righteous live by faith. This is how the righteous are defined. Yet, their faith is not in foolishness and it is not in themselves. The wise know well their limitations, not in fear, but in fact. The wise operate within their successful parameters and are not tempted by foolishness to attempt that which is outside their scope of achievement.

Granted, this is only generally true; it is the normal course of action. There are however those unique times when the righteous must rise to the occasion and do great deeds above and beyond the ordinary. Yet, when these opportunities avail themselves, the righteous with faith in their hearts and with the courage of lions will move forwards, still with the proper balance of rationality and emotion; even though that mixture and balance may be different in this unusual state than it would be in a normal state.

Many times the individual is not strong enough personally to cultivate the inner strength to overcome adversity and to find the right opportunities in one's life. In such a circumstance when one does not believe in oneself, one does believe in the power of another. This is why many will seek out a Sage and Kabbalist to ask for their blessings. A true master understands the realms of the mind and the mental influences one embraces and those that can cling to one. The Master knows what rituals to perform that have an unconscious influence upon the person to shake loose the subconscious negative influence that disables one from seeing proper opportunity. A true master imbues the individual with faith. This is the cure for the evil eye, evil speech, curses and the like. There is no magic here, no mystical mumbo-jumbo. All we have is grounded mechanical psychic activity that works.

A true master can remove the negative influence because the person believes it so. Faith here is the operating tool, the master simply wields it. Believe in the master and he will teach you to believe in yourself. Believe in yourself and your will come to believe in Heaven. Heaven is always found within. The Way of Heaven is not found in the pursuit of the desires of the human heart, but rather in a deeper place. The Way of Heaven is found deep within, with that which brings true fulfillment.

Dark "Other Side" practitioners endeavor to cloud the minds of their victims, making them desire the pursuit of fleeting things. Such pursuits are worthless and therefore all energies invested therein are destined to be wasted. This is the curse and how it operates. The Sage and Kabbalist, on the other hand, seek to inspire one to pursue more grounded and stable goals. In psychology we know that there is a "teleological direction to psychological individuation." Simply, this means, that even psychology acknowledges without ever having to get G-d involved, that there is something deep inside of each of us that guides us to a preconceived destiny and fulfillment. Being in tune with this is the greatest of blessings. Being out of sync with this is the greatest of curses.

Heaven ordains for us what our portion in life is to be. It has imprinted this knowledge within our very cells and psyche. When we pursue what is ours, we will find that path of blessings open to us, always. When, however we allow ourselves to listen to other voices and confuse those voices with our own, then troubles soon begin.

The dark "Other Side" works because the human mind works. Understand the human mind and you will master both the dark "Other Side" and the forces of holiness. All these powers are before us. All of them reside within us. We do not need elaborate rituals to unleash them. Unfortunately, not everyone can embrace this truth. Many still need to believe in myth, superstition and ritual. So they will continue to practice their voodoo and indeed, it will have its effects; but only upon those who are at some level open to receiving the subconscious influence. Those with faith in Heaven are like an impenetrable wall. All the psychic influences of even the most powerful projections will bounce off the closed minds of the righteous who know better than to listen to doubt or to be tempted by fleeting and foolish things.

The blessing of the Sage and Kabbalist carries with it great power and influence, but only for those who believe. Belief is everything. It is the ultimate power of the mind. Rituals can only help focus the mind. Yet, not everyone needs help to focus. Acting and living upon simple faith is more powerful than almost every ritual.

The righteous live by their faith; simple, pure, unadulterated faith. The righteous simply do not believe in myth and superstition. Therefore, the curses of even the strongest of occult practitioners simply bounce off their simplicity and disbelief. Of course, their disbelief is as complete and pure as is their faith in Heaven and G-d. They are therefore immune to psychic attack.

As it is with the righteous, so can it be for us, all we need do is join their number. And this is how we receive the blessing, whatever our unique blessing is supposed to be, and this is how we remove a curse, regardless of its source or power.

Chapter 13

◄O►

Creating Safe Domains

In our previous lessons we have discussed the spiritual powers of the mind used for both good and evil, the existence and presence of non-human entities and how we can be harmed by those entities, disembodied human souls and ourselves. Now, we must proceed into the realms of psychic self-defense. Prayers and faith in G-d are strong tools, however, like any other individual tools; they must be used in unison with other tools so that a comprehensive defense can be constructed.

The mechanics of psychic self-defense can be easily understood once we provide the basics. However, as with everything else, unless theoretical knowledge is put into practice, it remains worthless. Knowledge by itself lacks strength; it needs action to make it work. In the coming chapters, we will proceed to discuss practical steps one must take to protect oneself from psychic attacks as well as to safeguard loved ones and surroundings.

The strongest tool for psychic protection is obviously the strengthening of the mind. Mental exercises are one tool used to strengthen the mind. However, internal work must always be coupled with external work. A clear mind requires a clear environment. It is imperative to understand the relationship between the inner and outer realities. One must cleanse one's physical environment and transform it into a sanctuary of protection.

The human soul can be attacked in numerous ways. The final point of entry is the mind. Protecting the mind, therefore, is paramount. However, there are many ways to penetrate the mind, some less obvious than others. Any type of meditation is clearly an alteration of consciousness and thereby doors into the mind are opened. Any usage of chemicals such as drugs and alcohol also compromise brain chemistry creating openings in the mind through which other forces can enter in. Even sexual activity creates subtle changes in brain chemistry also allowing for outside penetration. This is why all these types of behaviors are regulated under religious law.

Torah laws are not parochial, rather, they are protective. What started at Sinai has for millennia been continued by our Sages. Laws are made to protect the individual from forces unseen, forces rising from within and forces surrounding us on the outside. Anyone who violates the laws that safeguard the soul by compromising consciousness might as well paint a big red target sign on his chest and invite all malevolent entities to come and eat.

Laws that defend consciousness do not begin with the mind and certainly do not end there. The mind must be protected at both the conscious and unconscious levels. Even if one safeguards oneself from chemical alterations of the brain, one can still attract malevolent forces through means that one would never consider to be dangerous. The definition of danger is not subjective, subject to personal interpretation. Danger exists in certain things, places and behaviors regardless of whether or not one wishes to believe it or accept it. Those who see dangers and take precautions against them we call wise. Those who deny the dangers or belittle their intensities are what we call fools. In our sorrowful state of affairs, fools abound far more than the wise.

Items can emanate dangerous energies and so can certain ideas. To embrace or possess dangerous items is to invite trouble. To entertain or be sympathetic to dangerous ideas opens one's mind to becoming attached to the source from where those ideas originate. Never forget the law of magnetic attraction. Everything in creation has attached to it something similar to "sticky tentacles" of psychic energy. Once you draw close to or embrace something, it in turn embraces you. This is true whether we speak of forces that we define as good or evil. Religious law has long ago taught us to embrace the good and to shun what is evil. This was no mere proclamation of morals. This was a psychic warning, instructing us how to safeguard our souls.

Unless we recognize and take seriously the psychic nature of the world we live in, we can never properly defend ourselves against the numerous forces out there that seek our harm. We are all aware of physical dangers. Most take the necessary precautions to safeguard themselves from these. However, when it comes to psychic dangers, most are unaware of them and even fewer take the necessary precautions to safeguard themselves. Being that psychic dangers are not so clear and immanent, many choose to follow the desires of their hearts unconcerned about what consequences could possibly arise from their foolish behavior. While this applies to the greater dangers of chemical and physical abuse, it also applies to the more subtle dangers of psychological abuse and careless connections.

We are taught that everything in creation is imbued with energy. Everything in essence has a soul or life-force of its own. Everything, including inanimate objects has a spiritual component to it. Nothing in creation is without its source. Even whole planets are alive and think and are conscious of themselves and of their Creator. There really is an energy force that we can call "mother nature." It is conscious and personal. It is a creation and servant of Heaven as is each of our souls.

Each place on Earth therefore radiates life-force energy. Yet, as we have learned, life-force energy (nefesh) can be harnessed and manipulated by countless powers for either good or evil purposes. When a place on Earth is used to congeal an enormous amount of life-force energy and use this energy for good, to help and heal others, we call this a holy place. On the contrary, when such a huge amount of life-force (nefesh) energy is congealed in a place that brings harm and pain to others, this becomes an evil place.

People who reside in a place actually imbue their locality with an energy field compatible to them. Even after those original inhabitants are long gone, the residual effects of human behavior lives on long after the people who lived there. Even if the behavior is no longer practiced there or if the peoples who performed such good or evil have long gone, their positive or negative energies still congeal in that certain place and that place will for a long time remain to be a place of good or evil.

It takes a long time and tremendous effort to cleanse such places. Once, when the whole world was contaminated in such a way, G-d had to send a flood to cleanse it all, and to wipe out any memory of past existence. Not for naught is Atlantis but a fuzzy memory, without any hard evidence to validate its existence. It did indeed exist, our Sages have said so and they revealed that pre-flood societal behavior was so unnatural, that Heaven had no choice but to wipe them all out. Only Noah and his family survived.

Legends about the pre-flood days have survived. Once, the ancients even tried to revive the pre-flood technologies. Their plans were thwarted by Heaven at the Tower of Babel. These ancient Bible stories have a side to them that most reading them are unaware of. No story can be taken out of its context, especially not Bible stories. When we lose the context we lose the message. This is true of the Bible and of everything else. When we embrace a thing not knowing its psychic origins, we open ourselves up to the danger of becoming attached to the psychic tentacles that are attached to such items and ideas.

Did you ever walk into a place and get a bad feeling about it? Have you ever visited a place you've never seen before and just feel very frightened or uneasy about it? It is possible that you are unconsciously picking up on the "vibes" of the area. Of course, it could also mean that you have a vivid imagination and are open to suggestion and mental manipulation. Getting a feeling about a place can mean that you are either wise or a fool. Often, without knowing the person or the place it is hard to tell which is which.

Physical places or items can also be imbued with powerful life-force energy. These become what we call holy. Anyone who is religious has gone to special locations considered sacred by their religion. Because the individual is psychically connected to the beliefs of the numerous peoples who believe similarly and who have visited this place, their collective mental energy has imbued the place with a significant power; one that is usually only felt by most sympathetic believers.

Is the place itself special regardless of the beliefs of the people? Most often not, however there have been exceptions. The Temple Mount in Jerusalem is considered so sacred by all three religions connected to it that it has served as a source of contention between the three for centuries. There is no compromise simply because the religious beliefs of each of the three exclude the presence of the other two. When three fight for one, only one can win in the end. This is not the time or place to discuss Biblical prophecy. However, the contentiousness of the Temple Mount is due to its psychic nature. It is important to realize this underlying fact.

Life-force energy is the sole commodity of value in the universe. When there is a reservoir of it congealed in a space, then that space also becomes valuable real estate. Holy places, or for that matter, assumed holy places, all have the congealed mental energies of countless believers focused there. This combined mental energy has empowered the physical real estate and made it special. Even if centuries go by and the land lies uninhabited, the mental energy therein lies dormant along with the land.

If believers were to return to the location and revive the ancient beliefs and practices associated with it, this could lead to a complete reawakening of all the energy lying there dormant. The manifestation of such would be a wave of consciousness spreading around the world, touching the unconscious minds of each individual who would be in any way sympathetic of the rites and ways that have been revived from that place. Mind you, this is a mechanic operation. It happens because it is natural to happen this way.

This is the way the powers of the mind interact with behavioral rituals and physical locations. Together they combine and form a living entity, a spirit or force. This works for both forces of good and evil. This explains how religious or political movements can spread across the Earth in relative little time attracting fanatic loyalists, who have become possessed unconsciously by its message.

Where we go and where we live both play a large role in our psychic lives. No one can say that where they live is void of any energy, this is not so. Every place has an energy to it- every place! Every nation has its unique energy pattern as does every geographical area, city, neighborhood and house. These energy fields are generated by numerous sources.

There is first the indigenous spirit of the place, be it land, water, mountain or air. Some will call these the "earth spirits" and I can think of no reason to call them something other. These entities are mentioned in the Bible. These natural and indigenous spirits technically own the land or domain that they inhabit. They view human settlement in their domain as a very unwelcome invasion. Yet, in many areas, humans have established habitation for centuries. Sometimes these entities leave in protest, sometimes they stay in quiet and sometimes they demand compromise from the human invaders in forms of what we would call sacrifice.

Sacrifice, in ancient times, always took the form of blood offerings. In more modern times other forms have been substituted. Nonetheless, the indigenous entity demands a sort-of rent payment from the humans inhabiting its turf. Failure to appease the local spirit usually leads to said spirit causing all kinds of mischief and harm, or the fear of such. Either way, in the end, the human guest often pays his host with some sort of offering. Do not think for a minute this is ancient history of which I speak. This still goes on today very much, especially in the circles of Santeria, Voodoo, Wicca and all other occult schools that commune with the spirits.

Let me share with you now a personal story. Many years ago, in the days when I was free and able to take week-long hiking trips off-trail into uncharted areas of wilderness, I had a most unusual experience. I do not wish to identify where I was, let's just say I was in a heavily wooded area in the United States. I went off trail with only my compass and the sun to guide me. The land was not very steep so I was able to travel inland at a good pace, going further and further out into areas that I was certain very few had gone before. I spent the entire summer's day hiking. I am not certain how far off-trail I was but it was certainly a good number of miles. That night when I decided to pitch camp and rest, I found a clearing with a large flat rock formation. I chose this to be the best place to spend the night. Traveling light, knowing there was not going to be any rain, I did not pack a tent, but only a lean-to, sleeping bag and other items necessary to cook and eat. I had my dinner, kept a small safe fire going to keep the critters away, and rolled up in my very warm and comfy sleeping bag, falling into a well-deserved, deep sleep. But, I was not to sleep for long.

It was dark. I could not tell exactly what time it was or how long I had been sleeping. I was awakened by a sharp kick in my side with what felt like a pointed boot. I awoke with a startle, weapon in hand, yet what I saw shocked me into silence and stillness. I was surrounded by what must have been 20 to 30 little people, no more than three or four feet tall. They did not appear to be human midgets, but rather like small people, almost like the fabled hobbits from the writings of J.R. Tolkien. Although I had nothing to say, they sure did.

They were all very angry with me. They asked me why I was there and why I was invading their territory. I was in complete shock, I had never known beings like this existed or that they had claim to any territory. I said I was just a hiker going out into the wild to separate from mankind so that I could commune alone with my Creator. I certainly meant them no harm. Apparently, my answer must have had some effect on them, for after consulting with his associates the one who appeared to be the leader turned to me and said, "this is our land, and you humans are not allowed here, your kind has taken from us for a very long time and we have retreated here to be safe from you."

Of course, I asked who they were and begged them for more information, but my pleas only seemed to anger them. Realizing that they could do me harm in an instant I silenced my tongue from questions and took another course of action. Standing up, I respectfully bowed to them and said with honest remorse that I had not known that this place belonged to them. Had I known, I would never have violated it. I apologized and vowed to leave the next day destroying the path notes as I returned to make sure that not I or anyone else could ever return to that spot. They accepted my sincerity and apology but told me that they would not leave me all that night and that at the crack of dawn I had better make good on my promise. All that night I certainly did not sleep, I heard all types of strange noises and saw strange things, the likes of which I will not record. That morning at the crack of dawn, I fulfilled my promise and left, never to return.

I have often spoken to my students about my encounter in the forest with those whom I have come to call the "wee people." Like me, some have asked if it was all a dream. Whether or not it was a dream can always be argued. Just let me add this, over the years I had two students who themselves are avid hikers who after hearing my story sought to have an adventure of their own. Indeed, they did, both came back and said that they too experienced something in the off-trail woods at night. Maybe we were all dreaming; then again, maybe not. Maybe there really are "wee people" and maybe there are also a number of other entity types that roam both woods and cities.

All places of religious worship or spiritual interest have a "presence" to them. Torah law prohibits us from entering any place of idol worship. This is because of the magnetic law of attraction. Anyone entering into any of these places, even as a tourist will nonetheless be touched by the sticky psychic "presence" there. Mind you, idol worship exists in domains far outside the practice of religion. Any place or environment that caters towards hedonistic pleasures, which can lead to cerebral chemical alterations, that are conducive to psychic penetration, are equally places of idolatry as would be any type of shrine. In modern society the most predominant of these types of places that overflow with demonic and otherwise evil activity are the night clubs, bars and rock concerts. In these places all types of drug and alcohol abuse occur and sexual promiscuity runs rampant. Anyone going to any of these places will not leave unscathed. They should all be avoided like the plague, for indeed, like a plague, one's mere exposure to these places can cause one to become a target for malevolent occult activity.

Not only must one be careful as to where one allows oneself to go, one must also be careful as to what one allows oneself to bring into one's home. Remember, everything has a meaning and a context; everything has psychic tentacles attached to it. Whatever you bring into your home brings along with it everything that it is attached to. How many clueless home owners have brought items into their homes totally oblivious of the psychic chaos that it such items cause. When all of a sudden strange, bizarre or bad things start to happen in a home (apartment or whatever), one should question whether something new has been brought in that is disturbing the psychic energy of the place. That which appears seemingly benign can actually be most malevolent.

How one decorates one's home is important. One should never surround oneself with items that represent ideas or elements foreign to what one wants to attract. Never allow yourself the fallacy to think that the things you own are benign and disconnected, existing only to please you and with a meaning that only you ascribe to them. Such an attitude is foolish and dangerous.

Everything is connected to something else. Therefore, ask yourself the next time you buy something, do you want this or that item so bad that you're willing to accept whatever it is also attached to? Mind you, this type of thinking can easily fall over into superstition, making you afraid of everything. This negative extremist view which is afraid of everything is just as bad and wrong as its opposite which is afraid of nothing. Be mindful and be careful but never allow yourself to be paranoid or fearful. A careful balance of rationality and common sense comes into play.

Certainly do not bring into your house popular music whose lyrics are demonic or speak about evil things. Such subliminal messages have destroyed an entire generation of listeners to popular music. If the individual artist is outspoken about immorality, violence and idolatry, stay away from anything that they do. Do not deceive yourself with the idea that you can still enjoy their music all the while that you reject their lifestyle. The laws of magnetic attraction disqualify all such opinions.

This caution should also be applied to movies and the like. If the prominent actor, director or producer represents certain ideas, philosophies or a lifestyle that you find most objectionable, do not allow their work into your house. More so, do not allow such movies and such music into your minds. You will be surprised how boycotting certain things serves as an excellent psychic protection for the mind.

Be careful where you allow yourself to go physically, and what you open your mind to entertain. Remember, whatever the physical eye registers, even once, stays in the unconscious mind forever. It can therefore be tapped and used against us. It is the often forgotten images buried deep in our unconscious minds that are somehow resurrected and shown to us in dreams, especially those that are nightmares. The forces that seek to penetrate our minds seek out any sympathetic element within us to exploit and use against us. While we may never be completely free of their influences, the least we can do is not to contribute to them.

Psychic reality, like I have often said, operates according to principles and rules of the laws of nature. The human psyche and soul also operate under these parameters and this is why our understanding the laws of consciousness is imperative. When we understand that there are certain domains, physical and otherwise and that they are by nature either places helpful or harmful, then we can make the concerted efforts to embrace the helpful and stay clear of the harmful. This should be common sense. However, in our modern world of psychic denial and our rejection of the laws of magnetic attachment, we want what we want when we want it. We proclaim how strong we are and how we are not subject to any such silly subliminal influences. What is actually silly is our denials or such truths. This is not only silly, it is dangerous. Before one can practice good, one must first stay clear of evil; this is a sound Biblical truth.

Be as mindful of paranoia and fear as you would of any real and sincere threat. When you acquire new things, make sure that they are benign, from a commercial source, whose sole purpose is that of making money. Transfers of monies do have the ability to neutralize psychic content. But this is only true of otherwise benign things. Your energy given through your money neutralizes the energy in that which you purchase. Unless, of course, you are purchasing items, be they music DVDs, movies, artwork, books and the like that contain within them contaminating messages. Most individuals have never developed the ability to become immune to these things, therefore they are best avoided.

Mind you, not all movies, DVDs or the like are bad. There are plenty of good ones out there. Do not be paranoid, but do be safe. When you learn to keep your mind on Heaven, in everything and in every place, then will you be able to ascertain what is helpful and what is not. This is true psychic self-defense and the pursuit of holiness wrapped up into one.

Chapter 14

◄o►

To Go On the Attack

So far we have discussed various ways of psychic self-defense. One must never forget that the best defense is a good offense. In other words, although one protects oneself in every way from psychic attack, one can still continue being a target. As with terrorism, it does not matter how many attacks one can avoid, it only takes one successful attack to cause devastating harm.

We cannot block every attack against us, unless we go on the offense and make the effort to destroy the sources of attack against us. No one will ever win in psychic warfare; no one will ever be able to rest securely in the confidence of sound protection unless one regularly goes on the psychic offense and routinely roots out the infestations of evil that try to gather around us to cause harm.

Today most acts of psychic self-defense have been dismissed and relegated to the realm of superstition. Needless to say, this mistake of the mind seriously diminishes the power of these psychic tools. One must always remember that there is no such thing as magic. What we call magic and see today operating in the hands of actual master occultists is not magical. They are simply using forms of technology based on the operations of the mind and have an intimate understanding of the actual usages of the forces of nature. This is the mechanics of all spiritual operations. These mechanics are simply usages of the forces of nature. We can even refer to them as forms of technology. There is nothing superstitious or magical about them at all.

I am placing emphasis on their scientific nature in order to demystify them. We must never allow ourselves to entertain ideas that are superstitious in nature. These are a poison to the mind; they blind the mind from seeing truth. Superstitions fill the mind with fear and thus put the individual on an unstable psychological footing. When we allow ourselves to fear, all the more so to fear the unknown, we surrender a part of ourselves that can otherwise reach out into the darkness of ignorance, turn on the lights of reason and see the truth that there really is nothing at all to fear. When we talk about going on the offense against the malevolent forces that use the psyche and the occult, many are held back by an irrational fear. This fear is very real, but it is also very wrong. It emanates from the dark forces themselves. They use fear to intimidate their victims, frightening them into not responding to the attacks against them in any efficient way.

There is nothing to fear other than G-d Himself; and He is definitely on your side in this battle. Indeed, we are the agents of Heaven, the soldiers in the army of G-d to fight the good fight against the forces of evil. Any soldier who is afraid to fight is certain to be killed in combat. Only the brave of heart will roar like lions and jump on their foes like a vicious animal seeking meat. Lions have no fear. Not for naught have our Sages told us to be bold like lions.

Fear is of the mind. Courage is of the heart. The tenacity of the heart when focused properly will always overcome the mental forces that seek to enslave and deceive. Not for naught were we commanded to place the Word of G-d upon our hearts, and not inside our minds or heads. When the Word merges with the heart, the power of G-d radiates within the individual enabling him or her to become very powerful indeed. However, one must learn how to focus that power and put it to proper use.

The power of the heart is projected through the spoken word. The power of the spoken word is augmented by symbolic rituals that add imagery and form. When the power of passion is spoken through the word and augmented by behavior symbolizing that which we seek to accomplish, it is energized and has a much greater chance of becoming real. This is not magical or occultic behavior that I am describing; rather, I am talking about the commandments of the Torah. G-d ordained that we perform specific rituals for it is through these rituals that we give expression to the inner core of our being. This is why Jews are obligated to observe the commandments of the Torah. This is no mere religious injunction; it is a psychological necessity. When the Jew truly touches the heart of the Torah, the Torah in turn will touch his or her heart and transform the individual into a lion.

Non-Jews have this same exact power, but in their own individual ways. The non-Jew is not supposed to follow the Jewish path and follow the commandments of the Torah. The non-Jew does not have a psychic connection with the commandments, in spite of whatever one wants to think. Therefore to mask oneself in Jewish garb is not only unnecessary, it is also untrue and therefore unwise and unhealthy. One cannot feign a legacy not one's own. Non-Jews have a power all their own in their own culture, environment and religion. "To thine own self be true" are powerful words, especially in the psychic warfare. When we are each true to ourselves, then as truthful individuals each expressing our own talents, origins and unique abilities, we can combine and work together for the greater good. One can never work with charlatans or with people who believe themselves one thing when in reality they are something else.

There are common rituals that can be used by everyone, common prayers that can be said and common behaviors to observe that create the strongest of individuals in both mind and body. Rather than place emphasis on factors of difference, I choose instead to emphasis factors that unite. Now beware, the forces of evil are always seeking to divide and conquer. Beware of any opinion or attitudes that try to create divisions and break up unity, often such forces are all working for the dark side. As long as good-hearted and right-minded people come together, without any basis of falsehood or self delusion, this should be a gathering of strength.

The right people gather but they do not have to be physically together. The right people gather but it does not have to be at the same exact time. Time and space are mostly irrelevant in the psychic world, therefore ritual observances can be here or there, now or later, with or without others, simply because we are creating and focusing psychic energy and it goes off into its own world and dimension, where time and space matters not. In the alternate dimension of mind, all our activities unite together and form a concentric whole. Together, our combined force weighs heavily on physical reality and continues to apply pressure on it until, inevitably, our mental creation becomes the physical reality. This is how psychic energy is stored and then shot out, like a projectile. It will accomplish its task, if the minds behind it are strong enough. I am talking about the power of prayer.

In Torah tradition, public prayers require a quorum of ten men and no less. There is power in numbers, but only if there is first power in the individual. When ten powerful individuals gather there is truly great power. Even one can have great power depending upon his or her faith and heart. Ten weak people gathered together may as well as be a hundred or a thousand. Weakness is weakness and regardless the number what is weak is not going to be strong. Indeed, one strong individual can overcome even a million weak-minded individuals. This is simple mental mechanics and the workings of psychic reality. This truth can be and has been used by both forces of good and evil.

All power of mind is channeled through the heart. The heart is actually the unconscious mind where feelings and thoughts merge as one. The projections of the heart, therefore, are the true key to power. All the academic acquisitions in the world cannot stand against one of a strong heart. To extend honor to those who have acquired knowledge is a backward thing. Those who are strong of heart are the ones worthy of praise. Yet, always beware: strength of heart is but a tool and a weapon. How one chooses to use it decides who is righteous and who is evil.

Here now we come to the foundations of psychic/occultic attack postures. One must be strongly charged with passion. It is this passion that takes the attack into the heads and hearts of the workers of evil. One must never fear their hearts and must allow their passion full reign. One must beware of all the religious philosophical deceptions that speak of how one must rise above their feelings and become totally stoic. True, one must never be swayed by emotions. Nonetheless, one must still have feelings. One must be in control of one's feelings and not the other way around. Mastery and control of emotion, not the denial of loss of them, are what we call proper balance.

One must also beware of the deception that tells people that they should seek to always be happy and that they should never focus on what is wrong and painful. True happiness and joy is the embrace of truth, however good or bad it is. It is not a state of drug-like fantastical rapture, where everything is beautiful, even when in truth, it is ugly. This type of thinking is a proverbial wolf in sheep's clothing. This is how the forces of evil infiltrate the teachings of religion, teaching the religious how to be passive and weak in order to prevent them from fighting back against psychic attack. Six million Jews died in Nazi Europe because for centuries their religious philosophy taught them to be passive and to accept whatever occurs as being the Will of G-d.

We can discuss philosophically all we want what is the Will of G-d; yet none of our talk matters much. What matters is what we do, not what we say or believe. Passion is power and aggression can be good. The heart of the lion is the Way of G-d; the submissiveness of sheep is the Will of Evil. Torah teaches that G-d is a "man of war" and we are taught that we must emulate the Divine Image. If G-d is a "man of war" how can we justify ourselves being anything less?

Aggression does not mean to harm the weak or innocent. Holy aggressors protect those who cannot protect themselves. The true servants of Heaven, those who use the mechanics of spirituality in the service of holiness and Heaven are warrior for G-d. They are humble, simple individuals, men and women, who do not tolerate the harmful attacks of the forces of evil on the weak and innocent. The armies of holiness do not seek out conflict, but if and when faced with it, they do not shirk their duty; they do not seek to make peace or compromise with the enemy. When the battle comes, the cry is simple, destroy and kill the enemy; no compromise, no surrender and most of all, no defeat. The holy warriors fight with all means at their disposal, even physical arms if conflict ever exits the spiritual plan and enters the physical.

The Bible is full of examples of such holy warriors. Unfortunately with the exile of Israel from the Holy Land, the holy warriors had to limit their warfare exclusively to the spiritual plan. Without a homeland and without a populace, fighting a physical war tends to be somewhat difficult.

Over the centuries psychic spiritual warfare was an area of expertise for most Sages of Israel. This expertise lasted in almost every community until the Renaissance period in Europe. Then, following in the footsteps of their Gentile neighbors, most Sages of Israel wholeheartedly embraced rationalism and discarded anything considered to be mystical. This led to an entire segment of the Jewish community, specifically those in Europe, becoming open and prone to psychic attack. When time came for the Holocaust, the Sages in Europe were spiritually defenseless to match the occult powers of the Nazi and the Thule. We all know the results of their not being prepared.

Philosophy and blind faith are no match for the psychic sword. The psychic sword is many things, but at first it is the words that come forth from a mouth on fire with the passion of heart. Yet, all the passion in the world needs to be directed. Without direction one is merely shooting off energy without focus. Such an endeavor is purposeless and fails to accomplish an activity.

One must allow oneself to be aggressive. One must allow oneself to become angry. One must allow oneself to hate. All these are actually taught directly in the Bible. King Solomon said it best when he said that there is a time and a purpose for all things under Heaven. Yes, all things, and these include anger, hate and warfare. Use them; yes, but never allow them to use you. This is the secret of successful balance.

No holy warrior goes into battle without the heart of the lion. He goes forth not with philosophy, not with long-winded sermons from the Sages and not with thoughts of forgiveness and love. No, the holy warrior goes forth as did King David to slay his thousands and tens of thousands. Like King David, the holy psychic warrior does not interpret his enemy to be some nebulous evil in the heart of his opponent. The holy warrior does not seek to root out the evil from an enemy's heart and thus turn them to good. No, the holy warrior is not a philosopher; his or her intent is to stop the beating heart of the enemy, period. Whether or not there is any good to be salvaged from the soul of a dead enemy, the holy warrior leaves this judgment up to G-d in Heaven.

For the holy warrior, the job is clear, remove the enemy physically from this Earth, period. Any Sage who does not see this or does not readily embrace it should not be considered by you to be a Sage. Such passive Sages are sheep; they no longer have the spiritual "image of Man" upon them. Like their spiritual predecessors in Europe, their fate is sealed. Lions are the kings of the jungle. Sheep are the food. Sheep are sacrifices. We are the ones who bring sacrifice, not the ones who are sacrificed. Remember this well; you will never succeed in psychic offense maneuvers until you first firmly embrace what I have said here.

When the battle is spiritual we fight it with full vigor just as if it were physical. If and when the battle does become physical, then we do not shirk our duty. We rise up with every weapon at our disposal, spiritual and physical. Yet, we also must beware that we never cross the line and translate a spiritual battle into the physical plane unless it is absolutely necessary to do so. When we chose to fight the spiritual battle in the physical world without paying attention to the psychic source of conflict, we enter an arena of battle in which we will surely be defeated. This is not the way.

You have heard how wise it is to forgive and forget. In truth, this is not wise at all. While we do forgive as long as the conditions for repentance have been met; we should still never forget. We must never hold a grudge or treat others unfairly or be unkind. Such behavior on our parts only lessens us as individuals and opens us up for psychic attack. Nonetheless, we must never let down our guards. When others treat us wrong, not due to weakness or lack of knowledge, but out of intent and with malice, we must remember that they are indeed capable of doing so. The wise therefore never let down their guard. When one violates our trust, even if and when the violating party repents and makes full restitution, this does not mean that we should be so foolish to openly and quickly trust that other person again. Remember, trust is not something freely given; it must be earned.

We have no moral or religious obligation to forgive someone who has harmed us all the while that there is no repentance for the misdeed. Repentance is not merely saying "I'm sorry." Repentance must include sincere remorse for one's behavior and then backed up by the violator fixing the damage that he or she has caused. There must be restitution in order for there to be repentance. If this involves money, then all monies must be returned in full. If this involves honor, one must resolve to show extra honor, in practical, not ridiculous forms. If this involves trust, what can I say?

Trust is something that cannot be easily restored. Once it is shattered it might very well be impossible to repair.

To repair a breach in trust requires the strongest of character. If the offending party is truly remorseful and has taken all steps necessary to repair the breach, then the long road of repair may begin. Mind you, the necessary steps to repair a breach of trust are not defined by the offender or by a third party. The offended party must be honest and demand what he or she feels is right to restore the broken bond. The violator has broken the sacred bond of trust; rebuilding it is very difficult. Therefore, the violator should expect the offended party to demand certain curtailments of behaviors and activities which will prove to be very invasive. True, the offending party does not have to accept such conditions. Then again, the offended party does not have to forgive. A state of war can exist between the two souls, which can indeed follow them from lifetime to lifetime. Eventually the offending party will make full restitution to the offended, if not in this lifetime then in the next. But beware, when justice and restitution is taken out of our own hands and placed into the Hands of Heaven, it is quite more severe.

To fulfill the Biblical commandment to love one's neighbor does not require of us to forgive those who have offended us. The Biblical commandment is fulfilled by our behavior towards others and not by our feelings. If an unrepentant offending individual is in need of food, drink or shelter, it is the honorable thing to provide for him his basic needs. One does not have to be fancy; yet one does have to be humane. We are not animals and we do not seek to harm others, even those who may otherwise deserve it. We may not have to like certain people, but we have no right to mistreat them or disrespect them.

When we are faced with an unrepentant offender, we should do our best to ignore him, to not speak with him or interact with him in any way. In the Bible, this was called excommunication. Remember the unrepentant attacked us, and without any true remorse may be looking for an opportunity to do it again. Why would one be so foolish to open oneself up to be attacked again? Mind you, most attacks are verbal. They can be a snide comment or unkind words, all the more so outright lies and slander.

When attacked in such a way, we must hold up our emotional shield and not allow ourselves to be hurt by such comments. If we must we defend ourselves before others, we simply provide a simple statement proving the facts to refute the lies. Be careful not to send the evil eye on to the offending party. Yet, it is totally righteous to silently pray and say something similar to this effect.

"Master of the Universe, You Whose Name is Truth; behold the injustice I have now endured; You are the True Judge; judge now I pray between myself and this other. Vindicate me and avenge me for the wrong

inflicted upon me, for this is the way of righteousness. I await your justice, Righteous King, Amen."

Once said, cast from your heart any feelings about the matter. Leave it in the Hands of Heaven.

When we hold others accountable for their actions they will be required to rise up to meet the challenge. Otherwise, they may live to face the Divine Judgment. This will in no way be an easy or pleasant thing.

When there is sincere remorse and serious effort to repair a broken breach, then the honorable thing to do is to accept back the repentant soul. Granted, they will have to earn back trust, but if that is accomplished, then we should embrace the penitent with open arms. We do forgive, and although we may never forget, we do not keep past misdeeds in our conscious minds. We may always be aware that slipups can occur and we are always diligent to watch for them. Part of the efforts to repair a broken breach is that the violator must accept that the one whom he violated will naturally be suspicious of his behavior. They must bear that suspicion forever. Mind you, such suspicion must never be misused by the offended party to make false accusations or otherwise inflict harm or punishment. Such behavior turns the offended party into the offender. This, too, opens one up for serious psychic attack.

Making peace is no easy task and requires great effort. It requires two mature individuals acting with maturity. When one begins to act like a child then no peace making can occur. This is true with two individuals or with two nations.

I have digressed here to discuss a valuable lesson about human relationships. This advice is important. It is the "nuts and bolts" of all spiritual/psychic mechanics. This is how the mind and personality must operate in order to properly wield the Heavenly power. Learn these lessons well and take them to heart. Do be a lion and do not be a lamb. Do not allow religion or philosophy to confuse your mind. In your heart, you know what is true. Now, learn how to properly act on it.

Chapter 15

—◀○▶—

Power Prayer- Invoking Heaven

Life is full of frustrations. With regard to most things, we are totally powerless to exert any influence. We cannot change the big things, like the course of world events. We often cannot even change the little things, like physical matters within our own bodies. We have often seen that good people, who devote their lives to helping and healing others, themselves, come to a most undeserved bad end. We also see people who cheat, steal and harm others prosper greatly. There seems to be no rhyme or reason why and how events unfold. Nevertheless life unfolds the way that it does, regardless of how we think it should.

While it is true we may work hard to help mold and shape our lives. We will still find that we have next to zero input, control or influence over the vast majority of matters that affect us personally. Many individuals waste their entire life's energy pursuing that which they cannot attain. Many people waste their entire lives wanting what they cannot have and despising that which they do have. The pursuit of more, regardless of whatever more it is, is always the source of personal grief, pain and frustration. Those who claim that life is beautiful and happy are either liars or totally out of touch with reality.

Life is full of frustration and suffering. We are partly at fault, true, but partial fault is not the whole. There are a great number of forces in our world that seek our harm and their betterment. The interaction with these other entities defines for us the practices of the dark "Other Side." Let it not come as a surprise to us that these other entities, like us, have their own problems. Like us, these other entities know well the meaning of suffering, frustration and loss. In a way, their lot in life is not so different from our own. In a way they are a lot more human than they are not.

Frustration leads to despair, despair leads to anger, anger leads to violence. Is it any wonder then that dark "Other Side" forces seek to attack with venom. Those who have less always seek to take from those who have more. The distribution of wealth and power is never equal. There are always those who crave more and are willing to do anything to get it and then there are those who could not care less and seldom miss that which is stolen from them. In the middle of all this is the vast majority of everyone else.

Most individuals just want to get along, live their lives and be left alone. No one seeks stressful situations. No one really wants problems or the need to have to face them. Nevertheless, we do not usually get what we want. There really is not much we can do about this. We have no choice but to accept it. And here comes the great challenge. How do we thrive in an unbalanced world that itself thrives on chaos? How do we thrive when everyday is simply a struggle just to survive?

Have we not seen the rich and famous suffer? Have we not seen the rich lose all their wealth? Have we not seen the mighty fall? It seems that the more one has, the more one has to lose. While there are those who seem to attract power and wealth, they are nonetheless not exempt from troubles. In many ways, even the rich and powerful are as powerless as is anyone else. Money can only buy so much.

Spiritual operations function because of the conditions of the human mind. The dark "Other Side" is a psychological phenomenon and should never be mistaken for anything other. At the same time, we must understand that the scope and borders of the human mind do not end with the limits of the physical human brain. Human consciousness is focused in the organic brain, this is true; yet from this organic base, the human mind/consciousness spreads out far beyond physical boundaries, even penetrating the dimensions of space and time.

With all the power inherent in the human mind to travel almost anywhere in space and time, we are still bound by a Higher Force that seems to corral us and severely limit our psychic spheres of operation. Those who live within these appointed boundaries are the everyday people subject as we are to the unforgiving forces operating our universe. Those who seek to break the bounds and to force change, usually for their own betterment, are considered by the Higher Power to be criminals who are interfering in the work of the Higher Force. Success in such manipulations may be short-lived. However, in the long term, those who push Heaven are usually pushed back with force and vigor. These too usually do not come to a peaceful end.

There is a right way and a wrong way to solicit influence in Heaven. Taking matters into one's own hands to impose a psychic solution to one of life's problems is not viewed with compassion by Heaven. Heaven has an agenda all its own and has no tolerance for those who interfere with its operations. The only recourse open to us is to properly solicit Heaven in those ways permitted to us. Unfortunately, most of these ways have become unknown to the masses, but not all of them.

One of the great tools granted us by Heaven is the power of prayer. While we are all familiar with prayer; many are oblivious to exactly what kind of prayers we can offer and exactly what kind of powers they may contain.

Prayer must be more than mere words. Prayer must be more than just a "wish list" addressed to Heaven. We must recognize that the words of prayer by themselves never ascend anywhere. It is only the intent of prayers that rise up to Heaven. Intent is power. Intent is the combination of the thoughts of the mind united with the passion of the heart. Prayer must be intentional and not just arbitrary. Those who merely recite words may fulfill their religious obligations according to the letter of religious law; however they have not fulfilled their obligations to pray to Heaven. The laws of man and the laws of Heaven differ greatly.

Prayer is a matter of heart, therefore, if there is no heart, then there is no prayer; it is that simple. Prayer is a powerful tool in our hands and some say, it is our only tool in the war against injustice and evil. I might tend to agree. Even if one were to perform all the permissible rituals to solicit Divine support and to banish evil, they all revolve around the usage of prayer. In our coming essays we will discuss many of these rituals, yet for now we must discuss the one thing upon which they all stand.

In previous essays I have discussed the power of the spoken word; here is where we learn to put it to use. In our previous lesson we learned about the importance to go on the offense and to attack our enemies; here is our weapon. So powerful is prayer that when wielded in the right hands, or maybe better to say, when spoken from the proper lips with the proper intent of heart, it can bring either life or death. There is a famous story recorded in the Talmud how one Sage was grievously insulted by another and then turned to G-d in prayer to address his grievance. No sooner than he finished praying did a voice cry out in the neighborhood that the offending Sage had suddenly died.

Prayer is not magic. The Sage did not use any magical or occultic means to strike dead his colleague. Rather, fearing G-d, he simply brought his case before the Heavenly Court and asked Heaven to judge. When one has the power to do this; the results can be most powerful, again, for either life or death.

In Torah tradition, when there resides amongst us an individual so evil and yet so powerful that he or she is untouchable by normal human laws, we have an alternative way to address their crimes. There is an ancient Torah ceremony where a group of Sages gather together to collectively call upon Heaven to judge the soul of the evil individual in question. Specific prayers of supplication are recited asking Heaven to intervene to save the community from the further evil deeds of the untouchable perpetrator.

The prayers are formatted very carefully to make sure that we here on Earth give proper allowance to the domain of Heaven. All these prayers do not, and I repeat, they do not call for the death of the evil individual, but rather, they call on Heaven to judge. Heaven, and not man, knows the truth that resides within the depths of one's heart. Only

Heaven can ascertain whether or not the evil individual is indeed acting with malicious intent, with the purpose of causing harm. Heaven is asked that if the individual is found wanting and guilty in the Heavenly Court, then may justice be served and may the evil individual be removed from the Earth without further delay and without causing further harm to the community. Then the congregants say Amen and wait for Heaven to enact its verdict.

Never is there a prayer for death. Never is there a curse of death. We do not have the authority to take a life outside of the proper legal means as outlined by Torah Law. Even to wish for another to die is the projection of evil, in the worst way. True Sages do not do these things. We have been given the right to approach the Heavenly Throne and to address our grievances. Heaven must then decide and Heaven must then act. We have done our share; whatever happens next is not in our hands.

What I have here described is a sacred and secret prayer ritual which was relatively unknown until the most modern times, when certain individuals for whatever political reasons chose to advertise their performance of this ceremony on certain political leaders. Indeed, on both occasions when performed, the results were dramatic. In one case, the leader was assassinated and in the other, the leader suffered a terrible debilitating illness which forced him out of office. Now, let us put politics aside. I do not support or condone the use of such prayer rituals against politicians or against any others who we may disagree with. I believe that this is an abuse of the ritual. Nevertheless, the media did report that the ceremonies were performed and the fates of the two individuals are on record. It is not for me to say anything else at this point. All I can add is that this ceremony is called in Aramaic the Pulsa D'Nora; rightly is it called the Lashes of Fire; the fire in this case are the words of sincere supplication and prayer.

Now that we have discussed how prayers can kill; let us turn to discuss how they can bring life, blessing and prosperity. Remember the old saying; "where you think, is where you are at." If you dwell upon the negative it will be hard, if not next to impossible, to see the positive. If you dwell on the positive, then no matter how negative actual events truly are, at least you will find a way to get out of them. Focus on bestowing life and good and our prayers can be transformed into weapons of power that can pierce even the strongest of evil's armor.

There are many different types of prayer. Of them all, the most powerful is the one uttered from a pure heart with sincere devotion and intent. This form is even more powerful than the usage of so-called holy Names and the invocation of angels. The Bible is full of such powerful prayers and the great results that have come forth from them. While we can analyze the mechanics of prayer, meditation and power thinking, we have no need to analyze the mechanics of sincere prayer. This is because sincerity is rather simple, it is

219

what it is and that's all there is to it. You either have it or you don't. You either feel it or you don't. I cannot say anything more about sincere prayer; we should all already know its power.

In Biblical days, emotionally based sincere prayer was recited in a position of complete prostration. In other words, one, as if, threw oneself down to the floor, completely humbling oneself before Heaven, and throwing oneself on the mercy of the Heavenly Court. So powerful was this act of throwing oneself on the ground that religious law actually taught us not to perform it, fearing that death of the individual supplicant could result through pouring out his or her soul in their anguish of prayer. To this day, ritual prayers do not include any form of full body prostration. This does not mean that individuals do not privately perform this ritual from time to time, yet, when they do, it is usually a rather serious thing and they do it alone, outside the context of congregational prayer services. Falling on the face prayer does not require one to approach Heaven's gates through the medium of the angels; no invocations are necessary. This type of prayer needs no further assistance or explanation.

Not everyone has such devotion and intent that their prayers can easily pierce the veils of Heaven's gates. Some prayers need assistance to ascend. To address these, various forms have been developed to assist the masses. We have previously discussed the repetition method and how this verbal technique helps focus the mind. Indeed, repetition of specific power words can arouse the heart and induce a state of meditative trance. "Where you think is where you are at" therefore, what you recite and repeat is what arouses the heart. Words are important, what we pray for and in what form we pray makes a great deal of difference.

Prayers of supplication should be repetitive poetry. Some of the best prayers ever written are the Psalms of the Bible. Yet, there are also numerous other sources one can choose from. Prayers from the heart are always the strongest, yet when someone cannot find the words, then whatever prefabricated prayer that they come across can work, as long as one can recite it with true devotion.

As I mentioned above, the world we live in is not a very nice place. There is more in the average day that can burden us then can set us free. Worries and concerns abound, be they great or small. Even the strongest of hearts can sometimes be overwhelmed by life's challenges. And so what? Our world is so grandiose; there is so much more going on than our individual lives with our petty personal problems, which are microscopic in comparison. Yet, for us personally, we cannot see the entire world, we can only see our own little portion of it. Therefore, our microscopic little problems grow to humongous proportions, often blocking out our entire scope of vision. How can we see the world and the true nature of things, when everyday is a struggle for survival; when every day we struggle just to make a living, to stay healthy, to stay safe and to maintain a semblance of sanity?

Prayer therefore serves as our glasses. Through prayer, our vision of the world is corrected. Left to our own devices, we can do nothing more than to succumb to the wills of fate. Prayer however is a ladder of ascent that can lift us out of our present travails and move us to another, more safe location. When we focus our minds on change and salvation, we open the doors to their occurrence. No one can promise anyone that they will always receive what it is they ask for in prayer. However, without prayer there would be no chance of receiving that which one could not otherwise obtain.

Prayers uttered with true intent and sincerity help calm a troubled heart. By doing so, they enable the mind to elevate its vision from the immediate, festering problem and to see new and different avenues. One may or may not like what one sees, nevertheless, with new options not previously seen, one can chose a course of action that might bring about the best resolution to the immediate problem. Here is where the Hand of G-d becomes revealed.

Many believe that prayers are supposed to work miracles; to somehow bend or change the natural order. Sometimes prayers can have this affect. Yet, this is the rare occasion. Long ago, our Sages taught us not to wait around and rely upon a miracle. Heaven rarely sends us magical miracles that are so glaringly obvious. That type of magic comes out of Hollywood and it is best left on the movie screen. Real miracles are what happen every day; these come from Heaven; however, they are not accompanied by all the hype and fanfare of fantasy. Real miracles are subtle and they are usually cloaked somehow in natural occurrences. Little things happen all around us at every moment, most of which we are totally oblivious to. It is in these little unseen things that the Hand of G-d works to answer our prayers.

We seldom recognize what is for our good. Only in moments of crisis do we recognize our immediate needs. For these we pray with earnest. Yet, what happens after we have overcome the immediate crisis facing us? Do we then go back to fighting our daily battles of taking on the forces of fate? Do we forget to carry our battle shield and sword? Yes, most of us forget these daily. The strong heart is one's battle shield and one's sincere prayers are one's sword. These should be with us at every moment of every day. Together, they can protect us from the most vicious of psychic attacks. Together these two also form for us a ladder of higher vision, enabling us a glimpse of the greater world beyond the boundaries of our personal problems.

While we might not naturally have what it takes to address an immediate problem the way we would want to, somehow, in some way, when we make our best efforts and open our hearts to Heaven, something miraculous does occur. We may not consider it a miracle when it happens. We might accidentally interpret it as something that we did ourselves, by our own strengths and efforts. Yet, in truth, all our personal efforts are no match if the winds of fate blow against us. We can never wage war against the harsh, natural universe and expect to win using only our mortal strengths. No, every accomplishment and every victory in life is brought about by the subtle, miraculous moving of the invisible Hand of G-d.

Thousands upon thousands of tiny unseen and apparently insignificant events take place around us at all times. One is the cause of another, one has an effect upon another, and together they build and form a course of events. These can work in our favor or they can work against us. While we may not be able to control the entire system, we can at least influence it, however great or small. This is the power of sincere prayer.

Prayer changes attitudes. Daily prayers should therefore not focus on one's personal wish list. Heaven takes care of one's personal needs, although maybe not in the way that the individual would want. Nonetheless, we each have a great deal to be thankful for. No matter how bad things are at the moment, they could always be worse. For this we have to be thankful.

In ancient times, all meditative prayers were repetitious recitations of praise. G-d was praised for this and for that and for everything else imaginable. An uneducated observer might think that G-d had an ego problem to be in need of such constant praise. Yet, we must always dismiss such primitive mythological thinking. G-d does not need for us to praise Him; it is we who need to praise Him. Praising G-d serves us by reinforcing within us a scope of consciousness that raises us above our petty little world and our selfish individual needs. When we praise G-d we divert focus from ourselves and place it on the Higher Power, the same Higher Power that is the true Mover and shaker in this universe.

Constant repetition of Divine praise is a good form to use in meditation. While we cannot manipulate prayer to change the world, we can still use it to bring change, big or small. One who feels oppressed by dark "Other Side" forces or simply overwhelmed by life's struggles should turn to prayer and to praise. This combination has yet to be beat.

Chapter 16

◄◦►

Calling Upon Angels

In all spiritual pursuits, be they for good or evil, we often find practitioners calling upon spiritual entities for their support. Be they angels or demons, we have ceremonies and rituals that call upon them seeking their advice and power to further our human agendas. Many dismiss these entities as being mere figments of our imaginations. Many more know that there are very few limits to the human imagination and that these limits expand far beyond our present boundaries of time and space.

We are not alone in our universe or on our Earth. While we cannot physically travel to the locations where these others reside, we can still make contact with them. Rather than travel physically, we travel mentally, and allow our thoughts to do the traveling. We begin with the realm of human imagination and allow our the images in our minds to take on a life of their own and in doing so take us to where we meet the others, be they good or evil. Our minds take us to where we are magnetically attracted. We therefore invoke and arouse good or evil entities depending upon whether we ourselves are good or evil. The defining factors of good and evil are defined by Heaven and never by man.

Here we come to one of the central points of all spiritual practices: the calling upon the Higher Entities. It is imperative that we understand how this is done and more importantly when and why this is done. Contacting Higher Entities is not something that anyone should take lightly. Higher Entities, good and evil, usually do not like to be bothered to have to deal with human beings and their problems. When we involve them with our issues it is usually at the cost of taking them away from other more important matters that they are involved with. Not to dissimilar from us, the Higher Entities do not like being distracted and taken away from important business to have to deal with childish and foolish endeavors.

There are so many numerous types of spiritual beings that we cannot possibly succeed in listing and identifying them all. There are those entities that are indigenous to our Earth and then there are those that are quite extraterrestrial. There are those that are benevolent and then there are those who view us as nothing more than cattle, good for nothing other than to be corralled and used as a source of food. Whenever we speak of angels and demons, we must understand that these two generic categories include within them numerous different races. We must also include within the category of spiritual beings those that emanate from within our own minds. Some may even take on an autonomous life of their own. Some are projections of our inner thoughts and some are manifestations of our higher selves. Even within us there are numerous expressions. Nothing about spiritual entities is easy or simple to understand.

Contacting spiritual entities is also an arduous process. This is not because the rituals themselves are difficult, for in truth, they are rather easy. Rather, because there is so much congestion in the spiritual dimensions, that unless one knows how to properly focus and direct one's invitation of connection, one's invitation might very well be intercepted. If this occurs, and it often does, then one had better know how to discern truth from falsehood. Without this, the entity who intercepted one's invitation or invocation presents itself in the guise of another and captures the soul of the one who called upon it. The results of this are not very pleasant.

In many circles of traditional Jewish mysticism any such types of invocations have long been feared. This has led the philosophical school of mystical study to boldly proclaim that any and all such invocations are prohibited. Needless to say, the ones of this school have no authority to make such proclamations and their edicts are only followed by those who adhere to their philosophy. There are today and have always been numerous other Sages who have never accepted such prohibitions based on fear. These Sages have long held tried and true methods of making spiritual contact. They teach their ways to their students, who in turn guard their secrets. We all know that politics is politics. The Sages who are masters of connection do not wish to enter into debate or conflict with those of the philosophical schools of mysticism. Therefore, they maintain their anonymity and certainly do not propagate their secrets. These Sages do however make use of the knowledge of spiritual connections regularly both for their own benefits and too help those who seek out their assistance.

Proper formulas for contacting spiritual entities are essential. If there is an invocation that mispronounces the name of an angel or other combinations of holy Names, then the right means, even in the right hands will cause things to work in the wrong way. Like I just said, the end results of this are not pleasant. Not having the proper information is what led the philosophical school to ban all such endeavors. Being that they have lost their personal connections they have no spiritual source with which to check to ascertain which procedures and names are the correct ones and which ones are not. By blocking off direct spiritual contacts, the philosophical school has also blocked off any chance they had to rectify matters for themselves. The other Sages have always refined their practices and their methods are safe and sure. Yet, the philosophical school has embraced a mind-set of fear and few have the courage to break out from it.

However important it is to have the right rituals, the proper invocation of angels and holy Names work not because of the ceremony itself but rather because of the one performing the ceremony. If, as the Psalm says, one is clean of hands, pure of heart and righteous of cause, only then he will be invited to commune with the angelic community. If however, the one approaching is just a curiosity seeker then his efforts will amount to naught. Those above heed not the words spoken by man; instead they watch our human hearts. If we generate the necessary magnetic energy to attract them, then they will indeed come. If however the heart is either weak or tainted, then the invocation goes to a parallel place of weakness and taint, the results again are not pleasant. Proper techniques and proper devotion must go hand in hand. Both are essential, one cannot work fully without the other.

Specific techniques for angelic invocation have for the most part been lost in history. Most of the forms today are terribly corrupted. I have seen the English translations of ancient Hebrew and Aramaic texts of magical formulas and angelic invocations. As a scholar of language I have not found a single one of the available texts to have any true value whatsoever. The translations are terribly inaccurate and the transliterations of angelic and holy Names seem to be more like guess work than any real scholarly attempt at decipherment. Nonetheless I see these English versions of old magical texts are very popular and modern occultists make use of them regularly. I find it amusing how the blind lead the blind. These books and those people who use them pose absolutely no threat to anyone or anything. It is rather amusing watching them as they think they are doing something that they so very much are not. Occultists of this nature are not occultists at all.

Real formulas for angelic invocations can only be used by those with a heart pure enough to use them properly. Therefore, I believe it would be morally wrong to publicly release any material that could be used wrongly and that could possibly bring someone psychological or other forms of harm. There are, however, certain formulas that can be publicly released and that everyone can take advantage of for daily usage, without any concern of harm.

In traditional Jewish prayers we have one such angelic proclamation that is recited by pious individuals before they retire to bed at night. This prayer is said to be a protection for one's soul as one sleeps the night. The formula is as follows.

"In the Name of Adonai, G-d of Israel, may Mikha-el be on my right and Gavri-el on my left; may Uri-el be before me and Rifa-el be behind me and may the Presence of G-d be above my head."

While this prayer is not meant to contact the angels mentioned therein, it is still considered to be a powerful prayer that everyone can use.

All prayers should always be addressed to G-d and to no other entity, angelic or otherwise. The Bible is very clear on the importance of this issue. Anyone with even the slightest knowledge of actual occult mechanics knows how true this is. G-d and G-d alone is the source of all power, and the L-rd over every angel, demon and spirit. No power in this universe lifts a finger without there first being given Heavenly consent. This is true whether it be for good or for evil. G-d is the Source and only the Source can alter that which is. Therefore, all angelic invocations are never addressed to the specific angels themselves but rather to G-d directly and to no other. All that we do is supplicate the Heavenly throne and beseech G-d to send His angels to be our support and help. This type of supplication opens us up to many different things.

Angels are not what we think they are. All the modern images of angels being effeminate beings with long human hair and wings are nothing but pure fantasy. Angels in no way look human at all. Although they may appear human to us for a certain time and purpose, nonetheless, such appearances are mere contrivances. These are done so as not to alarm us. When G-d sends His angels to become involved with us, they appear to us as human. We are meant to not be able to ascertain their true non-human origins. However, once they go back to where they come they adopt their natural forms. Indeed, they are something so totally from out of this world.

When we chose to invoke an angel and to bring it down to our side to perform our bidding, it does not go through the contrivances to take on human form. It comes as it is. Such a sight can frighten one into having a heart attack. In the Bible, the prophets Ezekiel and Isaiah both saw angels in their original forms and they were nothing less than terrifying. Demonic entities are no different in this respect. They are far from being human and when their presence is invoked and they are forced to come, their appearances are frightening enough to shock even the most strongest of hearts.

In ancient literature, we often find long lists of angelic names. However, angels do not have names that we can recognize all the more so pronounce. Angels are known to us by the service they provide. Their names are an expression of their present mission. When an angel is sent to bring healing, it is called Rifa-el, which means "G-d heals." It does not matter whether or not this is its actual name because the angel does not have any actual name that we can comprehend. The angels' names are more like a title than they are names. Therefore, the angel who today comes and brings healing from G-d and is called Rifa-el, might not be the same angel who came yesterday using the same name. Their titles are the same; their functions are identical, but they may or may not be the same entity. Both are carrying out the same mission, but their mission is more like a computer program. These angels do what they do and then that is it. They are reassigned and therefore given a new name, which is none other than a new mission.

While we can invoke angels in prayer, we may never pray to them directly. Praying to angels is a sure way to not have one's prayers heard or answered. Let me explain. Angels that interact with humanity are of a variety of species. Those that come to us in visions or on the performance of a Divine mission should be understood as something akin to an artificially intelligent computer program. They most definitely exist. They can think and act. They can come and go. In a way, they have a mind of their own. Yet, as intelligent as they are, they are still nonetheless only a program in G-d's Divine computer. They can only function within the parameters of their programming.

If we were to address a prayer or supplication to a computer program, regardless of however intelligent and capable that program may be, it still does not contain the potential for independent operations. If we want a certain computer program to operate for us, then instead of talking directly to the program, we instead need to talk to the Programmer. The Programmer writes the program and then it is executed. The Program, however artificially intelligent, does not write its own program. It does not define its own parameters. As it is with computer programs so is it with those angels who interact with us in the knowable ways.

When I wish to invoke Mikhael, Gavriel, Uriel or Rifael, I can all upon them all I want. There are numerous entities each sent out on their individual missions that daily take on one of these four names. This is how each of us can have the protection of these four angels every night. It is not that the four individual angels are everywhere, by everyone's bedside throughout the world. Rather, there are throngs of angels each of whom is given a mission to serve as Mikhael, Gavriel, Uriel or Rifael. Upon receiving their mission, the angel becomes the one called by that name. There is no one Mikhael, Gavriel, Uriel or Rifael; on the contrary, there could be millions or even billions of them.

Therefore, if I call upon Mikhael to assist me to become like G-d; there really is no individual Mikhael who can hear my request and answer me. I am addressing the computer program that is called Mikhael. It cannot answer me, for that is outside of its operational parameters. This is why we cannot call upon angels to answer our prayers. They are not programmed to function in that manner.

When I call upon G-d the great Programmer of the Divine computer I can supplicate and beseech Him to send me Mikhael so that I can become more like Him; I can request that Gavriel be sent to me to fight my battles against an unbeatable foe; I can request that Rifael come to me and bring to me (or a loved one) the gift of healing from Heaven. If G-d the great Programmer so ordains, then the program can be initiated; only then will the angel come to me and fulfill its task. Therefore, every invocation of angels must be addressed to G-d the Programmer. Instead of staying "I call upon you mighty angel Mikhael, come to me," we instead say, "G-d in Heaven, please send to me your angel Mikhael." The angel will either come or not come based upon the Divine decision. This is always influenced by the righteousness and faith that resides in the human heart.

There are long lists of angelic names, with most of them being corrupted and undecipherable. These ancients lists have almost no value whatsoever other than to scholars in the fields of theology and angelology. However, as corrupted as these lists and names are, I have seen sections of them published in English translation in many of those trashy books that I mentioned earlier. Certainly any invocations of any angel names on those lists will not bring the expected results. Yet, worse than this, as the invoked name is corrupted so will be the entity that responds to the invocation. It might appear as Mikhael or Gavriel and even claim to be called by that name. Nevertheless, the responding entity might just be an earthbound spirit or a demonic force who just so happens to have the name Mikhael or Gavriel. Yes, entities have names just like we do. If we are not careful who we call and how we call them, we can very easily "dial the wrong spiritual number." If this were to happen the chances are you would not even know it and you would not find out until it was already too late for you.

Angelic powers can be invoked by following a simple Hebrew formula. We grasp the concept of what we seek from G-d and then add it to G-d's Name El. These two combined give us the name of an angel, or better to say, the function of the program that we are requesting Heaven to put into operation for us. Therefore, for example, when praying for healing, we ask G-d for Rifa-el, which translates as G-d is my healer. When we seek enlightenment we ask G-d for Uri-el, which means G-d is my light. If I were to ask G-d for financial support I can request that He send me Oshri-el, which means G-d is my wealth. If I were to ask G-d to reveal to me His secrets I can request that He send me Razi-el, which means G-d is my secret. On and on we can go, there is no stop simply because G-d is the Cause and Source of all things. We can ask of Him everything, whereas we cannot ask anything of someone other than Him.

The only proper reason for invoking the names of angels is to use them as a tool to assist the focus of our minds and also to give expression to the passions of our hearts. When we combine the power within us with the power of our words, and then direct them both through a very specific formula of angelic names that specifies to G-d exactly what it is we are seeking from Him, we stand the greatest chance of having our prayers heard and answered. Reciting the names of angels is certainly not a necessary thing, but the mind works in funny ways. When one does ask G-d to send this or that angel to perform a certain function, it somehow makes us feel more empowered, as if we can at least ask G-d for specifics instead of just for general, generic help.

Angelic invocations can be very powerful, but only when done right. Of course, the problem exists that everybody believes that he or she is the right person doing things the right way. This is only reinforced when certain things start to happen that reinforce their beliefs. By this stage it is next to impossible to convince them that their encounters are demonic and meant to deceive them to their own harm.

In Hebrew prayer books, mostly of the Oriental/ Middle Eastern variety there are often found prayers that contain proper forms of angelic invocations. Usually these are associated with prayers for prosperity, protection and wisdom. Seldom are these even translated, although I have translated a good number of them in my other works. One can do some scholarly research and discover that many of the angelic names that we do have today come to us from ancient origins. From what we can ascertain many of the angelic names we possess can be documented to have been known during the days when the Temple stood. It is only by checking with our most ancient literary sources and comparing them to those that we have today that enables us to piece together the proper and true forms of angel names. Of course, unless one is a scholar with complete fluency in Hebrew and Aramaic, such an endeavor is impossible.

All spiritual mechanics operate according to the parameters of their laws; these are the laws of nature, the laws of the universe; the laws ordained by the Divine Creator. Angels are nothing more than messengers. There are angels who are nothing more than computer programs of artificial intelligence and then there are others that are living, sentient beings of a race very foreign to our own.

Biblical prophecy states that when the Mashiah is to come, he will descend from the skies with an army of angels. These angels will not be computer programs. These angels will be warriors, of a variety that we will wish that we never had to see. The army of Mashiah will be fierce and very much non-human. Their mere appearance will be enough to frighten many people to death. When this armada comes to Earth, they will take over in a matter of moments, dissolving any opposition, similar to melting an ice cube in a microwave oven. It will be quick, permanent and will not leave a trace of what once was.

When these angels come, we will know it. They cannot be called upon. These cannot be invoked, for to do so would incur their wrath. Angelic wrath is not something anyone would dare want to face. Are there those Sages who know how to peacefully commune with these warriors of Heaven? We are taught that there are such masters. Yet, they maintain their anonymity and their privacy. In time, these Sages will perform their tasks, and the armada will come in its time. Until then, let it suffice that we know that angels do exist.

They do not look like their popularly presented appearance. They do not work for us, but at times they are there invisibly to support us. Some perform their missions by rote; others program them to perform their missions.

We live in a great and very crowded galaxy. The multiple races of beings that we sum up and bundle together under the name angels are just some of the various species created by the Creator and seeded throughout our universe. There are many others, but we just need to discuss those that relate to our topic of defense against the dark arts.

Chapter 17

◄◉►

Mazal Angels, Magids & Earth Spirits

There are many spiritual entities that inhabit our Earth, some that are benign to us and others that are not. We have already discussed earthbound human souls. If they were evil when they were alive, they remain evil after they have died. Just as they posed a threat to other human beings when they were alive, so do they continue to do so after their deaths. These are the entities involved in what we call cases of possession. There are also the Shedim, (demons); they have their own indigenous lives and for the most part keep away from human beings. Many Shedim however do get involved in what I call "the cattle business" wherein which we human beings are the cattle. When Shedim activity is present, it is rather evident. We know what steps to take to teach people how to defend themselves against such incursions. Our previous essays have already discussed all this.

Now we must come to an entirely different species of entities, placed here by Divine command and who exert the greatest influence upon all things here on Earth. To best introduce them, I will quote the Midrash Rabbah (10:6) because it best describes their activity. The Midrash states, *"There is not even a single blade of grass that does not have an angel (mazal) over it striking it and making it grow."* Everything on Earth, down to the simplest blade of grass has a spiritual counterpart which is the source of life to the physical. This counterpart has been given many different names, the most common being one's "guardian angel," however I find this term to be most misleading. The term I believe most accurately describes the nature of these beings is one's "mazal."

A mazal is traditionally interpreted as having to do with the influence of the stars, like being one's horoscope. Yet, the Sages understood this in a different manner. While being well aware of astrological influences, our Sages recognized the Hand of G-d in the Creation of all. They saw in their spiritual minds the limitations of astral influences but yet also saw their earthly counterparts, that which channels generic universal life-force energy to all life. This channel is indeed a being of sorts and each being has its physical counterpart on Earth. The purpose for this being is to maintain the contact between its physical counterpart and the spiritual flow of Divine energy that comes into our universe. All life is allotted its appropriate share of life-force energy; the job of the mazal angel is to receive our portion from the greater universe and to ration it to us as we need it. Therefore the mazal angel plays a vital role in the life of everything here on Earth. As such this is why some call it one's guardian angel. In a way this is true, however, the definition of guarding must be defined from the context of the angel and not from our human point of view. One can also chose to refer to this entity as one's "higher self."

The role of one's mazal angel is vital in the understanding of defense against the Dark Arts. For all strength and weakness that comes to one, be it human or otherwise, comes through one's mazal angel. Indeed, when the forces of evil endeavor to attack a human being, instead of attacking the physical body, they often chose instead to attack one's mazal angel. If one's angel is blemished or harmed, their ability to channel life to their physical counterpart is extremely curtailed. The physical form therefore suffers greatly.

There are ways to strengthen our mazal angel; there are ways to commune with our mazal angel and there are ways to commune with the mazal angels of everything alive. Strengthening our mazal angel is a very good thing which we will discuss shortly. Communing with our mazal angel can be done and often is done through dreams. Communing with the mazal angels of others or other life forms on Earth is an area of spiritual communication that we have been prohibited to execute. Such forms of communication are dangerous and to be avoided. Let us delve into each of these three to understand them better. In order to do this I must digress for a moment.

In the beginning, G-d created the Heavens and the Earth. As simple as this verse seems it contains within a great secret. Heaven and Earth are clearly both part of creation. They are interrelated and interconnected. Today, we have better names to help describe their reality. Earth is the general name we use to describe our entire universal plane of physical matter. Heaven is the generic term that we use to describe a parallel universe made entirely of energy; an energy that is integrally connected to the matter of our physical universe. In other words, the dimension we call Heaven is the source of the physical universe we call Earth.

Like our physical universe, the energy dimension called Heaven exists everywhere that physical matter exists, as it were, to its side. Heaven can be considered to be beneath us or above us or alongside. The describing terminology matters not. The Heaven dimensional plane right alongside our own feeds our dimension like a mother lowering her breast to feed her newborn on her lap. The dimension that we call Heaven is the source of all life-force energy that gives rise to our physical universe. The connection between these two dimensional planes is therefore essential for our universe. If our universe did not have its source of nourishment, its life-force energy, our entire existence would cease to exist almost instantaneously.

Just as our physical universe is full of various forms of life, so too is the dimensional plane we call Heaven. Each of the denizens of the Heaven universe is the source soul and source of life-force energy for their physical counterparts here below on Earth. The denizens of this parallel dimension can view everything on Earth, whereas we for the most part are blind to their existence. We can compare our two dimensions to a large iceberg floating at sea. The vast majority of it is under the water unseen and unknowable. Only the smallest tip is seen above the surface. Nonetheless, it is that vast underwater portion that guides the iceberg and decides its direction. So it is with our two dimensions, the Heaven universe controls all that happens here. Therefore one who can influence what happens in Heaven dictates what happens here on Earth. Indeed, there is a way that Heaven can be rightfully supported. Then again, there are wrong ways that one can try to influence Heaven. These attempts can cause one great harm.

Our Sages have taught that when G-d created human beings, prior to what we call the Fall in Eden, our original physical form was made up entirely of a more refined form of matter than the bodies we inhabit today. This higher form of body was more like fluid energy than like rigid, physical matter. When we committed the error in Eden, we allowed ourselves to be tricked into the physical forms that we inhabit today. We have not yet been able to release ourselves from these, our physical and mental prisons.

Physical sensations and pleasures have long kept our conscious minds focused on living in this world. By reinforcing this, we seldom give our minds enough time to focus our consciousness on the different realities that we can also experience. Usually we only experience this vision of the parallel Heaven universe when we, either by choice or by force, deprive ourselves of the physical sensations that bind us here to Earth. When one chooses a regimen of fasting and deprivation one weakens the bonds of consciousness to this Earth dimension and enables consciousness to experience the alternate realities. This is why people who take long fasts often have visions. Also, when individuals are ill and weak, their attachment to physical sensations are weakened and in such states they often have dreams and visions. These experiences are mechanical and occur because it is natural for them to do so.

Since the beginning of recorded history religions have developed systems of meditation that enable consciousness to expand beyond physical limitations. Alongside these meditative practices, religions taught a code of moral behavior to guide human conduct. It is interesting that almost all religions worldwide that sought a connection to Heaven have a common denominator of morals and behaviors. Almost everyone agrees that behaviors such as theft, murder and adultery are wrong. While each culture has their own specific details of codes, nonetheless there are basic common denominators between them all. Those religions what were based upon meditative traditions understood that how we behave in this world contributes or detracts from our spiritual source in the parallel dimensional world called Heaven.

We all receive an allotted portion of natural life-force energy. We either add to it or detract from it. We add to it by performing those deeds that build it. We weaken and lose it by performing those deeds that Heaven knows are harmful to us. Here now is the key, spiritual protection is built upon the foundation of proper behavior as defined by Heaven. The side of evil exploits this knowledge by seeking to corrupt its chosen targets, getting them to indulge in harmful behaviors, thus weakening their life-force energy connections. Once such a weakness and breach has occurred, an agent of evil can come in and siphon off one's remaining energy until it is all spent up. When this occurs the human being dies. Proper behavior therefore protects the physical body by creating a strong spiritual counterpart body. Our deeds in this world become our reinforcement and support in the parallel dimension. This is how we strengthen our mazal angel.

We can commune with our mazal angel through both meditations and dreams. Remember our mazal angel is none other than our own higher selves, yet being that we are so absolutely disconnected from an awareness of that alternate side of ourselves, we often perceive our own higher selves as an outside separate force, something entirely other than ourselves. Again, this perception is false.

Connecting with one's own guardian angel is more a psychological process than a spiritual one. One simply needs to learn how to listen to one's inner voice. This is not as hard as one might imagine. Even in modern psychological circles there has evolved a form of meditation called active imagination where one uses visualization techniques to personify one's inner self and then engages it in conversation. While this process might begin as a flight into fantasy, over time it has the potential to develop into something much more actual and therapeutic.

In traditional Torah circles numerous methods of meditation have been developed since the days of the schools of the prophets. These meditative techniques enabled the adepts to become prophets. It also performed the same psychological function as do modern systems, but of course the prophetic path went much further. It is the psychological function that enables the mind to tap its own inner resources, the deepest of these being contact with one's own higher, inner self; the core of one's own being. One's higher self, aside from being called one's guardian angel, is also called in traditional Torah circles one's Magid (spiritual guide). It has often been mistaken that only the most righteous and holy of Sages can ever merit acquiring a Magid, however this is absolutely not true. The Kabbalists have clearly written that everyone has a Magid; it is just that not everyone's Magid is an angel of goodness and truth.

What a surprise that we should find that one's personal Magid will be nothing more than a reflection of one's true inner being. If one is good and pure so then will be the Magid. If one is rotten to the core, then so will be one's Magid. If one is a combination of good and bad and entertains a mixture of both truth and falsehood, then so too will one's Magid. Remember, a Magid is who you are; it is merely a reflection of you. It is your higher self and your higher self will only be a reflection of your lower self. Not everyone is good and righteous, not here on Earth and not even in the parallel dimensional plane we call Heaven.

Both the prophets of old and the psychology of today use the active imagination function to gain access into one's unconscious to become enlightened about the nature of one's true inner being. Whatever psychology chooses to do with such discovered knowledge might be radically different than those of the prophetic school. The righteous use their meditative descents into the depths of themselves to discover and expose any flaws or blemishes within their unconscious and personality. The adepts of the prophetic schools sought to cleanse themselves internally and externally to become so completely pure that indeed they could serve to function as conduit for the Voice of G-d, should G-d so decide to speak through them.

Of course, in Biblical times, there were false prophets. These were those who made a show of the cleansing process but did not perform all the necessary internal tasks. They too opened themselves up to something. However being that they were not pure enough to channel the Divine Voice, instead they were used by lying spirits. Sometimes these lying spirits were Shedim or earthbound souls. Other times the lying spirit was none other than their own inner voices speaking lies to them. Like I mentioned above, sometimes the experience of the inner self is perceived as something so absolutely foreign, the conscious mind perceives it as experiencing another being, when in reality all it is experiencing is an aspect of itself.

This type of self-deception happens to this day with all types of people from all walks of spiritual and religious life who claim they are talking to G-d and talking for G-d. In reality, nothing is more false. These deluded souls are simply having what psychology calls a numinous experience. They are merely talking with an inner aspect of themselves which reflects the world back to them in their own deluded image. Yes, one's Magid will be exactly who one is. One has to exert much mental labor to purify one's mind. Very few today even know how to do this much less accomplish it successfully.

While communing with one's inner higher self is often practiced, there is another form of communication with the higher selves of other forms of life. As the Midrash stated above, every blade of grass has its angel, so too then does every rock, lake, sea, mountain, desert and cloud. To everything there is a higher self that serves as its consciousness and its angel. The Earth is as full of these angels as it is with all other forms of life. These higher forms of all things natural, including animals, are called Earth Spirits. These are the entities that practitioners of various spiritual paths around the world seek out for their guidance, wisdom and protection. Torah however has prohibited such communications and condemns them for being a distraction both for the spirit entities involved and for us humans who should be focusing our spiritual attention on G-d the One Source of us all.

In spite of the Torah prohibition and the clear distraction these contacts make, many still seek them out and they are the foundation of many spiritual practices still practiced today worldwide. Indeed adept masters of the occult use these forms of communication to seek added strength for themselves and to find openings within an enemy. Little do they know the price they pay for their actions. Little do they understand the true nature of the Earth Spirit entities with whom they interact. These Earth spirits do not have human souls. They are not like us. Many times they are not even sympathetic to us, especially when their natural domain has been upset or harmed by human influence. These entities do have power, but they also know how to conceal it and to deceive prying human beings.

These entities have lives of their own. They have obligations and responsibilities. These Spirits are in many ways a higher life form than we are in our present mortal human state. These Spirits have little sympathy or patience with petty human beings. Even the angel of a blade of grass has no patience to reveal to a human being the secret of how it provides sustenance to its physical counterpart. The Earth Spirit knows well that if the human being would discover the secret of the flow of energy from one dimension to the next, the human could tap into that flow and divert it for his or her own nefarious purposes. Torah seeks to avoid all this and therefore prohibited the communications all together.

Earth spirits are considered by the ancients to be the gods of local places. In many native traditions one hears about the god of the mountain or of the lake and such. Many human beings have sought to appease these entities by making offerings to them, sometimes even sacrificing other human beings. These types of sacrifices are nothing more than outright evil. Nonetheless, offerings of this nature continue to this day in many occult traditions. Wicca, Santeria and Voodoo especially promote this type of activity. Wiccans have long practiced human sacrifice and in spite of their vehement denials, rumors of secret Wiccan human sacrifices still persist to modern day. As long as one is involved with an activity that is suspicious and dangerous by nature, it is hard to be completely free of any suspicions regarding it.

Local "gods" do indeed exist; the Torah speaks of them frequently. However, they should not be called gods, for gods they are not. They are angels, placed here by G-d to perform the tasks of guardianship and sustenance. These are the angels of the Earth plane. As such, they are not entirely pure entities. Like all other things here on Earth, they are a combination of both good and evil. This is another reason why communication with them has been prohibited. Even if one was able to establish contact, there is no guarantee that the information received from them would all be truthful. Earth angels can and do lie, unlike their Heavenly counterparts.

Even entire nations of people have their own guardian angel. This is the system established by G-d to maintain the proper order of things and to secure the proper flow of life-force energy to all areas of creation. While the Torah message has been to educate the world about the Presence of the One True G-d, nowhere does Torah deny the existence of the angelic governors, also known as the local gods. They do exist; they have their purpose; they do provide sustenance for that which is under their care; however we are not supposed to pray to them. Like us they are created beings and like us they too serve G-d. Therefore to confuse them with our mutual Creator is a big mistake. This is why G-d is called the G-d of gods and L-rd of lords.

Often people have a hard time dealing directly with the Divine Creator. Many times G-d does not provide for one exactly what he or she wants. In cases like this many times individuals will approach the local angels and ask them for their specific desires. These entities will most often ignore any human requests for interaction. They most certainly are not in any position to grant anything outside of their immediate sphere of influence. Any requests therefore made to them by definition cannot have much chance of fulfillment. Therefore, most times the angelic locals ignore human requests. However, this does not mean that these human endeavors go unnoticed. Our endeavors to make contact are intercepted and monitored by the various other malevolent forces surrounding us, most especially the Shedim and earthbound human spirits. These will often take on the guise of being one of the local gods and be willing to assist the seeker, usually for a high price, usually one of blood. This is another reason why we are prohibited from attempting any such contacts.

Local angels will sometimes communicate with human beings, but never to provide their needs, however they can from time to time offer advice or possibly even reveal some minor matters about the immanent future. These types of communion are still not sought after. Humans would have to initiate such contacts because the local angelic forces are way too busy involved in their tasks to be bothered with approaching us. Thus, whenever a troublesome human pops up, trying to make contact, rather than the local angel responding, many times a more malevolent force intervenes. Many Dark Arts practitioners and "wanna-be" practitioners attempt these contacts and end up getting involved way over their heads. The end result is usually that someone gets killed, sometimes the victim of the occult practitioner, but more often it is the occult practitioner him or herself who, in the end, dies or worse.

Communing with one's higher self is a good and beneficial practice. One will find such communions to be greatly rewarding. On the contrary soliciting such communion with the higher source of anyone or anything else is outside of permissible parameters. It is dangerous and prohibited and should be strictly avoided.

Chapter 18

◄○►

The Danger in Drugs, Burning Incense and Offerings

One of the great dangers facing anyone along the paths of spiritual pursuit is the temptation to take shortcuts to accomplish his goals. In occult circles, those who desire to cling to the sides of evil wish to make every effort to contact and commune with the malevolent forces that inhabit our domain. In order to quicken their way, many often turn to the use of dangerous mind-altering chemicals to open their consciousness to more easily perceive the other worlds. Little do they comprehend the dangers in these activities. Aside from this, many will also turn to offering plates of food or the burning of incense to Shedim and Earth spirits in what they think are benign offerings. However, these activities have their dangers. We must discuss them each in turn.

The human brain is a very complex organism. As much as modern science understands its operations, there is so much more that it does not understand. Human consciousness resides in the brain. From here it extends throughout the entire physical body. Yet, the brain is its point of connection that attaches it to the flesh.

The physical brain is subject to all kinds of influences arising from within consciousness; the mind/soul can and does affect the organic brain it inhabits. Yet, outside influences can also in turn affect one's consciousness. The brain is highly susceptible to influences from external chemicals ingested into the body and absorbed into the blood which then circulates into the brain.

Mind-altering chemicals make changes in brain chemistry. When these changes occur the paths of human consciousness are affected. The chemicals open doorways of communication between the conscious and unconscious minds. These chemicals can also break down portions of the barriers that keep our perceptions focused on physical reality. When these openings occur, allowing consciousness access to the other worlds, the first thing to happen is that the natives of that domain notice that the individual human now has the ability to see them. They see the opening in the human soul and recognize its true parameters far greater than does the human himself. These malevolent entities then take advantage of the unprepared open mind and show it all kinds of things that, unbeknown to the human, establishes a life-long connection between the human soul and the malevolent force that can now tap into it at will. The use of any hallucinogenic drug, even only once, will lead to this outcome.

Mind-altering drugs have become so popular today that their use, however illegal, is considered to be a recreational pastime. Little do those who indulge in this behavior realize the dangers they face. Whether it is marijuana, ecstacy or LSD, these hallucinogenic drugs alter brain chemistry and make their users targets for psychic attack. It should not surprise anyone, that those who make use of recreational drugs also become involved in many other types of harmful immoral behaviors. All of these drugs poison their souls and disable them from perceiving any forms of spiritual truths. Spiritual experiences they may well have; sometimes even making them believe that they are becoming more religious. However, when observed in the greater picture, users of drugs are clearly seen to have been seduced by the forces of darkness that seek to appear as light and then drag the human soul down to the depths of perdition.

Drugs work to open up the mind, but what is the mind opening up to? Is the mind strong enough to assimilate that to which it opens? In almost all cases the answer is no, and therefore the individual mind ends up becoming severely damaged. While there are those rare occasions in certain religious circles that drugs are used to enable one to commune with the local Earth spirits, even the masters of these systems warn of the dangers of this to those who are prepared for these journeys and all the more so the absolute disaster that awaits those not properly trained.

Compare the usage of drugs in spiritual pursuits to the use of military C4 plastic explosives. The only ones who use this most dangerous material are either terrorists or highly trained military specialists. Individuals like you or I would not even recognize the difference between C4 plastic explosives and children's play clay. We certainly would not understand how to use it or even properly and safely store it. Such things are best left totally out of our hands. We would love to keep it out of the hands of terrorists as well, because we know the damage and harm they cause. However military specialists are trained to know what to do and how to do it. We do not concern ourselves with their possessing such volatile explosives because we know they can be trusted with its usage. What this small, highly trained band of experts can do, the rest of us cannot. This is the same with the usage of drugs in the pursuit of spiritual growth.

Most people today, even those who are religious have almost next to zero training in meditative spiritual disciplines. In centuries gone by, meditators retreated from society and lived as hermits, to cultivate meditative skills and sharpen their minds. They spent extremely long periods delving into the depths of their own unconscious to explore inner space. Only after much training and practice was any type of hallucinogenic ever introduced. For the most part, these religious meditative systems have ceased to exist. No one today can practice, much less guide another in the ways of positively using drugs in pursuits of spiritual enlightenment.

Never has any system that did use drugs ever claim to put one into contact with anything other than the Earth spirits. No one ever claims that drugs could be used to experience the Divine Creator directly.

There are no shortcuts along the path to contacting the Divine. In modern times, new drugs have been developed and used recreationally. Some who take a drug-induced hallucinogenic trip believe indeed that they are experiencing G-d. Yet, how would they recognize G-d even if they were to experience Him? Without any spiritual background and training, they are easy prey for the dark forces to seduce and devour. Communing with G-d is not an emotionally based experience; it is far beyond the realm of emotions and even beyond the realm of conscious perception. I do believe that those who use drugs and claim to have had spiritual insights and experience are telling the truth. They did experience something; however that something is not what they think, in spite of what they believe. No one without training can accomplish such a spiritual communion, it is physically and psychically impossible.

The masters of the dark "Other Side" often ingest hallucinogenic drugs to open their minds to the spirit world. They invite whatever *shed*, soul or spirit to enter into their flesh and use it as a vehicle for communication. We have already discussed the extreme dangers of this practice in previous lessons. Yet, the Dark practitioners also seek to get others involved in illicit drug use to open up their souls to malevolent influences. It is no coincidence that we have termed the three great vices that are destroying western civilization as "sex, drugs and rock n' roll." All three of these abuse the body, alter brain chemistry and open the mind/ soul to invasion from malevolent outside forces.

Not one person who has been involved in this side of popular culture has escaped unscathed and unharmed from its influences. We all know this truth, in spite of the fact that we choose to deny it. Public opinion is very strong. The dominant social culture is overwhelming to many. This is why the wise and the holy chose to stay far away from it and accept with joy any scorn dumped on their heads for doing so. Better to stay safe from poison and be maligned for doing so than to ingest the poison and have it kill you.

All types of mind-altering drugs are simply bad news for everyone today. They should be avoided at all costs. We do not have the spiritual knowledge to know which ones were used for good and we certainly lack the training to enable the good ones to work in good ways. A firearm in the hands of a trained and disciplined officer of the law is a good thing. A gun in the hand of someone without such training and discipline is a danger to himself and others. Let me conclude this discussion about drugs by repeating: stay away from them! Do not be so arrogant to think that you can go against natural law and use drugs to your betterment. You have no idea of the harm you are causing yourself. All your spiritual experiences, however sublime and holy they appear are nothing more than demonic deceptions. The wise and experienced know this, but you dismiss their wisdom and wonder why they distance themselves from you. Cleanse yourselves in order to stand pure before Heaven and safe from the malevolent forces of the Dark "Other Side."

Another very popular practice today observed by many who are unaware of the occultic origins of the practice is the burning of fragrant incenses. This apparently benign form of introducing pleasant fragrances into our domains has a long history of association in both religious circles and occultic rituals. Some religious incense burning was performed because the spices when burned produced a smoke that when inhaled produced a hallucinogenic affect. In essence it was like taking a drug. I have already discussed above how dangerous this type of activity is to the unprepared.

Incense burning was not only practiced by the forces of the Dark Side, it was also burned in the Holy Temple in Jerusalem. The recipe for the Biblical Ketoret incense burned in the Temple was a closely guarded secret guarded within a single family of Temple Levites. When they died out the formula was lost forever. Biblical law dictated that it was forbidden to reproduce or use the Ketoret Temple incense outside of the Holy Place in the Temple. Violation of this law was punishable by death.

No one to this day knows exactly how the Ketoret was made, even though we do know that it was made with eleven specific spices. Yet, how they were mixed and in what proportions, this is what is lost. One thing about the Ketoret that has come down to us in history is that some claimed that it, too, produced an alteration in brain chemistry. Thus the inhalation of the smoke of the Ketoret incense combined with the special Priestly garments of the High Priest, along with the Presence of the Ark of the Covenant and the special location of the Holy of Holies in the Temple combined to create a spiritual/psychic window that enabled the High Priest to commune directly with G-d. Today, all these things have been lost with the passage of time. We cannot recreate the system because we lack the necessary details. Therefore, today, we have no Torah tradition of using any type of herb, spice or drug to alter brain chemistry for the sake of spiritual pursuits.

Today, people burn incense in their homes as a means of producing a pleasant fragrance. There is nothing inherently wrong with this. However, there have been Sages who have expressed concern with this practice. Knowing full well that the vast majority of individuals who burned incense did so as an offering to Shedim and spirits, the Sages became rather suspicious towards all incense burning. The Torah law code in fact states that one should not burn incense in one's house unless one is doing so to remove or cover up a foul odor.

Their concern with regards to apparently benign incense burning is well-founded and needs to be explained.

To this day in occult, voodoo and wiccan circles, incense is burned as an offering to the spirits and Shedim. Those practicing this know that by creating a potent fragrant aroma, they can attract these malevolent entities that have the innate power to extract from the fragrance a portion of life-force energy. Spiritual entities need to eat just as do human beings. Due to their being constructed of an entirely different form of matter than are we, so too the nature of their nourishment is different from our own, but only to a point. The fragrance was used for a two-fold purpose; it, in of itself, served to attract and nourish the entity and it also served to attract and invite them to a greater offering. This is usually something as simple as an offering of flowers or fruit, to something as elaborate as an entire meal. These classical offerings set before the spirits are spoken of in the Bible and prohibited by Torah law. It is a phenomenon that is not merely symbolic or mythical, it has a very real occult side to it that needs to be understood.

When we eat we naturally receive nourishment from the physical properties of the foods. However, within the physical properties is their psychic spiritual component. In essence everything has within it its life-force energy that enables it to exist and maintain itself. The spirit entities of this world have no need for the physical bulk of food as do we. However, like us, they too are nourished from the life-force energy contained within the foods. This is why throughout the centuries offerings of food, drink, fragrance and other tangibles have been offered as literal meals for the gods. Not that any god every came and ate a piece of bread or drank any wine. Instead, the entities would be magnetically attracted to the mental desires of those making the offerings; they would see the plates of food and the like and siphon the spiritual energy out of them. This left those items bereft of any positive component. In Biblical language these were called unclean. In other words, they were touched by a *shed* and maintained its residue. All who would partake of such offered foods would in turn become magnetically attached to the entity that drew the life-force out of it. This is why Biblical laws were instituted to protect the population from any type of food or beverages that had been offered to idols.

Another point very important for us to understand is the relationship of the sense of smell to spiritual entities. Smell is considered the one sense that makes the greatest connection between our physical realm to the spiritual realm of the demons and spirits. The nose is the place where G-d breathed into man the "breath of life" (ref. Gen. 2:7). Therefore, the nose and the sense of smell are very spiritual. The demons then are attracted to matters of smell more so than any other type of spiritual nourishment.

Indeed demons are attracted to fragrant aromas. These fragrances are their food. They "smell" them and thus extract the "life force" energy in them. Those individuals providing these demons this sustenance are then expected by these unholy forces to continue to provide for them. If not, they exact their revenge. Our Sages speak of human-demon relationships that span generations within a family. If one individual were to call upon and service a demon, this entity then looks to the individual's progeny to carry on the service. This explains why members of certain families may be seen to either have acute psychic powers, or seem to share precognitive abilities or more commonly to collectively share from some form of mental illness. All these signs are symptoms to a demonic presence attached to the family because of the activities of a past ancestor.

I cannot emphasize too strongly how the Shedim especially view human beings as nothing more than cattle, as a source for their nourishment. Whenever one endeavors to contact benign or even holy spiritual entities such as angels, their call is broadcast along the same frequency heard by the Shedim. These entities are immediately attracted to the spiritual caller. The Shedim look for any and every opening in which they can deceive the individual into believing that they are the angel or spirit conjured.

Usually the conjurer does not have the sophistication and experience to test the spirits and is satisfied that at least someone or something has answered her or his call.

Once this nefarious contact has been made, the *shed* then claims its territory and blocks any other force or entity from making contact with its prey. The unsuspecting individual is then reinforced into believing that she or he is in contact with some great and sublime spiritual entity seeking to reveal secret wisdom and powers to the individual. All the individual must do is pay a small price, such as the offering of incense or a meal. Usually the individual considers this something merely symbolic and does so without a second thought. Little does the individual realize that she or he is reinforcing the bond that they have made with a *shed*, who will then ever so subtly siphon off the individual's own life-force energy until such a time that the individual will become broken, mentally ill and eventually die.

Shedim especially act in this way. They are considered to be notorious energy thieves. Earthbound human souls act similarly but usually are not attracted to incenses and meal offerings. Unlike Shedim they do not siphon off such small pickings. Earthbound human souls instead siphon directly off human beings, often entering into them or tapping into them. These are the classical cases of possession spoken of in earlier chapters.

Earth spirits are not attracted to these types of offerings at all. It is a waste to offer anything of this nature to them. Most occultists however do not know this. This lack of understanding is due to *shed* influence. In order to deceive people into making these offerings, Shedim will often "whisper in human ears" that to make an offering to an Earth spirit is a good and proper thing to do. The unsuspecting and naïve human will listen and obey, not realizing that it is the *shed* who called for the offering and it is the *shed* who will take it, all the while that it is posing as the Earth spirit making all sorts of promises that it may or more commonly will not keep.

To avoid any openings to this type of *shed* activity, our Sages have long ago instituted certain laws to safeguard us. First, no food or drink should be left exposed and uncovered overnight. This applies to all foods that are normally not left out as such. This does not include plates of fruit which may normally decorate a table. But all other foods should be stored away in their proper places. Liquids that are left exposed and open over night are usually poured out rather than drunk the next day. Unless there is a dire need it is best to be safe than sorry. Food and drink should never be stored underneath a bed that someone sleeps on. These practices were ordained to protect us from any roving *shed* that might want to take advantage of an opportunity for a free meal. Unsuspecting as we are, these entities can enter our domains, do what they do and leave their trace upon our food and drink. When these are then ingested by human beings, a tap and connection is made, whether or not the individual is aware of it. These subtle connections can serve as a point of influence to turn a good person to act in bad ways.

While we have no room to entertain superstitions or fears, still we must take appropriate steps to safeguard ourselves. We live in a very crowded universe and in spite of our arrogant beliefs, we are not at the top of the food chain. Unless we protect ourselves we should not expect G-d to do it for us. We have to do what we can before G-d does what we cannot.

Drugs are a poison to the soul and should be avoided like the plague. They should not be experimented with even once any more than one would experiment with committing suicide even once. Incenses can be burned for the pleasant fragrances, yet be very careful what type you purchase. Many types of incense are manufactured for religious purposes and are intended to be offered in the name of a certain god. Many times this is actually written right on the package itself. Be careful what you let into your homes.

Never, ever follow any spiritual practice that offers flowers, fruits or anything else as an offering of thanks to anyone or anything. This is surely a *shed* plot, with the practitioners themselves often totally oblivious to what they are doing. I have personally seen the results of such nefarious activities. I have seen with my own eyes good souls become poisoned and blind, unable to see G-d's truth and unable to return to Light. They walk in an illuminated darkness thinking it is light and seek to attract many others. This is how cults work. Beware of them and stay far away.

The malevolent forces of the dark "Other Side" are all around us. Our present society is full of traps that seek to ensnare our souls. Only the most careful will avoid them all. It is up to us to become familiar with the mechanics of the occult, to recognize its operations, so that we can avoid them ourselves and to educate others how best to protect themselves.

Chapter 19

◄○►

Ritual Spiritual Remedies (Segulot)

Almost everyone agrees that there is a pressing need for spiritual defense against psychic/occultic attack. Unfortunately, so few know actual techniques that can be performed that successfully work to protect themselves, their families and environments from intruding malevolent forces. The remedies that I will shortly describe have a long track record of success. However, they only can work in conjunction with all the other necessary behavioral modifications that I have discussed in previous lessons. Unless one's behavior is morally proper, one's attire is modest and one stays clear of drugs and other negative influences, including other people who allow such negative forces into their own lives, no set of protective rituals can ever work. In essence, one cannot be spiritually safe no matter how many locks one puts on the front door, all the while that the back door remains open.

I often have individuals come to me and ask me to remove from them the influences of some evil eye or other malevolent power that has infected them. I have no magic mumbo-jumbo to offer them. I do not believe in deceiving people and telling them that for a large sum of money I will perform a ritual that will change their lives forever. Normally such rituals are meaningless nonsense and those that perform them are at best powerless, wishful thinkers and at worst deceptive thieves. While there might very well be a need for a financial investment in the performance of certain rituals, true Sages who perform such rituals do not require any personal financial compensation and certainly do not keep any monies offered them. All financial elements of a spiritual remedy are for charity purposes alone; to provide for the poor and needy. Anything other than this is highly suspect.

Most spiritual remedies to psychic/occultic attack are simple acts of piety. Specific prayers are recited. Fast days are observed. Monies are given to charity (and not as payment for services). There is even a proper order for burning a combination of herbs that create a smoke and aroma that is said to cleanse an area from malevolent influence. We will discuss each of these in turn; some in this chapter and some in the next. However I must again and again remind you, none of these will be effective as long as one's behavior does not completely change to comply with the directives of Torah and religious law.

Everything works within a context and outside of its context nothing works properly. Like I said above and will repeatedly remind you, you cannot protect the front all the while that the back is exposed. All the rituals in the world will be of no avail, indeed they can even cause harm, all the while that one's heart is far from G-d and one's behavior is far from righteousness and holiness. There are no short cuts and no tricks. The Dark Forces operates mechanically. These are natural laws that we are dealing with. Like the law of gravity that pulls and attracts regardless of one's personal beliefs about it, so too the occult can cause harm if one does not take the proper safeguards, regardless of one's personal beliefs.

Step one in addressing any psychic/occult attack is acknowledging its presence and its reality. Denial is the greatest of open doors. One who does not believe is unable to see that which one denies. Such blindness allows easy access. With such easy access caused by a blind eye, no ritual of any kind can fill the breach. One's denial, therefore, will be one's undoing. Usually the Dark influence becomes so overwhelming that one can no longer deny its presence. Unfortunately, usually by this time, it is too late to successfully help the inflicted soul. The damage done may be permanent. Therefore, from the beginning, if one senses a problem, he or she should immediately turn to a Sage and not a psychologist to seek a real spiritual remedy and not just some psycho-babble mumbo-jumbo as a patch. Even psychologists and psychiatrists need the help of a Sage from time to time. The bold and honest amongst them admit to this freely.

When one feels that there might be a problem due to Dark influences, the first thing to do is to ascertain where one has an opening to such a malevolent attack. One must first seal the breach before anything other operation is put into effect. Once one has made the necessary changes of behavior, one has closed the open doors. If one is not honest and sincere with this then the further actions I am about to describe will be useless.

When one makes a change and closes the openings, one still has to remove the negative influence that has already entered. This is accomplished by a combination of prayers and proclamations. One may also have to cleanse one's house (or domain) with a purification ceremony based upon the Biblical offering of the Ketoret spice. This ritual usually succeeds in removing most negative influences. However, cases of possession and poltergeist usually require more efforts. I will discuss the details of the house cleansing in our next chapter.

The beginning of removing any negative psychic/occultic influence starts with one cleansing one's mind. One cannot clean one's domain all the while that one's mind is still filled with contaminations. The proper way to cleanse the mind is to call upon G-d the Creator. Without Divine help we are all but hapless weaklings ready for the slaughter. Yet, with Divine help we can embrace the power and strength of Heaven itself. With Heaven working for us, nothing can work against us. Calling upon G-d requires of us certain proclamations. The purpose of these proclamations is to bind our minds to truth and to generate sufficient mental/psychic force to accomplish miracles. The initial proclamation should be as follows.

"I acknowledge that there is only One true G-d, creator of all existence. The One true G-d alone is the Creator and the source of all power; there is no power greater than He and ultimately no power other than He. G-d the Creator alone is the source of all things good and evil.

I acknowledge the existence of good and evil and pledge myself to the service of good and to fight the forces of evil. I acknowledge that this is my role in the Divine drama regardless of how much of it I understand. I do not need to understand everything; I just need to always do that which is right.

I acknowledge that I have nothing to fear from any force, spiritual or physical. No angel, spirit, soul or demon can ever approach me or harm me without the explicit consent from the One true G-d. The One true G-d alone is the One to whom I pray. I do not approach

Him in the name of any other. I do not approach Him in any form other than how He Himself has ordained.

I acknowledge myself as being created in the image of the Divine form. I have a natural connection to the Divine because it is within me. I acknowledge my human limitations and acknowledge that only the One true G-d can do for me that which I cannot do for myself.

I denounce any and all spiritual teachings or beliefs that deny any of this."

This proclamation as can be seen is like a combination statement of faith and a pledge of allegiance. Both of these aspects are necessary, for when making a proclamation to be heard by spiritual forces, one must be comprehensive to create a mental construct and a verbal barrier that is complete from all sides. When such a proclamation is made with intent and sincerity, it can be very powerful indeed.

First, one begins by correcting any behavior that creates psychic openings. Second, one can recite the above proclamation to create a mental picture for oneself, enabling one's mind to focus on G-d and the Divine power. As long as one is strict not to include or add the names of any additional gods, then calling on the One true G-d, Creator of all, will have the affect of focusing one's mind on that reality. However, if one calls upon the Name of G-d other than in its traditional and generic form, one stands in danger of inviting in a malevolent, deceptive figure that intends to deceive one into believing that it is G-d. Mistakes of this kind have happened throughout history and are the known cause for the disease of false prophecy. Once one is focused and certain, one can remove any taint of idolatry from one's spiritual practices. It is the idolatrous connection to idols and false spiritual beliefs that opens one up to occultic attack. Removing these is imperative.

Now let me address specific Biblical passages, the recitals of which also have strong power to cleanse both the mind and one's environment. At this point I will be providing Biblical passages and prayers and describe their individual usages.

To protect oneself from occultic attack, the above proclamation is very powerful. One should add to this the recital of Deut. 6:4-8, the famous Shema Yisrael prayer. The first verse, *Shema Yisrael, Adonai Eloheynu Adonai Ehad* is considered to have special psychic power. Our Sages compare this verse to a sharpened sword and say that those who recite this verse before going to bed at night will surely safeguard their souls. This is part of the nighttime prayers recited nightly by the Torah faithful. Another excellent form of psychic/occult protection is the recitation of two Psalms, Psalm 91 and Psalm 3. These are often recited at night after the recitation of the Shema.

The Sages of the Kabbalah have also devised a prayer of forgiveness, excusing all those who have sinned against them. They say that when we can forgive the sins that others have done to us, we can break the chains that bind us to them. If we excuse their debt to us we will no longer be required by the natural law of compensation to have any kind of relationship with them. This protects us from the possibility of them harming us anew. This is the prayer.

"Master of the Universe, behold I forgive and pardon all who have angered or provoked me or anyone who has sinned against me, be it against my body, my possessions, my honor or anything else that belongs to me, whether they did this accidentally or willingly, intentionally or unintentionally, whether they did this in word or in deed, whether in this life time or in a past incarnation. May no person be punished on my account. May it be Your will L-rd my G-d that I may sin no more and whatever I have sinned before You be wiped clean by Your great mercy and not by me having to suffer or be ill. May the thoughts of my heart and the words of my mouth be acceptable before You L-rd my rock and redeemer."

To recite this prayer with sincerity is the heights of piety. Now, do not think for an instant that when we forgive another for the harm they have caused us that such a one is not punished for their crimes. On the contrary, we are only proclaiming that we desire no further dealings with the individual(s) in question. We are requesting that Heaven deal with the imbalances caused by the malevolent individual(s) and leave us out of the equation. This lightens up our load and enables Heaven to execute retribution in a much more severe manner.

Do not underestimate the power of forgiveness and never be deceived into believing it is an act of mercy. Divine retribution is a natural occurrence; it cannot and will not be avoided. We simply wish not be to around when it happens. Therefore we remove ourselves from the obligation of having to execute judgment on those who have wronged us. If we become the executioners we embrace the danger of not being fair and balanced. This causes us to become offenders in equal measure worthy of punishment. In order to avoid any further harm to ourselves it is better to let it all go and allow Heaven to have its way and to execute justice in that way Heaven knows best. Letting go is often the best way of getting even. And never, ever, underestimate the power of sincere prayer.

Torah-faithful Jews have an entire order of bedtime prayers found in the traditional Orthodox prayer books (siddurim). For everyone else the above order is excellent. One begins by reciting the prayer of forgiveness, one then recites the proclamation of faith, one can then recite Deut. 6:4, followed by the two Psalms. This order may take all of five minutes to recite. This is a simple and small investment of time and effort which can yield tremendous results for safeguarding one's soul throughout the entire night and following day.

Torah faithful Jews also have an entire order of morning prayers which consists of a number of readings for various purposes. Little do most know that a good portion of these prayers were instituted specifically to defend against psychic/occultic attack. When recited with sincerity they become powerful; when recited without sincerity unfortunately they are little more than empty words. For everyone else not obligated to follow the Torah path, there can also be a small and simple order of morning prayer rituals, something as quick and easy as the night time order.

I will outline this in a moment, but first let me emphasis that as we go through our busy days and become all so involved in our regular affairs, it is all too easy to ignore the Dark dangers we face. We become distracted and therefore become open targets. If policemen or soldiers were to allow themselves to be distracted in their line of work, even for just a moment, it could lead to certain death. Do not think of yourself as any different in this regard. We are all on the front-lines of the Occult War and if you lose sight of this, then you, too, can become a primary target. Never forget the underlying realities of the world we live in. Stay alert and stay safe. This is why we take the precious few moments each morning to pray. We are, in essence, covering our minds with battle armor, to shield and protect it throughout the day.

Prayers are just words, true, however, when spoken with sincere intent, they can echo in one's mind and consciousness for a long period, especially coming to the forefront of consciousness at a needed moment. Psychic/occultic dangers are everywhere and can assault one without forewarning. Your unconsciousness mind will be the first to pick up on such dangers. It will naturally bring into consciousness the words of your prayers, to remind you of their power. With your mind momentarily remembering or thinking about your daily prayers, it is not open to the psychic/occultic assault. The mind therefore repels the negative influences seeking to inflict harm upon you. By thinking about G-d and prayer, you create an impenetrable barrier through which the forces of evil cannot pass. Reciting one's simple prayers, daily with devotion, trains the mind and enables it to remember the words and all the more so the concepts that the words represent. These will protect you in your hour of need. Do not underestimate the power of prayers. Even when you are not praying they can protect you from serious psychic harm.

In the mornings one can recite the proclamation of faith and the first verse of the Shema, Deut. 6:4. Then instead of reciting the Psalms, we instead recite another selection from the Torah; this one outlines the commandment for offering the Ketoret Incense in the Holy Temple. We have spoken of the powerful effect this Ketoret Incense had on the person of the High Priest. What we did not yet discuss is the power the Ketoret had on everyone else.

The Ketoret was designed to be burned for the sake of cleansing the Holy Temple and essentially the entire city of Jerusalem from negative and malevolent psychic/occultic forces. In its day, it worked wonders. Now that it is no more, the Sages have revealed that even the mere recitation of the commandment requiring it can have a profound affect for spiritual protection.

The arrangement was therefore established to recite the portion from the Torah speaking about the Ketoret (Ex. 30:34-36) followed by some of the words of the Sages that speak about the ingredients of its makeup and how they were mixed. This sacred knowledge is all we have left of the one-time great secret. We know the ingredients of the Ketoret, but not the secret of their mixture. Nonetheless, we recite the Biblical text, followed by the words of our Sages for the very words contain sublime mystical secrets of power and protection. We conclude the reading of the Ketoret with reciting three verses from the Psalms which seal in the psychic spiritual power. This order is recited three times daily by Torah faithful Jews. Let it suffice for everyone else to at least recite it once in the morning.

The order of the Ketoret prayer can be found in every Torah (Orthodox Jewish) prayer book. Many of these include a small running commentary alongside the text of the prayers. For those who seek more insights into the meanings of the Biblical text and all the more so the accompanying sayings of our Sages, I would highly recommend that one acquire one of these prayer books.

The reading of the Ketoret is considered so powerful and sacred that its recitation is attributed to provide numerous blessings, far more than just protection. It is said to also serve as a blessing for one's livelihood, health and domestic tranquility. In Torah circles, the Ketoret reading is specially written on animal parchments, similar to the writing of a Torah scroll. The faithful safeguard this spiritual remedy and carry it with them wherever they go. Its power is profound. Yet, its power will only be realized when one performs the recitation daily with true sincerity, with faith and trust in G-d.

The malevolent forces of this world have true and dangerous powers. Yet, the Source, the Creator, G-d Himself has much greater immeasurable power. When we cling to the source, we have no need to fear any of the branches. When we keep focused on Heaven, then Hell has no room to enter our minds, or our bodies. By being full of Heaven, we can become clean of Hell. This is a simple recipe and its works! Spiritual mechanics are simple. All we need do is learn the rules and follow them. We can save ourselves a lot of trouble and pain by doing so. Learning the mechanics of the dark "Other Side" therefore means learning about G-d. We do this for the sake of Heaven, yet we ourselves benefit from this here on Earth. This alone is the secret to having a successful and good life.

In Hebrew there are books that contain long lists of verses from the Torah and especially the Psalms that are recognized as having significant power to repel malevolent forces. To enumerate them all would require a separate book of its own. I have already translated a number of these spiritual remedy prayers and rituals and most recently published a selection of them in my book, "*Walking In The Fire.*" For those who are interested in these prayers and practices, I would recommend that you acquire this book.

The Ketoret prayer is also used as the basis of a ritual performed for cleansing an area from a malevolent or frightening presence. The prayers are recited in combination with burning a specific combination of herbs. This order is a ritual of cleansing and can be performed successfully only by those who are, as the Psalm says, are "*of clean hands and of a pure heart.*" (Psalms 24:4). We will devote our next chapter to this procedure.

Chapter 20

◄o►

Ritual Cleansings

In spite of our best intentions, malevolent forces can still permeate and dominate in certain locations. Within domiciles, past actions can leave indelible psychic stains on the place that can last for centuries. Indeed, even after a building has long vanished the psychic sense of the place can linger. This is the rule, whenever something happens in a place that releases a strong amount of emotional/psychic energy, that place captures that energy as film captures light to create a photograph. The place becomes marked. This happens with both good and evil forces. This is how holy places are established; and how places of evil also come into being.

Of course, there are yet other places that are the natural or adopted habitats of "Other" entities. Earthbound souls choose their own. Shedim have other domains that they call their own. Nature spirits each have their respective domains. No one can enter into any of these places and not expect to fall under the influence of those who are in possession of those places. If and when we find ourselves in a hostile psychic environment in nature, it is simply best to physically relocate. Move on and the spirit of the place will not move on with you, but rather it will let you pass, mind you, not necessarily in peace.

The realms in nature are not necessarily subject to psychic cleansing unless the cause of the problem is due to the area being polluted by malevolent human activity. For example, on numerous occasions sites in nature have become places of murder and carnage. Many times the souls of the dead have not found rest. They do not rest because they have not yet achieved appropriate vengeance against those who have wronged them. Wronged souls become earthbound because their anger and rage does not allow them to move on and pass over into the other dimensional planes. Souls of this nature die in a state of outrage and that emotional image becomes burned into that place, making the place one that provokes similar emotions. If further activity of a similar kind is enacted there, then this only reinforces the nature of the place. Cleansing such a place requires that the souls that are entrapped there by their own rage be somehow appeased and released so that they can continue along their paths of spiritual evolution.

Many times domiciles such as haunted houses and the like are actually locations where something bad has happened in the past, be it recent or distant. Although many will not experience the types of haunting phenomena made famous by Hollywood movies, nonetheless certain places definitely can make one feel very uncomfortable. Even individual items in a place where there had been a release of tremendous psychic energy will maintain that energy. When those items are then relocated they carry with them a portion of the absorbed psychic energy. In this way the item itself transports the energy to a new place thus enabling psychic/occultic activity to flourish in a new and previously clean environment.

Yes, there is such a thing as haunted pieces of furniture or other personal items. It is for this reason that Sages will never wear used clothing unless they know who used to own them. The same goes for receiving used furniture, especially antiques. If there is any concern that a previously owned item might contain an element of negative psychic energy from its previous owner(s), it is best to avoid it entirely. This is also true of jewelry. There are procedures that can be used to cleanse such items and we will discuss them in future chapters.

We just have to remember that psychic energy is as real a phenomenon as are physical object. Psychic energy is the life force within everything. Just as the physical attributes of a thing can be altered and made better or worse, so too can the psychic component. One cannot escape this inevitable fact of natural law. Strong emotional content does transfer psychic energy into an item or place. Yet, even the simplest of presence can instill a mild influence. The masters of occult know this secret well and when in pursuit of a victim will always seek to touch something of their victim, be it their person or property. By doing so, the mere simple touch is used to transfer negative psychic energy. On the other hand, when one wishes to bestow a blessing, one places one's hand upon the other or upon something that the other will embrace. Psychic energy is always passed on by touch.

Cleansing of one's possessions and one's domain will only be successful if one's physical self is also first cleansed. Needless to say, one must be physically pure of any type of drug or alcohol influence or abuse. Yet, more than this, one must also be cleansed of psychic contamination that comes about through illicit sexual intercourse. On both the physical and psychic levels when one engages in sexual activity with a new partner, one is tapping into and being attached to all the psychic energy that the sexual partner has been exposed to. This is why religious teachings have always taught rules about sexual conduct. This is also the reason why the occult has so strongly pushed for the dismissal of traditional Biblical and other religious restrictions on free and wanton sexuality. The masters of the occult know that the entry way to the soul is through the psychic energy transferred during illicit sexual activity, and the more forbidden, the better for them.

Physical cleansing of the body begins with sexual abstinence from prohibited sexual activity. This does not mean that sex is bad or wrong. It is neither. Yet, like everything else, it has its proper time and its proper place. One who wishes to write one's own rules and chart one's own course will end up having to deal with the consequences of one's own actions. Sexual promiscuity has led to nothing other than heartache, bitterness, depression and many other bad things. It hinders one from finding one's true soul-mate and causes numerous other physical and psychic health problems. Stopping this type of behavior is the first step along the road of cleansing.

Mind you, pornography in all its forms is equally dangerous and evil. One who has any forms of these should destroy them immediately. The best way to dispose of these items is to burn them in a safe environment, such as in a backyard BBQ grill or the like. As they burn one should curse them and repudiate them and what they stand for. One should be ashamed for allowing oneself to succumb to such depravity and vow to be stronger. Sexual activity is great and sublime and should be properly enjoyed. Pornography and promiscuity should never be included within the definitions and contexts of healthy sexual activity.

In Torah circles, after sexual activity one cleanses one's body in a ritual pool of naturally gathered water. Yes, this can be done in a lake, pool, or even the ocean. One should take caution while bathing to do so privately and not to be exposed to others. If there is no body of natural water in which one can completely immerse, one should then simply take a shower or bath. While this cleansing is only skin deep, it still expresses a desire to be cleansed deeper within. The inner cleansing however takes a much longer time and is not subject to assistance by ritual. The cleansing of one's psyche and psychic energy is a process that takes time. It is only accomplished after one has a true change of lifestyle.

One who is not pure of heart cannot cleanse something that is equally impure. Only the inner desire that is pure can overcome the outer psychic reality that is impure. Those who endeavor to cleanse an area, an item or another person, must be careful that they themselves are not subject to the subtle influence that such an area, item, or person might try to cast upon them. There are many different rituals used that have both symbolic and actual power creating a protective barrier around an individual who is carrying out a cleansing. Yet, the most powerful defense is one's inner state of being. All the protection rituals in the world will not suffice to protect one who inwardly is afraid or otherwise impure.

Impurity and purity are not ritual states, they are psychological states of mind. I cannot over-emphasize this. One can take rituals baths daily for the rest of one's life and still remain spiritually and psychically impure. It is not the flesh that needs to be cleansed but rather, the spirit. Only inner transformations of moral character and personality can accomplish this. It is the inner transformation that enables the external ritual to accomplish its task. Things do not work the other-way around. One must first cleanse one's heart from fear, improper desires and inappropriate beliefs.

Only when this is accomplished will one become pure at the psychic level. One who has accomplished this creates a psychic barrier around one's soul that almost no occult force can penetrate. With the help of G-d in Heaven, called upon properly with sincerity and humility, one becomes impregnable.

Now, once one's heart is strong and firm in faith, knowing that G-d is in control of all things and that no evil force can cause any harm unless permitted to do so from Heaven, we can proceed to confront malevolent emanations and remove them. Ritual cleansings require two specific functions; one is the recitations of proper Biblical verses and related texts and the second is the proper mixture of incense, the mixture of which has been handed down for centuries and is proven to perform the cleansing action.

When cleansing an area, be it a house or the like, we must differentiate between cleansing it from malevolent forces bent on perpetuating evil and non-malevolent earthbound souls who have become entrapped in that place due to the nature of their deaths. Chained souls simply need to be released. They are not malevolent and do not require a transformation. All they need is to be shown the way. This is accomplished with the simplest of methods, that being simple sincere prayer to Heaven requesting that spiritual guides be sent to guide the lost souls and to protect them along their journey to a better place. Reciting Psalms, especially the famous ones, such as Psalm 23 (the L-rd is my

Shepherd) and Psalm 121 (I lift up my eyes) work very well here.

Whenever there is a major loss of life due to natural or man-made causes it is always best for those with the knowledge to go to the place of disaster and to say prayers for the souls of the dead. In Jewish tradition, there is a regular prayer to be recited for the dearly departed. This prayer, called the Kaddish, is actually an Aramaic praise to G-d. The Kabbalists however have revealed all types of subtle secrets and codes concealed within its letters and words. Regardless of the secrets therein, even an English rendition of this prayer is of great value for both the living and the dead.

An English translation of the text here follows. Traditionally this prayer is recited by a quorum of men in ritual prayers in the Synagogue. However, in order to help elevate lost souls I believe anyone can recite this in a whisper just about anywhere.

"May G-d's great Name be exalted and sanctified in the world which He has created according to His Will and may He establish His kingdom.

May His salvation blossom and His anointed one come near, in your lifetime and in your days and in the lifetimes of all the House of Israel speedily and soon and say Amen.

May His great Name be blessed forever and for all eternity. Blessed and praised, glorified and exalted, extolled and honored, elevated and lauded be the Name of the Holy One, blessed be He, beyond all the blessings and hymns, praises and consolations that are spoken in the world; and say, Amen.

Let the prayers and supplications of the entire House of Israel be accepted before their Father in Heaven; and say, Amen.

May there be much peace from Heaven, good life and satiety, salvation and comfort, saving and healing, redemption and forgiveness, atonement, relief and deliverance for us and for all His people Israel; and say, Amen.

May He who makes peace in His heights, in His mercy, make peace upon us and upon His entire nation Israel; and say, Amen."

The intent within the prayer should be clear. Anyone should be able to recite it to acquire the solicited results. When one focuses on G-d the Divine Source of all, one can thereby nullify any and all negative forces. One can bring true spiritual healing to those souls that are in such desperate need. This simple act of prayer can release numerous souls by opening up for them a vortex of light that will enable them to find their way to where they need to be. This prayer can bring peace to those souls taken before their time, whereas at the same time it does not at all forgive the criminals who ripped them out of their bodies in such frightful and horrible ways. Vengeance will come upon those who perpetuate evil.

G-d has arranged natural law so that evil doers are always punished. Whether in the present lifetime or in a future one, those who have harmed another and have never made redress will pay back in like kind for what they have done. Payback is often two-fold or five-fold. It is not pleasant, nor easy. We often ask why terrible things happen to apparently innocent victims. While they may be innocent in this lifetime, in a past life, they may have been something very different. Thus they receive in this life what they dished out to another in a previous life. This is why bad things happen to apparently good people. While this is not absolutely true in every case, it is still the rule in most cases.

Now that we have explained how to deal with the trapped lost souls, now let us deal with how to deal with the malevolent forces, be they earthbound souls, Shedim and their kind. Unclean forces cling to their domains and they are not removed with ease. I must emphasize that I am talking here about removing malevolent forces from places and not from people or things. We will have to deal with these later on in the following chapters. For now, let us focus on the cleansing of space.

First, the domicile in question must be cleansed of any unclean or evil content. Books, CDs, and DVDs, art work and the like that present messages that can cause psychic harm should be removed, as well as any other item that projects a negative message. Once the area has been cleared of such subtle but real malevolent influences the process of cleansing can take place. Mind you, once the process has been performed, you must maintain the cleanliness of the area by not allowing back into it items of negative influence or act in negative ways that can open up the area to invite back into it any malevolent force.

To cleanse an area one must begin with a proclamation stating that this is what one is doing. One should offer a prayer to G-d soliciting Divine support in removing all harmful influences from this domain. One should then always pray to remove any lost souls that are trapped. One should then make a bold proclamation proclaiming this location to now belong to G-d and to holiness and therefore no further malevolent presences will be tolerated. When making these proclamations, one should be careful to solicit the Name of G-d, but never the name of anything that is not G-d. Such a proclamation can be made in one's own words, but this version can also be of help.

"I call upon G-d, Creator of Heaven and Earth to hear my prayers and assist me in my task. I hereby declare in the Name of G-d the Creator that this

domain is from now and forever to be a place of holiness and righteousness.

I declare in the Name of G-d the Creator that no further malevolent forces may be allowed to dwell here. I call upon G-d in Heaven to release any entrapped and lost souls imprisoned here. And I call upon the L-rd of Heaven to send His angels to cast out from this place any and all malevolent entities, be they earthbound human souls, Shedim, fallen angels, and all other types of spirits of anger, harm and deception.

I call upon the L-rd of Heaven to hear my prayers and assist me in this proclamation to cleanse this area and make it safe again for all those who seek the true Light of Heaven and to walk the path of righteousness and truth.

Behold I now will take this incense of cleansing and pass it throughout this place. May its fragrance be acceptable before the L-rd of Heaven and also have the effect of making this domain most uncomfortable and unpleasant for the malevolent forces.

May they immediately be removed from here now and forevermore, with the help and assistance of G-d the Creator and His angels whom He sends now to assist me in this great undertaking. Amen, may it so be His Will."

After making this proclamation, one should take an incense burner, preferably one of those that come on a chain and can be held by a handle while the burner swings in the air. One prepares a small charcoal disc and puts it into the burner. Once the charcoal is hot and ready, one places the proper incenses on top of it allowing it to be burned. One then takes the smoking incense and passes it through every corner of the haunted domain. Allow the smoke to fill the place completely. Only after the domain has been filled with smoke should one open the windows and doors and allow the smoke to dissipate. The malevolent entities always exit via open doors and windows. As they are shut-in during the procedure, they desperately seek to leave as quickly as they can. By not allowing them immediate exit only reinforces their desire to leave and to not return. When the windows and doors are opened, they depart, and we pray that they never return. Please note that when performing this ritual one had better disable any smoke alarms operating in the domain, or they could trigger an alarm that would hinder your concentration.

Now, two things I have mentioned here which I have yet to explain. First, one must have sincere concentration and devotion when performing this ritual. I cannot over-emphasize that one's intent makes all the difference whether or not this works or does not. Faith and sincerity are two powerful weapons that no malevolent force can stand against. Doubt is a poison that kills both body and soul. If you sincerely believe that there is evil in a place that needs to be exorcised, then you must equally sincerely believe that your performance of this ceremony can accomplish this task. The task of ritual cleansing is one best done alone. One does not need an audience and one does not need company. If one is fearful of doing this alone, then one should first overcome one's fears and then do what one has to do.

When performed properly, one can cleanse one's domain. Cleansings of items and exorcisms of other human beings also need to be addressed and we will proceed to do so in coming chapters.

Chapter 21

➤⬧◦⬧➤

Cleansing Objects & Persons

One must never forget the magnetic law of attractions that binds things together regardless of physical distance or passage of time. Contact on any kind- physical, emotional, mental or spiritual- creates a bond that is not easily broken. Even a mere physical touch can create a link between two parties, even if one is unsuspecting.

Sometimes these connections can be good and become a source of blessing. Unfortunately sometimes these connections can be bad and become the source of a curse. When a connection is good, bonds expand; when the connection is bad, the bond must be broken. We must now discuss how it is that we break the bonds that entrap negative spiritual energy within objects and then proceed to discuss how it is we can also free human souls trapped by the power of a curse, the evil eye or outright possession.

Harmful psychic energy is certainly not a new phenomenon. It has existed for as long as we have. Dealing with this problem is thus nothing new. Even in the Bible itself ways are discussed how we are to neutralize the harmful psychic energy that may exist in any physical object. The Bible teaches us that whenever we are to absorb something new and foreign into our lives and homes, we should first pass the thing through the "fire" or the "water." Literal fire and water have the ability to remove harmful psychic energy. While these practices are psychic in nature, they are at the same time, sanitary and physically cleansing as well. The rituals of the Torah always serve dual purposes, having both physical and psychic benefits.

Whenever we acquire new utensils used for cooking, Torah law requires of us to first immerse them into water prior to their first usage. The religious reasons for this are many, but we need only pay attention to the psychic reason underlying this. Water has the property to cleanse. This is true both physically and psychically. When we immerse something in water, we disconnecting the thing from the air and the psychic essence being transferred through it. Water is a dampening field. There is no requirement for a lengthy submersion or for more than one. A simple single immersion does the trick. Torah law requires this be done regarding all cooking items because foods are most often used as the conduit for channeling energy, be it good or bad. Vessels that cook food also absorb from the food's energy. The Sages chose to refer to this energy as the food's "taste." However, this is no physical taste but rather its spiritual taste, or in other words, its energy.

Not only is it a wise safeguard for all of us to appropriately cleanse our new cooking tools in this manner, we also learn from this how the process of cleansing can be used with regards to other items not food-related. As a matter of cleanliness, whenever we purchase new items from outside we should always wash them before usage. New clothes can be put into the wash, and other appropriate items can simply be rinsed off in a sink. Granted, one cannot do this with every purchase. It would not make much sense to run brand new paper towels and toilet paper under water for this would ruin them. Besides, who would project the evil eye (negative energy) on to these in the first place? Evil energy usually only resides upon that which the eye craves. It is the spirit of jealously that can create the evil force. Yes, water, can have an effect to weaken or remove such energy, if it even exists upon such items.

While we must always be aware of the true psychic nature of the world around us, we must never allow our desire to see deeper into things leads us into a state of paranoia and fear. This mental state alone is much worse than any negative energy that can be projected onto or into an item. Our own minds play the greatest role in psychic self-defense. Granted, our minds cannot make negative psychic energy go away all by itself, but by our not entertaining the fear of its existence, we do prevent a portion of it from penetration our minds. Of course, if we deny psychic energy all together, then we face the danger of falling under its influence unknowingly. Proper balance must always be the key. You must know that such things exist and you must know that you have the power to neutralize them.

Brand-new store-bought items, such as clothing, jewelry, furniture and the like, usually are not subject to adverse psychic influences. Being that no one has ever before previously owned them, the chances of them becoming absorbed with psychic energy from anyone other than the manufacturer is highly rare. When we wash or rinse new items we do so as a precaution and also there is a health benefit here. New clothes for example, contain dyes that can be absorbed through the skin. One does not need to understand spiritual mechanics to recognize that this is not a good thing.

When items are purchased second-hand or passed-down, this is where strange energies begin to surface. This law of magnetic attraction should not be underestimated. At the time of this writing I read an interesting story in the news that I believe will show us this concept in action. This is a story about a man who committed suicide. Years before he was the recipient of a heart transplant. The man from whom he received his heart also was a suicide. The two chose to end their lives in exactly the same way. Now, here is something even more strange: the recipient of the heart transplant married the widow of the man from whom he received his heart. So, the recipient had both, the man's heart and the man's wife and he ended up the same way the man did, dead from a self-inflicted gunshot wound to the head. This is not a joke or an embellishment. This is a true story.

The recipient of the heart received a lot more than just a benign organ of the flesh. He received a very strong part of the soul of the recently deceased. So strong was it, that it motivated the man to marry the widow so that part of the deceased soul could maintain its relationship with his wife. While this may not be so bad, apparently the evil influence that led him to take his own life also followed along and entered the second man. The same influence that led to the death of the first repeated itself with the death of the second. This story is sad, but true. It is bizarre and should serve as a warning to us all.

As a side note, it is a story like this that underlies the philosophy of why certain religious adepts strongly oppose all types of organ transplants from the dead. The souls of the dead live on through their organs. This is true of the physical DNA still in those organs as well as true of the psychic energy within them. There are numerous stories of organ recipients developing new tastes and interests (not all of them good) after their life-saving surgeries. The religious believe that all healing ultimately comes from G-d and that the souls of the dead must be allowed to rest in peace. I do not wish to make a statement for or against organ donations and transplants. These are highly personal decisions that one should contemplate with the help of one's family and minister. Awareness of the psychic dangers should be known, but these do not necessarily override the immediate dangers to physical life. Do not draw conclusions here, merely be advised and be aware.

I have heard of numerous other ways to cleanse objects of negative psychic energy such as immersing them in salt and leaving it there for twenty-four hours. I have never heard this ritual from my teachers, therefore I cannot state with certainty that it would work. I believe that we should always use methods that are tried and true. Whenever there is a question whether or not something really works, I chose to proceed with caution and to stay away. I always say, better safe than sorry.

Cleansing with water is well known and ancient. It has been practiced in cultures around the world. Therefore, whenever something new comes into our domain and we can dip it in water, then it should be so. This ritual cleansing is the source of two very famous religious rituals, the mikveh in Judaism and the baptism in Christianity. Mind you, just a sprinkling of water does not accomplish the necessary purification process. A full immersion should be done. After one performs a ritual immersion one should dismiss any further thought of psychic contamination. Such fears can actually re-open any closed doors.

Cleansing physical objects with water is easy. However, not everything can be immersed. Larger objects cannot be washed. They should be cleansed in similar fashions as are domains. The incense should be burned around them allowing the smoke to imbue the object(s) all the while that one is reciting Psalms 3 and 91 or other similar prayers like those we have previously laid out. Following these procedures one should be able to cleanse just about anything with the possible exception of the most malevolent forces. Removing these might require the assistance of experts. If the items in question are not of great value, it may just be better to discard them.

The best way to discard of items with negative energy is to first break them in to pieces. Using a hammer can actually be very therapeutic in this respect. Then one can actually utter words of a curse over the malevolent force that I will outline later in this essay. Just be careful never to use foul language or to utter the holy names of G-d when expressing your rage and anger. One can then take the pieces and if one can, one should either burn them or bury them. Do not just throw them into the trash. A ritual of banishment, death and destruction helps the mind heal from the malevolent influence. Do not underestimate the power of such rituals.

Dealing with persons who have a malevolent force either influencing them or outright possessing them is a much greater task that merely cleansing physical objects. Being that human beings are a direct resource of psychic energy, wanton behavior will often lead to a magnetic attraction between a person and some malevolent entity. These entities can become strongly attached when wanton behavior is performed repeatedly. Even when one has thoughts of changing one's ways, the malevolent entity almost always puts other thoughts into a person's head to compel the individual to act in the old wanton ways. Malevolent entities do not like to surrender what for them is a source of food. Getting them to leave a person alone takes great effort.

The first step in cleansing a tapped or possessed soul is for the individual first to strongly desire to be freed from what possesses them. Without this heart-felt, strong desire no cleansing of the soul can be made possible. Once the desire to be free is sincere and firmly expressed, one must also be completely remorseful of one's wanton ways. One must find one's own previous behavior to be repulsive and disgusting, and nothing less vile. One must really come to hate what one once was and one must be willing to do anything, even die, in order to change and distance oneself from one's own past. When the level of conviction is this strong, then the magnetic pull that attracted the malevolent entity in the first place can indeed be broken.

If one's own mind truly desires to continue in the ways of one's wanton past, the magnetic attraction is not severed, therefore neither will be the malevolent force that comes along with it. I cannot over emphasize the importance of a contrite and broken heart in the matter of cleansing. This is well known in religious circles. Little do most religious individuals realize the psychic, occultic nature to these things. Cleansing begins within. Once this most difficult of all steps is accomplished we can then begin to address the ritual aspects to cleansing the soul. This may or may not include the ritual of exorcism, depending on how difficult the level of contamination is.

Cleansing an individual begins with their personal desire to be cleansed. Thus all rituals begin with the individual. Only when individual rituals are exhausted and the problem still exists do we then turn to others to perform rituals that require their presence. However, as with all malevolent psychic attacks, we must have relative certainty that the problem we face is not one that is psychological or psychiatric. Organic problems in brain chemistry often manifest forms that can easily be mistaken for psychic issues. Whereas psychic issues can be addressed through ritual, psychiatric issues cannot. If rituals are performed, and the individual still believes him or herself troubled by some outside force, the experience of such a troubling force is most likely an indication of the psychiatric nature of the problem. Needless to say, under such circumstances one needs to seek out qualified medical help to address this issue.

Before I discuss ritual cleansings, let me digress for a moment to discuss psychological and psychiatric interventions. I do believe that both of these can be positive and helpful interventions. Yet, I must emphasize that usually the two must work in conjunction with one another. If there is an organic, chemical imbalance in the brain, one needs to go to a psychiatrist who is also a medical doctor to receive the appropriate and necessary medications. However, meds by themselves might not be enough. Often, even when medicated, some semblance of strangeness might continue. These have to be explored and examined.

Unfortunately, most clergy, including Rabbis and Kabbalists do not have a clue as to the workings of the inner mind and do not have the ability to discern the subtle differences between a mind disturbed due to psychological issues and one disturbed by a malevolent force. On the surface the two often look identical and only with proper investigation with the proper tools can one ascertain which is which.

Ritual cleansings, aside from the psychic value of actually ridding one of a malevolent force, can also play a role in psychological cases as well. Simply, even if one believes oneself to have such a psychic problem, then one should also equally believe that by performing a psychic ritual cleanse that one's problem should dissipate. Sometimes this can work, but I must emphasize that many times it does not. This does not mean that one should try over and over again to perform psychic ritual cures for a psychological problem. If it did not work once, it will not work again. This is the nature of psychological problems.

The only true solution for psychological problems is the long road, which includes counseling and therapy for the mind. One must learn to recognize one's own psychological issues and to address them in the appropriate forum and not fall back upon the mystical and psychic for a magical cure that does not exist. Psychiatric problems are not different; they must be addressed with the proper medications. When the organic brain is helped into balance through the use of psychotropic medication and the mind/soul is helped through counseling with a good, honest, moral and insightful counselor, then the process of healing actually begins. When this process is complete, only then can we truly ascertain if there really is an external malevolent force that is causing the disturbance.

Often in the process of psychological therapy it can be discovered that the individual is suffering from some form of external malevolent influence. Under such cases, it is wise and appropriate for the professional counselor to seek the assistance and support of professional clergy who know the arts of exorcism. Unfortunately, in our overly-secular world, psychology has fallen into the hands of those who deny the existence of anything spiritual and dismiss the existence of any real external, malevolent psychic threat. One should dismiss any such counselors. Their own prejudice and ignorance can cause one (and themselves) serious psychic harm. There are numerous good, religious, spiritual counselors practicing around the world. One does not have to settle for a secularist who essentially denies spiritual reality.

Exorcisms are no laughing matter. They are very serious and can also be quite dangerous. They should only be handled by practicing professionals who are experts in the ways of the occult and dark arts. Not many religious, spiritual clergy have this level of expertise. Therefore, in the worst case scenario, where an exorcist is required, one should be cautious and find the right person. This task, I assure you, is not an easy one. Exorcists are not listed in the telephone book and they do not promote themselves on the internet. Nonetheless, with faith in G-d and with prayer, almost anything impossible can be done. If one needs to find a proper exorcist, then somehow G-d will send one. Let this suffice for now.

Under less extreme circumstances, where the disturbed soul is not in need of psychological counseling or psychiatric intervention, and yet a malevolent force is present, there are rituals we can apply individually to help the person in question. As always, we begin by turning to G-d in prayer. We recite specific verses from the Bible in accordance to a specific formula. The format is as follows.

First, one has cleansed one's life of wanton behaviors. Second, one is truly remorseful over them. Third, one has cleansed one's domain of any offending paraphernalia. Only then can one practice this oneself. The purpose of this is to remove any invading malevolent force, which in most cases is an earthbound human soul, looking for a new host. Such souls can be dislodged and removed only when their previous homes have become uncomfortable. The new-found moral and righteous behaviors the person has instilled in himself have now made it uncomfortable to the malevolent force. Still, it does not give up and continues to emotionally compel individuals to fall back into their wanton ways. Such temptations must be rigorously avoided.

At times of such temptations, when one feels compelled to act in wanton ways, this is what one should do. One should in essence curse the malevolent entity by reciting this verse from Psalm 109:6, which states, *"Place upon him an evil one and let the Satan stand at his right side."* If one can do it in the original Hebrew, this adds to it extra spiritual power. The transliteration of it is this: *"Haf'ked Ah'lahv Rasha V'satan Ya'amohd Ahl Yemi'no."* The formula is to recite it both forwards and backwards like this.

"Haf'ked Ah'lahv Rasha V'satan Ya'amohd Ahl Yemi'no."

"Yemi'no Ahl Ya'amohd V'satan Rasha Ah'lahv Haf'ked."

"Place upon him an evil one and let the Satan stand at his right side."

"Side right his at stand Satan the let and one evil an him upon place."

One recites this as many times as need be until the compulsion ceases. One can then recite these following words:

Tamey Tamey B'rakh Lakh M'khan

Unclean one, unclean one, be banished from here.

These words can also be recited at night if one awakens suddenly and feels a frightening presence.

There are many other similar procedures, but sometimes more is not better. Simplicity and focus of intent is what works best. One does not need numerous rituals. One usually will suffice. Yet, one must be diligent and strong. One must never waver or doubt. If one is to wage war against the occult and malevolent psychic forces, one cannot tolerate doubt, not about oneself or about one's mission. One must stay focused, disciplined and determined to strengthen one's personal resolve. One must make oneself to be better and to no longer be a viable victim for malevolent forces. One must make the determined effort to cleanse one's behavior, then one's domain and finally one's soul.

One who follows the procedures properly and correctly will see for themselves the rewards of proper personal refinement. Cleansings are physical, psychological and psychic. One should never forget how all levels are intermingled are united. When we do what is right, then what is right will be done to us. This is the promise of Heaven.

Chapter 22

◄○►

Staying Physically & Mentally Healthy

After spending many chapters discussing how to defend oneself from psychic attack and occultic influence, it is now time to focus on how we can practically use the powers that we have previously discussed for our own good and betterment. Just as the power of the mind can be used to cause harm, so too can they be used to create good. Every good defense must also include a good offense. Psychic offense does not include attacking others, however it very much does include invoking Heaven and the inner powers of our minds to create circumstances and environments that serve our pursuing the higher good.

Just remember this; all psychic activity absolutely needs to materialize in a physical vessel. Unless the physical vessel is both present and strong, there can be no actual manifestation of any psychic energy.

We have simple rituals, which are mostly prayers, that when recited in the proper ways can have a tremendous impact in helping us manifest certain realities in our lives. These rituals are called Segulot, which best translates as spiritual remedies for psychic ailments. There is nothing magical or mystical about them. They are merely the vessels through which we channel the spiritual/psychic energy into physical space. Segulot operate based on the power of faith that they are imbued with. We introduced this material in Chapter 19. Now, in this and the coming chapters, let us turn to applications for specific usages.

The three greatest pursuits that most seek individuals out are simply health, wealth and family, although not necessarily in this order. There are numerous Segulot enumerated in a great number of books that help one to solicit the attainment of all three of these things. All of them, however, share one common denominator: they all rely upon the blessings of Heaven, and never seek to manipulate some lower force to bend to one's will. The powers of the occult, like we have always learned are mechanical; as such, they are neither good nor evil, holy nor profane. They are merely a technology, and operate according to the scientific principles that underlie their reality, not too dissimilar from the science and technology that we know and use today.

Technological instruments, like the laws of nature that enable them to operate are neither good nor evil; they are what they are, mere tools in the hands of the users. The powers that the occult provide should not frighten anyone, especially if one is religious. Religion rightly condemns the occult, but this is not because of the occult operations, but rather because of the occult operators. In and of itself the occult, when not embellished with foolish make-believe satanic symbolisms, is neutral, being neither good not evil. It all depends upon how it is operated.

Remember this: yesterday's occult is today's science. Many people harbor a baseless irrational fear of the occult, based upon the occult practitioner's use of demonic symbols. This fear is both foolish and dangerous. The occult practitioners who seek to harm another can do so because they manipulate and take advantage of one's fears. Without fear, the powers of the occult are severely curtailed. In the end, G-d did create the mechanics underlying the occult just like He created all the other forces in nature. Religious individuals seeking to serve Heaven therefore have nothing to be afraid of from the powers the occult provide.

Indeed, spiritual technologies and occult mechanics are one and the same creations of the Creator. They only become good and evil depending upon how they are used. This is why the Tree in the Garden of Eden was called the Tree of Knowledge, Good and Evil. It is what we make it to be. In the hands of evil doers, we already know what they can produce. What is often overlooked, if not altogether unknown, is that these same spiritual technologies used for evil are also used for good. As such these same principles and spiritual technologies have forever enabled holy souls to serve G-d. These principles are the same ones through which miracles become manifest here on Earth. Again, the problem arises not because of the tools, but rather because of the operator. This being said, we can turn to Segulot prayer that operate according to so-called occult mechanic principles and not be afraid of the words that I associate with their usage. Part of successful operations of strengthening oneself in the service of Heaven is to see and recognize G-d in everything and to use the innate power of G-d within oneself to shine the Divine light out to the world.

Segulot for physical health, like I said are numerous. There is no one source for them all. Therefore, I will just outline the basics. First and foremost, let me be upfront and clear; no one can recite holy prayers with Heavenly invocations and expect them to work all the while that one is sabotaging their performance. In other words, if one is seeking blessings for physical health from Heaven, then one had better be doing whatever is necessary on the physical plane to safeguard one's health. There is an old saying, not recorded in the Bible, but whose wisdom is Biblical, and that is "G-d helps those who help themselves." You must do what you can for yourself, only then will G-d fill in the blanks and do what you cannot. If there is no healthy vessel, there will be no reception of Light.

To safeguard oneself both psychically and physically, proper diet is essential and physical exercise is an absolute necessity. The great Sage and physician of medieval times, Maimonides, wrote that exercise is more important than diet. Even if one eats all the proper foods, he writes, unless one exercises vigorously they will never be free from illness. Here is where psychic attacks and occult manipulations often rear their ugly heads. One of the easiest ways to psychically attack and kill an opponent is to infiltrate the mind using all the methods we have discussed up until now and then implant a thought which will find a comfortable reception in the mind. This thought is usually one of laziness. The malevolent forces always seek to weaken the physical body knowing full well that a weak body will often lead to a weak mind. Every truly spiritually-minded doctor knows this to be true.

When we fail to eat right and are too lazy to exercise, these things alone can kill us. Add on to this a psychic attack targeting these two specific areas of natural weakness and one can be pushed over the edge to oblivion. Therefore, the first step to both natural good health and to defend against psychic attack is for one to cultivate proper rigid discipline of self, to eat right and exercise vigorously, like Maimonides said. One who does both of these will close windows of opportunity that one's psychic enemies seek to exploit. Once the body is closed to attack, then one can work to strengthen the mind/soul.

Spiritual remedies for physical health are simple. Usually they are a formula of certain Hebrew letters recited with specific vowels. These formulas are usually considered to be "magical" Names of G-d; however, as we know, there really is no such thing as magic. Rather, there are only levels of natural law and technologies that we have not yet fathomed or understood. For physical health, there are many such formulas or Names. We can learn one of them here. It can be recited within the context of a greater prayer, or better it can be contemplated and meditated upon to unleash their inner energies into one's mind. By doing this, one embraces their power and encases oneself in a coat of spiritual armor.

This formula/Name is based upon Numbers 12:13, which states, *"And Moshe cried to G-d saying, please G-d, please heal her."* In the original Hebrew text, there are ten words in the verse. If we take the numerical value of the first letters of each of the ten Hebrew words, we have the basis of our formula/Name. The numerical value of the ten initial letters of this verse adds up in Hebrew numerology (Gematria) to be equal to 418. The number itself is what is significant here. The number 418 is also the numerical value of the phrase, "Almighty G-d Lives." In Hebrew, this is Elohim Shadai Hai.

The procedure for using this information is as follows. First, one should pray for one's own health daily. Aside from maintaining one's health, one should never forget the spiritual component underlying all physical reality. One should daily thank G-d that one has health and can properly physically function. The power of praise goes a long way to offset and neutralize negative psychic energy. One can thank G-d in any language and use any prayer that one can speak for oneself. One can then contemplate the above verse, "*And Moshe cried to G-d saying, please G-d, please heal her*," and simply say something to the effect, "*G-d, just as you heard the cry of your servant Moshe to bring healing, so may you hear my cry to heal me.*"

After such a simple supplication, we then use the ten Hebrew letters that begin the words of this verse as a sort of meditative device. The ten Hebrew letters are Vav, Mem, Alef, Yod, Lamed and Alef, Nun Resh, Nun and Lamed. Together these ten can be joined together to form two "Names" that are pronounced as follows, "*Va'me-ah Yola* and *Eh'Nar-nalah*." One can actually whisper these words as a meditative device because they contain within them the Torah power of healing. Together their numerical value signifies their meaning, which again is, "Almighty G-d lives" (Elohim Shadai Hai). When we pray for healing, be it for ourselves and for others, we can use our own words and couple them to this special formula Name to augment the intentions of our heart, to add strength to the spiritual component of our prayers. The following can be used as a prayer guideline.

"May it be the Will of the Creator, the L-rd of Heaven and Earth to grant me health and strength so that I may accomplish my appointed tasks this day and everyday throughout my life here on Earth.

May the Creator, L-rd of Heaven and Earth grant me wisdom that I may recognize the need to discipline myself to safeguard my physical and mental health.

May I always have the wisdom to recognize that the Creator has bestowed upon me the ability to make the right choices for my life. May I always make those right choices regardless of how hard they may seem to be or however I am tempted to do something other.

I call upon the Living Almighty G-d and proclaim Him Ruler and L-rd over my life and health. My body belongs to Him and my health is my obligation to Heaven.

I proclaim and reinforce my discipline to do that which is right and by doing so I solicit the power inherent within the formula and holy Names which are "Va'me-ah Yola and Eh'Nar-nalah." Almighty G-d lives and I too wish to live, healthily, with strength and with vigor.

I hereby commit myself to do all that I have to in order to accomplish this, Amen."

This type of prayer/spiritual remedy can be recited daily. However, I must again emphasize that talk is cheap without action. Do not expect G-d to work miracles with you and to answer your prayers unless you back up your words with proper, healthy behavior.

Now that we have addressed how one can help heal oneself, let us address the important issue of how one can help others to heal. In order for the psychic and physical healing processes to function they must be firmly grounded in realistic practices and not fantastical illusions. One of the greatest of these fantasy dangers, in my opinion, is the modern pop attraction towards the alternative medical practice of so-called energy healing. I have followed this phenomenon for many years and have been rather concerned with what I have found to be glaringly true. I clearly see that the majority of these so-called energy healers are nothing more than deluded charlatans who claim to be working with ethereal energies and to be performing miracles when in actuality all they are doing is selling false hopes. I find this package of make-believe goods to be dangerous from both the psychic and physical points of view.

It is true that underlying all physical and psychic activity there is movement of life-force energy; in Hebrew we call this energy Nefesh, in the orient, it is called Chi. It is also true that life-force energy can physically be moved and manipulated through the power of thought, but not necessarily thought alone. I believe that there are numerous medical studies that have come out of oriental universities of Traditional Chinese Medicine that clearly document this scientifically. Now, just because there is such a phenomenon as Chi movement, such as we see in acupuncture, this does not mean that those calling themselves energy healers can perform this delicate work without the necessary years of training and testing to prove it.

In order to verify that the invisible Chi is truly being manipulated and to prove that such manipulations are in fact providing actual benefits there must be clear and verifiable evidence that shows these things to be true. Traditional Chinese medical institutions provide these tests and their results. The charlatans, on the other hand, who claim that they are naturally-gifted healers, without the benefit of professional medical training provide only illusions and lies. There are even entire schools dedicated to teaching this sham of energy healing, charging thousands of dollars for their programs. Yet, their students generally have no medical degrees and when practicing these so-called energy techniques are certainly not practicing any true form of medicine.

In Traditional Chinese Medicine there is an ancient art of energy healing called Chi Kung. This is not the forms practiced by pop modern healers, but rather by professionally trained and licensed Chinese medical doctors. These physicians, I have seen with my own eyes, are highly trained, skilled and licensed professionals. They are not necessarily spiritual people and for the most part have no particular religious or spiritual interests. Yet, they are committed to healing and know how healing really works. These doctors are the acupuncturists and the professional herbalists; they also learn the Chi Kung methods, along with the rest in professional and competent medical schools of Traditional Chinese Medicine. Chi Kung has a long documented history of proven successes. Different forms are used in different ways to solicit and support natural healing of the body. Professional traditional Chinese doctors I highly recommend.

Authentic energy healing is meant to be an actual form of medicinal practice. For example, if one has broken one's arm, authentic energy healing, such as acupuncture and Chi Kung can produce verifiable results that show the bone's mending. In China, surgeries on the brain and even open heart surgery are performed using only acupuncture as anesthetic. The patient is totally awake and without pain or fear during the entire procedures. This dramatically helps the healing process as all good oriental doctors know. Other less radical forms of such energy healings are practiced throughout oriental culture. They are not religious practices or even spiritual. They are completely medical in nature. Such factual energy healing simply manipulates body energy, sometimes using the famous acupuncture needles and sometimes without them. Qualified and licensed professionals are familiar with these techniques and use them with verifiable success.

The pop forms of energy healing should never be compared to those coming out of licensed professional universities of Traditional Chinese Medicine. Uneducated peoples might be confused between the two, but a lack of education should never justify making an error that can have grievous consequences. Patients of the pop forms of energy healing believe they are being healed, but from what are they being healed? What is their medically diagnosed illness? How is this energy healing verifiably helping heal this medically-diagnosed malady?

In most cases, the pop forms of energy healing are nothing more than an emotional placebo. The patient believes he is being healed and therefore regardless of the fact that there is no verifiable healing performed the patient nonetheless believes he is being healed and that is all there is to it. One believes and one feels and as far as one is concerned that is all that matters. Yet, as all practicing medical professionals know, what you feel and believe is fine, but that alone cannot change the course of an illness or heal a malady. Only real medicine can do that. If and when a person had a really serious condition and went to one of these charlatans, such a session could create a false hope of healing, thus preventing the person from seeking out a proper and true intervention that could indeed save one's life.

Energy healing is not simply a benign, make-believe, semi-massage-type of experience. There are some healers who can actually make one feel something. However, again, without clear and substantial evidence of actual medical improvements, we must be suspect as to what energies are actually being manipulated here. Many so-called healers, trained in what today are considered benign and even spiritually pure and some-what holy forms of energy healing are actually tapping into malevolent, dark forces that are disguising themselves in the proverbial wolf in sheep's clothing. These so-called healers and the ones they train are completely oblivious to the dark forces they are involved with. Yet, those of us with an open eye can clearly see the harm these people suffer.

Energy healing in general should be avoided, for in most cases the energy that is channeled through the healer is coming from a nefarious source disguised as something benign and good. Ultimately this same source taps into the so-called healer and siphons off their own life-force energy. Over many years, I have known many healers, some legitimate and many frauds. I have not seen one of them (and this is no exaggeration) have a happy, balanced and good life. In general I have found that it is the healers who themselves are in most need of healing. I cannot over emphasize how much I strongly condemn these modern pop forms of energy healing.

Psychic illnesses can and are treated within the framework of Traditional Chinese Medicine. Their system is so ancient and experienced that they have witnessed most occultic forms of psychic attack and have learned how many of them can be healed, including attacks on the mind. Psychic attacks are handled with psychic protection and psychic healing. Yet, once the psychic wound becomes physical, then the proper knowledgeable medical doctors should be called in. We never separate between the physical and the spiritual. While the spiritual can cause physical illness, it can seldom alone heal it.

The first step in healing another is to provide for them proper and correct information that will guide them along the right path to seek out their own healing. The art and science of healing must be left in the hands of properly trained and licensed professionals. It is far too dangerous to trust one's physical and psychic health into the hands of an amateur, all the more so, with someone who has questionable ties to malevolent occultic forces disguising themselves as benevolent. The best segulah for health is to always do what is right and practical and at the same time to shy away from everything that at best has only questionable benefit.

Chapter 23

◄○►

Segulot for Making Money- or Not

Everyone would love to have a segulah through which they could assuredly acquire new wealth and financial gain. After all, who doesn't want to be rich? We all know the good that we can accomplish if only we were to win the big lottery or somehow seal that business deal that will clench us millions. We have a hard time understanding why it is that Heaven just cannot see the simple goodness in our all being millionaires and why we all do not have abundant financial resources. If only we could make Heaven understand; if only we had the right segulah.

How many of us think just like this? How many of us feel cheated by Heaven? How many of us know so much that G-d wants us to be rich and yet we have a hard time understanding why G-d is having such a hard time fulfilling His own Will by making us rich?

Does any of this sound familiar? It should. These thoughts are indicative of a common mental illness, one that is prevalent throughout society today. It infects, religious and secular equally, men and women, even the rich and poor. This mental illness is called greed and it is the source of so many other psychic illnesses that it would be very difficult to enumerate them all.

Whether or not one is wealthy, moderate or outright poor, it is one of those rare things that in spite of one's best personal efforts, financial success still seems to be squarely in the Hands of G-d.

Reality has shown us in, I believe, every occasion that an individual's finances are truly in the hands of Heaven. Every successful businessman knows that there are times when money just seems to roll in and yet other times when money just seems not to flow at all. Logically there does not seem to be any rhyme or reason as to why things move either fast or slow and how they fluctuate between one and the other. Granted, some market trends can be foreseen, but this does not mean that one can always see the future to know how economic markets will be and how one should act within them. Only a psychic can see the future and yet, no psychic accurately predicts either the stock market or other ways how to elevate one's financial status.

There is a unique verse in the Bible which is always associated with soliciting Heaven to provide financial support. This verse is Psalm 55:23, which states, *"Cast your burden upon G-d and He will sustain you."* This one verse pretty much sums up the greatest segulah one can use to solicit financial support. One must ultimately trust in G-d and surrender to Heaven. If and when one does the best one can, Heaven indeed will bless one's activities. One may not become the next millionaire, but at least one should rest secured knowing that one's needs will indeed be taken care of.

The greatest psychic hindrance today to one becoming financially successful is avarice. Today, more so than in the past, money is the chosen god worshipped. Self esteem and personal value tend to revolve around the size of one's wallet and finances, much more than on the size of one's heart and the nature of one's character. Having financial needs and fulfilling them is one thing; craving more, getting it, and still wanting more is an evil sickness.

The nature of our present capitalist, consumer society is that the more one has the better one is. Status is defined by the brand of one's clothing, the maker of one's automobile and the neighborhood in which one lives. These superfluous, meaningless things have become the status symbols upon which self-esteem is built. As long as one has a shred of interest in any of these things, he or she will always be open and subject to psychic attack. Nothing, however holy, righteous, magical or occultic will be able to defend one from harm. Greed creates an opening in the soul so wide that evil, both great and small, have no problem entering in.

The true secret of acquiring wealth is the redefinition of what wealth is. As long as one pursues garbage and nonsense, then one should not be surprised that garbage and nonsense is what one's acquires and finds surrounding him. When wealth is redefined and one instead pursues what one needs, instead of everything that one desires, then one stands the chance of acquiring true wealth. More than this, when one has the proper attitude adjustment to focus on proper and balanced acquisition, then one stands the chance of also becoming balanced internally and thus actually finding true happiness in life.

Once one is of the proper mindset, one can then turn to Heaven and supplicate one's needs in purity of mind. It is vitally important that when approaching Heaven and asking for anything that one needs, that one do so with an appropriate spirit. The proper attitude is called humility. This simply means that one has to realize that Heaven owes nothing to anyone. Heaven reserves the right to reject any and all prayers without ever having to explain why. Heaven is pretty much all powerful and we, on the other hand are pretty much powerless. There really is not anything that we can do to influence Heaven and to persuade G-d to act in our favor. The ratio of balance is considerably one sided. This is the true spiritual reality. One may chose to like it or dislike it;

one may even chose to deny it; however one cannot change it and one would be foolish to ignore it. Truth is what truth be and we can only live by what is true. If we chose to live by a falsehood then we stand the chance to die by it as well.

This being said, we come to approach Heaven with a spirit of humility, knowing full well that G-d has no obligation to answer our supplication and to grant us our requests. Therefore, rather than approach Heaven to inform G-d of all our merits and why we deserve to receive His blessings, we instead approach the Heavenly Throne in humility, acknowledging our shortcomings and our lack of any true merit. We essentially throw ourselves upon the mercies of G-d and His Heavenly justice. Unlike our fellow humans, G-d is both just and merciful. A contrite heart is never rejected in Heaven. G-d looks for those who are honest, sincere and humble. These are the ones whose prayers are heard and answered.

Yet, this being so, we might ask then, how come the honest, sincere and humble are all not very rich and financially successful? The answer to this is simple. The honest, sincere and humble do not ask for riches. They simply ask for their needs. In their wisdom, they know the right things to pray for, and thus in their humility, the right things are provided for them. It is the arrogant who supplicate for that which is not their due and therefore they never receive it. G-d weighs the heart of every supplicant. Prayers are words; alone they seldom rise through the Heavenly gates. Yet, the power of a contrite heart pierces all the veils and enters into all the Heavenly palaces. There the truly humble one is heard and answered.

At this point, let me share with you an abridged form of an ancient Jewish prayer for financial sustenance. I believe that everything within it is clear and needs no commentary or explanation. This is a prayer that can and should be recited daily, by everyone regardless of one's present financial status; for as the rich know all too well, fortunes can turn on a dime and one who today is rich can be in poverty tomorrow. In spite of one's best personal efforts, it is the Hand of G-d that guides all.

"May it be acceptable before the Ancient One, You are the L-rd, the G-d who feeds, maintains and supports all Your creation, in Your abundant grace, large and small alike, as it is written "He has given food to those to those in awe of Him, He will forever remember His covenant" (Psalm 111:5). "You open Your Hand and satisfy the desire of all living" (Psalm 145:16).

Master of the universe, in your holy word it is written, "He that trusts in G-d shall be surrounded by mercy" (Psalm 32:10). You give life to all. You L-rd G-d are truth. Give to us blessing and prosperity in all the work of our hands and in all our business, so that we may be able to support ourselves and all the members of our families with ease and not difficulty; with the permissible and not the forbidden; with profit and not just enough to get by.

Grant us Your blessings from the abundance of Your blessings and prosperity; from the abundance of the supernal blessing of Your Hand, and not by the hand of man. Fulfill in us the verse "Cast your burden upon G-d and He will sustain you." (Psalm 55:23) "Open your hand and give to all living their desire." (Psalm 145:16) G-d will reign forever and ever.

May it be acceptable before you L-rd my G-d that you send blessing and prosperity to all the work of my hands. For I have trusted in You, so that I will be able to support myself and my family with ease and not difficulty, for life and peace. Amen, may it be Your will."

The pursuit of wealth and financial gain is one of the greatest attractions that draw people to the occult. Rather than humble oneself and rely upon Heaven for sustenance and support, there are those who chose to try to take matters in their own hands. They will take whatever measures they can to try to be in control of their lives and fortunes, even seeking to make both greater and more secure, regardless of the price they have to pay. These selfish souls easily and willingly sacrifice others to meet their nefarious whims. They seek occultic forces to enable them to take control of the reins of power and then to pay off their demonic masters by sacrificing to them whatever is demanded. Total societies have been molded and built upon a ruling elite and the crushing burden that they place upon their populace just to keep them in power.

I cannot emphasize strongly enough how the attitude and lust for power and wealth has driven some individuals mad, so much so that internally they cease being humans. Their human soul is, as if, eaten out of them, and what replaces it is the soul of a devouring animal, a beast that is both hungry and cruel, caring for nothing other than its next meal.

All of us have natural needs. All of us on top of these have desires, some however want more than others. Fulfilling our needs is Heaven's promise, as long as we are doing what we need to do. There is no such promise for Heaven to fulfill our every desire simply because we want it to be so and we pray for it. Therefore, one who turns to Heaven and expects G-d to grant their heart's desire and then gets angry at G-d and Heaven when this does not happen, such a one becomes a primary target for occultic attack. In this case, the attack comes in the form of temptation; a temptation to seek out other sources of power and influence that will indeed promise to fulfill one's every desire, but for a hefty price.

I have seen all too many otherwise good people become seduced by the dark side because of their pursuits of financial gains. Little do they know that the activity they become involved with is completely demonic in origin. When shown to them, they go to all extremes to deny the nefarious connection their "dabbling" has produced. Self-deception can be a powerful force, one that blinds one's eyes from truth in all its forms. I have seen those who are religious in every sense of the word who nonetheless involve themselves in activities that strip their souls of holiness and unwittingly make them to become agents of evil.

When it comes to the pursuit of financial gain, one must be ever so cautious how one proceeds. There are numerous entities out there that look for the opportunity to attach themselves to unsuspecting humans. There is no greater opportunity that the spirit of greed. The greater part of western civilization is built upon this very premise and it is this very pursuit that has led to the disintegration of families, the abandonment of children and an entire generation (or two) growing up without any moral compass or guidance. Do not underestimate the occultic influence in this most prevalent of modern social norms.

There is no proper and holy way to guarantee financial success. Heaven does not concern itself with our financial desires for wealth. Heaven concerns itself with what is best for our souls and for the development of our humanity. Often, greed interferes with this progress. Heaven will never support or condone greed. When some individuals get fed up with Heaven's limitations upon their greed, they will turn to ready-to-help entities that will provide for them their desires and at the same time suck out of their souls any semblance of their humanity. Greed is a serious disease and one must be on guard against it at all costs. This advice alone is the secret of financial success.

Long ago, the great Sage Ben Zoma (Pirkei Avot 4:1) once said, "*Who is truly wealthy? The one who is satisfied with his portion.*" Here you have the secret of true wealth. When you surrender to the guiding Hand of Heaven and allow G-d to provide for your needs and you then accept this and embrace it willingly, then you will discover the true happiness that comes through being truly wealthy. When you pray and ask that Heaven's will be done and not your own, you will find that Heaven will indeed answer and that you will not be disappointed.

Trusting in G-d for all one's financial needs is the true key to financial success. One must work and work hard to accomplish all that one is able. Then, once you have accomplished all that you can, G-d will fulfill for you that which you cannot. He may not give you the winning lottery ticket or make you a millionaire in the stock market. But if you look at what you do have, instead of what you do not have, you will find that indeed your needs have been fulfilled and then some.

The one final thing that one needs to concern oneself is the danger of the evil eye that having a lot of money attracts. Rich people are usually ostentatious. They usually like to show off their wealth with the cars they drive, the clothes they wear, and the houses they live in. They naturally attract the evil eye. Frankly for those who live such a life style and are proud to show off their greed, I have very little remorse or pity when the effects of the evil eye strike them. There is nothing wrong with being wealthy, as long as one acts responsibly with one's wealth. There is everything wrong with being greedy and wealthy and showing off one's wealth as a status symbol of power. For those who do this, there is no cure for their psychic malady. They become natural targets of psychic/occultic attack and no magic, voodoo, Santeria or Wicca can save them.

Learn a lesson, if you set yourself up a as a target, don't be surprised when you take a hit.

True wealth comes from Heaven. It may not be what your greed desires, but it is what is best for you. Trust in Heaven and make yourself worthy so that Heaven can trust in you.

Chapter 24

◄O►

Healthy Male/Female Relationships

Never underestimate the power and importance of human marital relationships. Not for naught did the Torah state that no man or woman is complete unless the two are joined together. This union is not one of flesh, but of soul. The male psyche and the female psyche are markedly different from one another. Recent scientific studies have even proven that male and female brains work differently and process information and address problems differently. This should come as no surprise to anyone.

One of the greatest areas of psychic/occult attack is in the domain of male/female relationships. When this sacred bond is broken, holes in the soul are present, which are very difficult to fill and heal. On the other hand, when the male/female bond is complete and secure the strength derived from it is seldom matched. One of the greatest defenses against an occultic attack is to be in a healthy and committed heterosexual monogamous relationship.

Spiritual energy is neutral. It can be used for either good or evil. Psychic and occult powers simply make use of this most elemental reservoir of natural resource. Psychic/occultic power operates according to the laws of nature as does every other power in the universe and like every other power in the universe it can be harnessed and exploited through an appropriate technology. Spiritual energy is by nature magnetic; it operates according to positive and negative polarities.

Humankind is also magnetically based. Our mind/souls are naturally either charged positive or negative. When we manifest on Earth as human beings, our inherent magnetic polarity directs the DNA forming our physical bodies to materialize the proper form that matches our essential being. This is why all souls are born either male or female. While we are born to become men and women, our souls prior to birth and after death are either male or female. We are only born what we already are.

Granted, sometimes the system does not operate according to the normal standard. There are numerous times when male and female souls are born into the opposite sexes, in contradiction to their own inherent natures. Yet, these incidents are by no means a mistake. The Guiding Power above all souls directs them into the bodies that they will inhabit in each and every lifetime. For reasons known in Heaven, sometimes a male soul is born into the body of a female, and the soul of a female is sometimes born into the body of a male.

This reversal again is no accident. We do not believe in sex change surgery or gender confusion. A soul is born into a body to be who it has been born to be and no one else. Any attempt to challenge or change this matter is an attempt to thwart the directives of Heaven. Those souls that succumb to such social confusion and adopt a course opposite than the revealed Will of Heaven will eventually have to learn their lesson and then return to Earth to correct their mistakes.

Male and female form two halves of the same whole. There really is such a thing as soul mates. Yet, the reality of this issue is far from what is popularly believed. Although every soul has an opposite half with which it must bond in order to be complete, this does not mean that this missing half is limited to manifesting exclusively within one physical body. In other words, souls can take on multiple manifestations, even in the same life-time. Indeed, even within a single lifetime elements of souls can actually move from one body to the next.

As physical human beings we may very well be composite souls, with one or more "other" souls traveling "piggy-back" alongside us. These other souls are sent to us sometimes from birth and sometimes later in life, sometimes they stay for a long while and sometimes just for a short time. Heaven ordains how souls are distributed. Knowledge of how this works is far beyond present human understanding.

What we learn from this is something rather profound. Granted we each have a soul mate, yet that very same soul mate can come to us in the form of a number of different human partners. More than this, even if we are in a marriage with a partner not our soul mate, Heaven can ordain that the element that makes one to be our soul mate actually incarnate within such an individual making that one to become our soul mate. Therefore there is no such thing as one missing the opportunity to be with one's soul mate. Even if one's soul mate were to die, the element within the departed one comes back and can inhabit any physical body so ordained by Heaven. Soul mate bonding is so important that Heaven rarely denies us the opportunity to find it. If one is living without one's soul mate it is usually due to his or her own fault rather than because of an edict from Heaven.

Living with one's soul mate should never be considered a "happily ever after" situation. Many believe this false idea that living with one's soul mate means that one will be happy and balanced. This does not necessarily have to be true. Soul mates complete us, this is true, but the definition of completion should never be considered such a simple thing. Sometimes a human soul needs to lean much. The best teacher to learn from is one's soul mate. He or she reflects back to its own other half valuable lesson of whatever Heaven ordains. Sometimes, soul mates fight like "cats and dogs." This does not mean that they are not soul mates. Rather, it usually means that they truly are soul mates and that they are in a state of learning together. Heaven works in strange ways as compared to simple human thinking and outlook.

Energy is energy. Human souls are not exempt from this equation. How we cultivate our personal energy and balance it is of vital importance. The relationships we cultivate define for us the flow of our own human energy. Sexual intercourse is a simple exchange of energy. Whenever one has a sexual encounter, one exchanges soul energy with one's partner. One receives energy from that partner and gives energy to that partner. Therefore, every time one has sex with another, one is, in essence, receiving a portion of soul energy from every sexual partner that one has ever experienced. The more partners one has the greater the contaminating influence such a sexual encounter contains. Receiving multiple sexual energies from a promiscuous partner sullies one's own energy and weakens it. This psychic weakness often manifests itself in outright psychic harm to the individual and many times even physical disease results. We see this prominently today in our promiscuous society, where sexual contamination runs rampant like an unchecked epidemic.

Nothing blocks the acquiring of one's soul mate more than sexual promiscuity. The more partners one has the less and less one's magnetic draw for one's soul mate becomes. Because one's own sexual energy becomes contaminated by so many other energies passed through the sexual encounter, the magnetic attraction that naturally draws one's soul mate is almost entirely overwhelmed. It ceases to function until such a time that one cleanses oneself of such intrusive energy and refocuses on drawing towards oneself what one should naturally be attracting.

The lesson to be learned from this should be obvious. One who wishes to attract his or her soul mate, to marry and settle down must as a first step stop all promiscuous sexual behavior. For those who will have a hard time understanding this, let me be perfectly clear. If one wishes to be psychically pure and magnetically attractive to one's soul mate, one must be completely sexually abstinent. This means no sexual activity outside of marriage. As contradictory as this is to modern secular standards, its psychic and occultic validity is as natural as nature itself. Sexual promiscuity, even only once, is the cause that blocks one from finding one's true soul mate. Sexual abstinence is what helps both you and your soul mate find one another.

Sexual energy is psychic/spiritual energy. They are one and the same. This is why the malevolent forces of the occult try in every which way to promote sexual promiscuity amongst humans. When humans are sexual promiscuous, going from one sexual partner to the next, they waste a tremendous amount of psychic energy. They are constantly giving away good energy and receiving contaminated energy in return. The contaminated energy clogs the psychic system causing it to be psychically sick. Without its own pure psychic energy the soul cannot properly strengthen the physical body. This is why many people who are sexually promiscuous, at present or even in their past, often suffer from medical problems related to immunity deficiencies or to general overall weakness and fatigue.

When promiscuous people are so weakened it is easy for them to become a target for psychic or occultic attack. Therefore, the malevolent forces seek to weaken human beings through sexual promiscuity in order that they can then tap into their souls and drain off their psychic energy, regardless of how contaminated it is. The malevolent entities are stealing this energy; they do not care if what they steal is purely yours or whether it belongs to another or to many others. They simply steal what they need and use it how they wish. This is why we call these malevolent forces unclean. They embrace that which contaminates us and by doing so it in turn contaminates them.

When we safeguard our sexuality we are safeguarding our life-force energy, that which keeps us alive. When I speak about maintaining purity, I am not speaking from a religious context, but rather from an energy standpoint. Think of sexual energy as being like gasoline in an engine. How well and how long will an engine continue to operate if only watered-down gasoline is injected into it? Ultimately the weakened fuel will cause engine damage. Then the whole vehicle begins to have trouble and it all began with the lack of purity of the motor fuel. Purity is a natural state required for all levels of peak performance.

Another extremely important safeguard that protects one from psychic attack, the evil eye and from unwanted and unnecessary sexual temptations is modesty in dress and appearance. Modern secular standards sets a norm of dress that make women look like whores and men look like bums. It is no wonder that our children fall into so many psychic snares when even the clothing they are taught to wear entraps their minds in webs of poison. Know and accept this great lesson, you are indeed what you wear. If you follow modern norms and dress in what traditionally has always been a provocative style but today is considered acceptable, you may find acceptance among your fellow human peers, however the higher forces, including the malevolent ones are much enticed by your actions.

Although times and norms change here on Earth, in the psychic/occultic planes there are no such changes. What was once provocative and whorish remains so, regardless of social trends and fashion statements. When fashions shift and embrace what was once unthinkable, the psychic domain views such shifts as a cultural affront. It is as if the entire society has shifted into a position of challenging Heaven. It is as if the entire society has embraced the malevolent dark side. Although the everyday people do not consider it so, Heaven interprets their actions as a provocation to war. Heaven never acts kindly to provocative societies.

History has clearly shown us that any society that begins to walk down the path towards such debauchery eventually stumbles, collapses and is destroyed by a combination of natural and unnatural forces. Why should anyone be so arrogant and misguided to think that modern society is any different from all those that proceeded it. Why would anyone believe that the inevitable destiny that our modern society will face will be any different from all those who have been just like us in the past. In the psychic realms, there is no escape or change. What you sow, is what you reap. Heaven bestows its mercy only upon those who do not antagonize it with their intentionally wanton behavior.

Rather than concern ourselves with the apocalypse, we should rather focus on the here and now. Modesty in attire is one of the greatest psychic weapons against occultic attack. Now, there are those so-called psychics who will challenge this and claim that they can dress and act anyway that they choose without any negative consequences. I have even heard the foolish claim that negative consequences exist only in the mind and that only those who believe in them attract them. Look at the personal lives of those who makes claims of this nature and you will find a collection of misery, failures, hardships and illnesses. The proof of a thing is clear within a thing. Those who deny the dangers of provocative behavior are the very proof that such dangers are very real.

If one wishes to attract a mate, then one must do so in accordance to the natural laws as ordained by the Creator. Divine laws that regulate sexual behavior and stipulate modest standards of dress and behavior were not instituted to be restrictive. Rather, they were instituted to be liberating. Indeed, only one who is emancipated is truly free. One must be free even of one's own wanton lusts and one's enslavement to societal norms and standards. Sexual freedom is the ability not to become contaminated. Sexual freedom is to be sexual in the natural way as ordained by Heaven. We human beings are not just animals following our whims and desires without concern of consequence. We are higher beings; we possess a soul; indeed, we are our souls. Behaviors that are appealing to the flesh but which harm the soul are undesirable and therefore avoided. Only an animal, which never had the ability to act as a human being cannot see this and act with the necessary discipline.

Attracting a mate first means rising to the level of being a mate. One must become mate material. This means that one must know how to live in the context of a partnership. One must realize that one is not the center of one's universe. One must live to serve, not live to be served. A partnership is a bond between two human beings. As such, even sexuality is thereby transcended. Husbands and wives become partners at a level that transcends their individual sexualities. Partners work and live together, sharing all things, responsibilities and privileges. The attitude that motivates the partnership is "one for all and all for one," not, "I for me and all for me." When it comes to establishing a relationship or maintaining one, proper attitude comes first. It is more important than anything else.

Many people like to turn to mystical formulas to attract a mate. They are led to believe that if they light candles or recite prayers that somehow magically Mr. or Ms. Right will suddenly appear and make everything all right. This recipe works well in Hollywood fictional accounts, but has absolutely no legitimacy in the real world or with real people living with real problem, all as ordained by Heaven. Marriages, contrary to popular belief are not made in Heaven. Rather, they are made here on Earth, between two hard working human beings who are invested in one another and make whatever sacrifices necessary to establish and maintain a stable home.

Marriage is true soul-building because it requires of one to live outside of oneself. Any marriage where one considers his or her own needs to be paramount over those of the relationship or the family will, in the end, fail. Marriage is a partnership and no partnership can ever succeed standing on the selfishness of one of the partners.

Marriage is not about good looks and prestigious living. This is the fantasy, one that is completely open to psychic attack and that magnetically attracts malevolent occultic forces. Marriage is about two real people, living real life in a real way. In such a real world, neither partner is perfect. All of us have our flaws. Real partners do not have to love or even accept the flaws of their partners, but they do have to live with them. Real partners do not nag and manipulate one another to change and become molded in the image of the other. Real partners work to develop one another, even their differences, even those differences which one may not agree with. Whatever is best for the individual and the partnership together is what is supported; whatever works against it is not. The best Segulot for finding a proper mate and maintaining a successful family afterwards is living a live based upon kindness, blended with just the right amount of tolerance and acceptance.

Single people looking to marry should date with serious intent. From the very first meeting with a potential, one should be forthright, open and honest and declare outright that one is looking to get married and that one is only dating for serious reasons. Those with fears of commitment should never date. One should enter a date with the knowledge that this is business. Your business is to get to know the other person and to get to know him or her well enough to see if this is the one partner above all others with whom you would like to live the rest of your life. Singles should be social and meet members of the opposite sex only in appropriate environments that do not promote promiscuity and other lewd behaviors. Bars are just bad news and should be totally avoided. Date with wisdom and with caution. Keep your mind open, your heart guarded and your pants closed. Date like this and you will see the wisdom of it automatically.

Sometimes finding the right partner is a very hard challenge. Sometimes one dates numerous individuals and finds none of them to be suitable. When we have such a one who is so hard to please, rather than place blame and fault upon the myriads of failed suitors, maybe we should look back at the individual and ask if there is anything really wrong with him or her. Sometimes one is not looking for the proper things and therefore fails to see them even when placed right under one's proverbial nose.

Always know this, whomever we do pick as our partner, there is always someone else out there who may be a better match, at least so we think. Once we make our choice, we must cast aside any such ideas. Commitment means being true to one's word and to one's self. There is no room for "what if" or "if only." Real commitment says, "I am here and that's that." Real commitment is, like the words of the old song, *"if you can't be with the one you love, then love the one you're with."* You might then find that the one you're with has been your soul mate all along. It is funny how these things happen, but they do happen like this all the time.

Finding one's soul mate and living happily married is all about proper relationships that are formed and lived in here on Earth. Relationships do not follow our souls after our bodies are placed in their graves. The love between souls, however, does last forever. Love is not something that we feel emotionally. Love is what we do, how we behave and how we act. Feelings actually do not play much of a role in real love. Love between partners transcends emotions and feelings. It transcends good looks and so many other superficial things. Real love in a marriage is not a miracle; it is a hard earned reward. It comes about only after much true effort. Finding one's soul mate is easy when compared to the hardships of having to live with him or her after the wedding. It is easy to get along with anyone while in bed. It is when we are out of the bedroom that we must really get along.

One can never be a good partner in a marriage before one is first a good human being, whether or not one is in a relationship. A healthy marriage requires two healthy people who are in the marriage. If one is spiritually, mentally or emotionally ill, this will affect the stability of the relationship. In such circumstances, only the strong will survive. Specifically, only the strong who love honesty and truly the other human being, regardless the other's faults, will have the strength and stamina to survive all. One with such commitment and discipline will never have to fear the dark malevolent forces. For although those forces will seek to attack the weak partner and through him or her the strong partner, nonetheless the strong partner, because of their tenacious nature to always do what is right will naturally repel the forces of evil and help bring natural healing to his or her weak partner. This is what soul mates do.

When one is ready to do all this, only then will the opportunity be allotted one from Heaven. If you are single, then prepare now for marriage by being the best human being that you can possibly be. Guard your sexuality and your sensuality. Save them for your partner. Do not waste them; however you try to justify doing so. Do what is right and what is right will be done to you. Trust in Heaven; do the right things, prepare yourself and you will see that Heaven will indeed guide you to Mr. or Ms. Right, all in the right time and in the right place and most importantly, in the right way.

Chapter 25

◄O►

The War Against Evil

W e live in a world where we are under constant psychic/ spiritual bombardment and attack. In the previous chapters of this book I discussed numerous ideas, concepts and techniques that can enable you to properly see this problem and to deal with it. However, I must say that all the training of the mind and all the techniques to neutralize the occult will still never make it go away. Occult mechanics, like I have said throughout this book are simple technologies. They use the natural, Divinely-created and ordained powers that are inherent in the universe. Even if all these powers and forces were never created and thus nonexistent, the force that motivates their malevolent use would still, nevertheless, exist.

The one final issue that we must address is the actual and overt presence of evil. Evil is manifest through behavior. However evil exists beyond the realms of action; it also exists in the realms of the heart and the mind. Where righteousness can go, so too can evil be found. As long as there is a human being, evil can be found within him or her. It is and has always been a matter of choice.

The true dark "Other Side", unlike the nonsense portrayed in the popular media, is not in of itself an independant force bent on fighting G-d. The Torah is clear; G-d Himself is the author of all things, light and darkness good and even evil. Isaiah (45:6-7) thus states, "*In order that they know from the shining of the sun and from the west that there is no one besides Me; I am the L-rd and there is no other. Who forms light and creates darkness, Who makes peace and creates evil; I am the L-rd, Who makes all these.*"

However, the Divinely-ordained spiritual forces, created by G-d to serve purposes that only Heaven can understand can be stolen, abused, and used by malevolent individuals to serve their own selfish nefarious purposes. This is not an evil from G-d; this is an evil of humanity's own doing. The problem therefore is not the occult mechanics, but rather those who would unscrupulously use them. Evil people do evil things, this is the simple truth. If they did not have the occult to use, they would choose whatever other tools they could find to assist them in working their nefarious plots.

One can confront the occult and totally miss the point of the attack. One cannot defeat evil just by attacking an opponent's weapons. One must take the battle directly to the enemy and defeat its evil heart. In order to do this, sometimes soldiers use the very same weapons as their enemies are using. The enemy does not make the gun bad. The enemy shooting the gun is what is bad. The solution is not to ban guns, but rather to use the gun against the enemy and "take him out" with the same fire power he is using against you. One of the great rules of occult mechanics is that in order to neutralize a thing, one does not use its opposite, but rather more of the same thing. The desire and love of peace will never stop the evil one with a gun. The only thing that stops an evil one with a gun is a righteous person with an even bigger gun. Argue this point all you like, nevertheless its truth is still valid and self-evident.

One way the malevolent practitioners of the occult work to neutralize their enemies is to get them to believe that all occult is evil and demonic and that whoever goes near to it will be forever tainted and blemished. This standard fear tactic has been used for centuries, it is even found in military manuals teaching psychological operations. The idea is that if one side can control the mind and thinking of the other, then that side will also be able to control the choices that the enemy makes. Obviously the intent is to limit the choices the enemy has and to manipulate them into making wrong choices from which the enemy benefits.

This is exactly what the forces of evil do in their fight against righteousness. They endeavor to instill fear into the minds of their opponents and then to manipulate them into a position of powerlessness. This is why we see so many people in religious communities attacked regularly by forces of the occult and their clergy totally unprepared and unable to provide any assistance or defense. As long as certain clergy continue to believe that all mention of the occult is bad, evil and from the Devil, they will never learn how to pick up the true and righteous mantle of G-d to fight evil for real and to defend their flocks of souls.

Another great lesson taught by spiritual mechanics is that one must learn how to individually distinguish between good and evil, right and wrong, and most importantly, between reality and illusion. One of the greatest evil devices used against the righteous is the facades of falsehood. Illusions, deceptions and lies are powerful tools in the hands of any soldier on the battlefield, especially when that battlefield is the domain of the souls. Soldiers for holiness and G-d do not have the luxury and liberty to debate and choose what weapons they will or will not use. When it comes to the war for souls, let me share with you the age-old proverb, "all's fair in love and war." Those who love their fellow souls will do anything to protect them. Those who recognize that they are engaged in a war against the true and real forces of evil must also do anything to win the good fight.

Illusions, fear and lies severely limit the soldier on the battlefield and could more seriously contribute to his defeat that his being out-gunned by the other side. Correct intelligence information is vital for military operations. We must focus and remember we are at war against the forces of evil. We can no longer tolerate and condone fears and myths of the past that have placed taboos on the very holy and righteous tools given to us by no one less than G-d Himself. The occult mechanics must be properly learned from the side of righteousness and holiness and then engaged and used against the enemies of light.

One serious problem does exist for the righteous: the sources of information necessary to learn about these realities and vital techniques are extremely rare and hard to find. Most often, nothing on these subjects from a Torah/Kabbalah point of view ever get translated from the original Hebrew/Aramaic. Most, if not all of the books on "the occult" available today in most bookstores are expressions of the dark "Other Side" of these forces. Where can one go to learn about the true side of things?

The answer for this is both easy and hard at the same time. The best place to learn occult mechanics is the last place in the world one would think of looking into. The best text that outlines all one needs to know, however not in the most overt and direct fashion, in none other than the good old Bible. Yes, the Biblical texts include within them all one ever needs to know about how to deflect all means of psychic/occultic attack and also, how to use such powers for the cause of righteousness.

Unfortunately all too many people approach both the Bible and the occult from a mythological point of view. Rather than recognize any mechanics or technologies underlying the teachings, most expect things to work like magic. Just a simple *hocus pocus* or an *abracadabra* and "poof," magic is supposed to happen, be it from G-d or from the forces of evil. Such simplistic ideas, whether they are from the traditionally religious or from those who dabble in the occult is ridiculously infantile. Our world and universe is a far greater place than what our feeble human minds can imagine. Unless we take the necessary steps to build our minds and expand their horizons, we will forever remain enslaved in a mindset of limitation, superstition, fear and prejudice. One in such a mindset, however religious or righteous, is always an easy and open target for psychic/occult attack.

Evil begins as a blemish in the mind. Enlightening one's mind, which means expanding one's consciousness, is how one can begin to heal the blemish of misguided thoughts. I have seen all too many individuals who are not trained how to think properly, to diagnose and analyze situations within appropriate depth and insight. Because of the weakness of the mind I have seen countless numbers of individuals get caught up in all too many cults and ridiculous religious or spiritual organizations, beliefs and practices.

Those individuals so involved in one of these groups believe that they are enlightened and that they know the truth and especially they know that everyone outside their little group are unenlightened and in need of the salvation that the group offers. Sound familiar? It should. I have just described practically every cult in existence and a couple of world religions as well. It is fine if you wish to believe yourself unique or chosen, but since when does this mean that everyone else is less? Different? Yes, but less?

Torah teaches a code of moral living and righteousness, it calls the Jewish nation to rise up and serve as priests to minister and teach this Light. Yet, unlike other religions, Torah never condemns the non-Jewish unbeliever to an eternity of hellfire and damnation. Torah does not require everyone to be a Jew or to follow Torah laws. Torah only insists that all humanity act humanely towards one another following the universally accepted codes for morality and behavior. No theology here, just simple, pure, logical morality. One does not need religion too teach us these basic truths, which everyone should know and embrace regardless of one's religious beliefs.

It is the mentality of exclusivity that is a sure sign of cultic thinking. I guarantee you this: one who suffers from cultic thinking is definitely involved in some sort of a cult. Such an attachment and bond could never come about unless that person was first somehow subjected to one of the many forms of psychic attack. The attack could have either slowly or quickly broken down his rational mind, leaving left him or her open to influence and subject to submission.

Independent rational thinking, coupled with one's own ability to experience spiritual reality personally, without any preconditions, is how an individual becomes spiritually/psychically strong. Yet, it is not enough that one simply think and question. Minds are an easy thing to confuse and deceive. One must also stand on the firm foundation of faith. One must learn, know and put into practice the rules of occult mechanics. The first of these is the acknowledgement of the One True G-d, Creator of all. Without this foundation of faith, even the most spiritually sophisticated individual can be toppled and become subject to ruin.

Remember Adam and Eve in the Garden of Eden. They were on a higher spiritual plane that any other human being ever. Still they were corrupted and suffered a great fall, all due to a successful occultic attack. The serpent in the Garden attacked their hearts through their minds. The serpent led them to believe something that they knew was bad could actually be good.

Adam and Eve were told directly by G-d not to eat of the forbidden fruit. They knew this was wrong. Yet, this does not mean that they still did not want to take just a small taste. It was this desire festering in their hearts that allowed the serpent to cloud their rational judgment. We all know the outcome. We are still suffering from the aftermath.

A firm foundation implies that one does not even enter into discussion with the malevolent forces, however benign they wish to appear. We have to know who they are and what they are and not allow our eyes or our hearts to lead us to question that which we already know to be true. We must have firm and sound knowledge based upon the Good Word and not based upon superstition, fear and spurious interpretations that do not make real sense in the light of scrutiny.

Psychic self-defense, however, can never be based on logic alone. Indeed, logic alone is very much subject to psychic attack. This is why the forbidden Tree in Eden was called the Tree of Knowledge, Good and Evil. Knowledge alone, without intuitive insight can be a dangerous thing. While it can be good, it can also be bad. Occult mechanics is knowledge. Without a proper connection to G-d, righteous behavior and holiness, this knowledge is perverted and used by the agents of evil to pursue their nefarious causes.

The solution to knowledge devoid of morality is also found in the Biblical story of Eden. There was a second Tree in the Garden, known as the Tree of Life. Adam and Eve were never commanded not to eat of this Tree. Indeed, if they did eat of this Tree prior to their eating the forbidden fruit of the Tree of Knowledge, they would not have died. Rather they would have been able to transmute the poison of the Tree of Knowledge. Unfortunately, they did not do this. We too have all partaken of the metaphorical forbidden fruit. Yet, even for us the solution is the same.

The Tree of Life today is a metaphor for the teachings of G-d's Word. When one lives by the religious standards as laid down from ancient times, one is metaphorically eating of the fruit of the Tree of Life. While this alone cannot take away from us all the poisonous effects of the forbidden fruit of the Tree of Knowledge, it can still filter knowledge through the light of the word of G-d and transmute the evil therein and turn it into good. Pay attention to what I have just said, for I have just summed up the secret of psychic defense.

As long as you believe that you cannot be harmed by the occult, you are an easy and open target. As long as you deny that you can be harmed by the occult, you are an easy and open target. When you realize that you are vulnerable to attack and that yet you can take steps to defend yourself, through your behavior, through your actions and most of all through your faith in G-d, then you have done all you can to seal the open breaches. This alone might not be enough to defend you completely. Yet, once you have done all that is humanly possible to be done, then trust in G-d that Heaven will do all that is humanly impossible to be done.

Knowledge when combined with faith becomes a strong thing. The two together create an impressive barrier, the likes of which almost no psychic attack can penetrate. Knowledge and faith defend the mind and heart. Proper, moral behavior coupled with righteous action adds strength to one's spiritual defense. Do not underestimate the power that G-d has already placed in our hands. We must do all that we can to defend ourselves and then some.

Knowledge of spiritual mechanics is essential for anyone who wishes to be safeguarded against psychic attack. While one must never succumb to superstition, still one must make whatever efforts that are necessary to defend oneself against such powers as the evil eye, jealously, anger, and energy theft. One must be learned in the ways of occult mechanics to recognize how the forces of evil use the fruit of the Tree of Evil Knowledge. One must have the knowledge of the fruit of the Tree of Good Knowledge to offset the use of evil. Simple faith and belief is not enough here.

When we say that G-d expects us to do our share in defending ourselves against psychic attack, this means that Heaven expects us to learn and to put into action the knowledge that we acquire. Merely calling upon G-d's Name and expecting Him to act, all the while that we act foolishly and dangerously is a sure recipe to become a victim to the very thing we seek to avoid. Remember the old saying, not from the Bible, but equal to Biblical wisdom, "G-d helps those who help themselves."

Let me sum up some points. When I use the term psychic/occult mechanics, I am not speaking about the occult as it is portrayed and practiced in the world at large. Most such expressions of the occult have little to do with the real occult and have more to do with idolatry and the worship of demons. Any such practices and the beliefs emanating out of them should be avoided like the plague. They can do nothing other than harm all those who would approach them.

Modern occult as seen in the books in the bookstores is mostly New Age philosophy and/or Wiccan magic. Their practitioners will deny that there is anything malevolent or evil in their practices, yet they will have no compunction to place a spell or a curse on you because you do not support their religious or other social agendas.

To be safe, stay away from the circles of the New Age and/or Wicca. In spite of their proclamations of innocence and purity, they are neither. The New Age teachings, Wicca and all others like them deny the One True G-d and certainly do not seek to submit to the Will of Heaven. What more than this can be said to properly identify their source of origin?

True psychic/occult mechanics do not have to be learned from any unclean or compromised source. There is enough legitimate information out there, from legitimate sources. Judge in this vein, if the source seeks to serve the One True G-d and teaches a code of righteous, moral and modest behavior, then you may possibly rely on it. However, if any of these elements are lacking, I would avoid them and consider them suspect. It is not enough that a source claims to be serving the Light; it actually has to be doing so.

The criterion of judgment here is to see what type of behavior code the source advocates. If it does not endorse any type of moral or behavioral code, then you should be suspect why such a vital element would be missing. Any source of information about the occult that does not include as one of its foundations a moral code of Biblical proportions, I would not entertain as a source to be relied upon.

We must always recognize that evil exists all around us. Its nature and intent is to ensnare us. That is what evil does; and it is well seasoned and good at what it does. We have the obligation to watch out for it. We will never protect ourselves from evil all the while that we cannot recognize it. There is a great danger in not recognizing evil when it is before us. Remember this; evil is disguised in two different ways. The easy way is that it dresses up as something benign and innocent. It fools us into not seeing its malevolence. We therefore embrace it, thinking it to be good, only later to find out that we have indeed harmed ourselves.

The second way is more nefarious than the first. This second way seeks to keep us away from that which is good by trying to convince us that it is bad. This is the same first principle, but in reverse. When we consider the good to be bad and therefore distance ourselves from it, we in essence weaken ourselves by our pushing it away. This is, of course, evil's intent all along.

When we reject good as being evil and embrace evil, thinking it good, we have become so confused that we end up becoming unintentional agents of evil. This is the result of our eating the fruit of the forbidden Tree of Knowledge. We have confused the good and evil therein. As long as we entertain fear and superstition, prejudice and ignorance, we will forever be under its domain.

The Bible teaches us, separate from evil and only then can you do good. One does come before the other. Psychic/ spiritual mechanics helps one see the world as it really is; it helps one to recognize evil and to defend against it. The whole purpose of this book is to help you in your personal recognition of evil and your personal fight against it.

Review the lessons I have already written; they will teach you much of what you need to know. Then you can proceed onto this next and last chapter, wherein which I will speak again about the greatest conclusion of them all, the fear (and not the love) of G-d.

Chapter 26

━◄○►━

Conclusion: Summing Up, Fearing G-d & Doing What's Right

The end of the matter, when all is said and done, is simply this: fear G-d and observe His commandments, for this is all there is.

(Paraphrase of Ecclesiastes 12:13)

Psychic self-defense and personal character building are really one and the same thing. Even though there really are numerous groups and individuals out there who practice all sorts of occultic arts and even witchcraft, still one who trusts in the Higher Power of G-d has nothing to fear. This does not mean that the fearless should be foolish. This only means that the fearless should be bold, yet they should be cautious and wise in their boldness. Fearlessness should never be an excuse for foolishness.

368

There will always be those out there who seek our harm. We will never be able to placate all enemies all the time. Even to seek to do such a thing is a terrible waste of time. One cannot go on the offense and try to attack every perceived threat. Such a diversion of attention takes one's eye off the true goal of simply defending oneself.

Psychic self-defense is just that- an act of self-defense; it is not offense. Being that the number of offensive targets are legion, it is unwise to select just one and attempt to target it. We cannot afford to waste our time with such petty concerns. One who trusts in the Higher Power of G-d keeps one's attention focused on Heaven and allows G-d to avenge one's wrongs. Living like this enables one to keep focused on Heaven and upon doing what is right. This type of proper focus leads one to perform proper behavior. Proper behavior is one's best protection against those who would seek to manipulate one into improper behavior to cause one's own harm.

The Biblical book of Ecclesiastes summarizes the wisdom of ancient King Solomon of Israel. He was considered to be the wisest man of the ancient world. I see in his words a wisdom that is sorely lacking today. Indeed, his ancient words are very much applicable to (and needed by) us in these modern times. I highly recommend one studying and learning well the Biblical books of Proverbs and Ecclesiastes. Regardless of one's religion or lack of one, these books contain sound good advice and direction on how one should live and think.

Solomon summarizes his wisdom in my paraphrase of the second to last concluding statement in the Book of Ecclesiastes. He says all life can be summed up into two arenas- the fear of G-d and the observance of His commandments. In spite of how religious this might sound, it bears such a simple and pure wisdom to it that it transcends religion and indeed transcends even the belief in G-d. Living with an attitude of responsibility and discipline and always seeking to do the right things are the best ways that one can live. It not only creates for one a psychic shield to defend against any negative intrusions, it also creates good will from others. Yes, doing right creates for us a good reputation. Such a reputation might attract jealously and attack, yet, at the same time, such a good reputation is its own best defense against such attacks.

Doing what is right is always a double-edged sword. On the one hand, doing what is right solicits Divine notice and blessing. On the other hand, it is also noticed by the dark forces who then may possibly target the righteous individual. This is why I have always warned you to do what you do under the guise of privacy and modesty. No one in the world has to know just how righteous and good you really are. We do not perform our righteous actions and behave properly for the sake of being noticed and praised by others. If this indeed is your intent, then indeed you will be targeted for negative psychic attack.

The world we live in is not a safe and idyllic place. Only simple-minded fools believe this. Our world is a jungle and in most places literally a war zone. You had better get used to this being true and live accordingly. Competent soldiers survive wars and mighty lions do not fear being eaten by small predators. Choose wisely if you are a lion and a warrior or a fox and a victim.

Faced with the real pressures that life brings, I have seen so many people turn to the "love and peace" movement. Since the days of the "hippy-60s" we have heard chants of "let's give peace a chance." Tell me, how many innocent men, women and children have been murdered around the world all the while that we are "giving peace a chance." Things in the last few decades have been no different than they have ever been from the centuries and millennia before them. The escapist illusions of the hippy generation were nothing more than just one more occultist plot to blind the eyes of many to turn away from the harsh truths of real life and to, in the words of their "guru," Timothy Leary, *turn on, tune in, drop out.* No greater recipe for occultic destruction could ever be spoken. Here was a man, who with all good possible intentions became an agent of evil and corruption.

The hippie mentality of the 60's was a poison that corrupted not only the United States but all of western civilization. The movement was clearly supported by the occult forces in this word as is clearly evidenced by the fact that the hippie movement spawned the New Age movement. The New Age movement is nothing new. It is simply the return of many ancient occultic practices repackaged and presented to the public in a more benign, less threatening package. One can take a poison and package it as candy. Still, once ingested, it still kills; even if it is sugar-coated.

Now, fifty years after the birth of the hippie movement, we see its children and grandchildren. They are the proud members of the secular, atheist society whose only commandment is, "*I am the lord, my own god, I shall have no others interests above my own.*" Selfishness and hedonism are the laws of this jungle. One can see this message everywhere one looks, on television and in the movies, and certainly in the way big business acts and promotes its products. Buy, buy, buy, spend, spend, spend, even if you do not have the money. Now we have invented a new thing; before you could only spend until you ran out of money; now you can spend even beyond that. We have been given the almighty credit card. Did you know that the majority of individuals living in western civilization spend beyond their means and live by credit? How successful has the occultic penetration become! We are all under its spell.

We cannot change the world. I believe it is foolish even to try. However I believe the commitment to righteousness demands of us that we at least reach out to those around us, those who have an ear to listen and to communicate with them, on an individual basis, to try and safeguard as many individuals that we can reach. We cannot change the world, but we can have a significant influence on the individuals within it.

Reaching out to others is never meant to be done in a way that makes one a "show-off." One is supposed to lead by example of behavior and not just by word of mouth. The truly righteous are not preachers; they are doers. They are not talkers, they are doers. They live by what they believe. They walk their talk. The great influence of the righteous is in their sincerity and their humility. We have discussed these traits earlier. Review them well and adopt them in every way possible. Remember to not be a "show-off" and to do what good you do for the right reasons and not to solicit the approval and praise of others.

King Solomon summed up life and told us the most important thing is to fear G-d. Yet, this simple advice is also subject to such ridiculous misinterpretations. How many foolish children's tales have we been told that if we do not do this or that thing that G-d is going to punish us? Granted, Divine retribution does come down on both individuals and society, but not because of foolish infractions of ritual, rather because of serious violations of the natural order. When we act perverted and thereby thwart the natural order, then the Divinely ordained laws of nature respond and reorient the world to restore justice and balance. We call these events natural disasters. They are both natural and supernatural.

Fearing G-d does not mean to live subject to one's religious credo, but rather to live a righteous and moral life. Religious theologies separate us from one another. Moral and righteous behaviors, common to all our religions are what unite us. What you believe is always secondary to what you do. I believe that this concept is the foundation of all true religion.

Fearing G-d means serving Heaven. One serves Heaven by doing what is right here on Earth. Essentially, serving Heaven means to serve and to provide for one another. Fearing G-d means doing the right things, simply because they are what is right. It is the natural and normal thing to do. One does not need a religious credo to recognize this. One does not need a preacher to know it. One knows deep within one's heart what is right and what is wrong. When one does what is right simply because it is the right thing to do regardless of what others might say or think, it is the fear of G-d in action. In my eyes, this is what King Solomon meant when he said to fear G-d.

The shield that protects one's heart from corruption is the same shield that defends one from all kinds of psychic occultic attack. Psychic self-defense and building good character are one and the same.

Observing G-d's commandments takes on different meanings depending upon one's chosen path of religious observance. One simply need not commit idolatry or serve the malevolent forces of evil in this world, however benignly disguised. Rather, let one worship G-d, the Creator of the Universe alone, as one will. We do not have a one-world religion and for right now we do not need one. When G-d so ordains to intervene in human evolution like He has in the past, then He will send His messiah along with an armada of angels. They will take control of our world and usher in the messianic age. When this great day comes, then so be it. But, until that great and blessed day, we have to make the best of what we have. We must recognize the common denominators that we have and build together based upon that which unites us. We must not tear down based upon our differences.

Building comes from G-d. Tearing down is the path of the malevolent forces. Remember the old adage, "*united we stand, divided we fall.*" This is why the hippie-New Age-secular adage of self indulgence and self worship is nothing more than a victory for the malevolent dark forces that enslave first the mind and then the body. "Give peace a chance" does not work during war time, and yes, we are very much at war. During war times, the troops rally together and fight as a united front, using every wise tactic of guerilla warfare. The forces of evil know this strategy well and have been using it successfully against the righteous for decades. This is why the numbers of the righteous dwindle.

The time has come for the righteous to regroup and to go on the offense. Our battle is not one to be fought with guns and bombs. Our battle is in the arena of attitudes, ideas and behaviors. When we do what is right, for the right reasons in the right way; we win a victory for our cause, regardless of who sees it or knows about it. Remember, in the psychic realm everything is connected. Whenever we do good, however small or insignificant a thing, it ripples through the entire collective unconscious of humanity. The more we do therefore, the greater our influence. It really is this simple.

I have now come to the conclusion of this work. I have shared with you everything that you need to know to face your daily challenges. I have even taken you beyond this and given you a glimpse of what it looks like behind the veil that separates our world from its mirror image on the other side of consciousness. Sometimes more words can offer no more direction. I have now reached this point. Let me conclude with my personal blessings to each of you, my readers.

Be strong, be wise, be humble, be sincere and strive to do what is right. Keep your feet on the ground and your eyes on the goal and as always, open your heart to Heaven. May G-d bless you and be with you. Shalom.

About the Author

Born and raised in New York, Ariel Bar Tzadok left for Israel in 1979 and studied in some of the finest Sephardic yeshivot in Jerusalem, including Porat Yosef. In June 1983, HaRav Bar Tzadok received his Rabbinic ordination from HaRav Ya'aqob Peretz, Rosh Yeshiva of Collel Hekhal Pinhas. While studying at Hekhal Pinhas, HaRav Bar Tzadok was blessed to become the private student of the renowned Mekubal, HaRav Meir Levi *zt'l*, the foremost student of the Head Kabbalist of Jerusalem, HaRav Mordechai Sharabi *zt'l*.

Upon returning to the United States, HaRav Bar Tzadok augmented his education with studies in Jungian psychology. HaRav Bar Tzadok expanded his education to include many of the world's religions, philosophies and psychological systems. Following the example set by ancient Sages, the Rav also explored the teachings of many occult systems and practices to recognize their dangers and to teach others how to avoid their snares. After developing a working understanding of the parameters of human consciousness and how it touches both seen and unseen worlds, HaRav Bar Tzadok began his career in Rabbinic/Life Coach counseling.

After teaching privately for many years, HaRav Bar Tzadok officially established Yeshivat Benei N'vi'im in 1992 to serve as an anti-missionary, anti-cult organization; to address the growing concerns of spiritual misguidance and misinformation that is pervasive in the Jewish community at large. Following in the footsteps of the great Sephardic Sages of the previous century HaRav Bar Tzadok began to use the teachings of Kabbalah as a means to draw wayward souls back into the Torah way of life. After many years of mixed success, HaRav Bar Tzadok withdrew from his position of publicly teaching Kabbalah. He realized that while many people are drawn to the myth of mysticism, not that many were ready and willing to apply its sacred teachings correctly in proper coordination with a life of Torah and mitzvot observance.

Recognizing that not everyone attracted to the message of Kosher Torah is of Jewish origins, HaRav Bar Tzadok welcomes to KosherTorah.com and to his Yeshiva any non-Jews who wish to embrace the Benei Noah code and live moral and decent lives as G-d fearing, righteous human beings.

Over the years, HaRav Bar Tzadok has been featured in numerous newspaper articles, radio talk shows and television programs. He has lectured in numerous yeshivot, university groups, synagogues and other forums around the USA and abroad.